THE PSYCHIC TOURIST

William Little

THE PSYCHIC TOURIST

A Voyage into the Curious World of Predicting the Future

ICON BOOKS

Published in the UK in 2010 by
Icon Books Ltd, Omnibus Business Centre,
39–41 North Road, London N7 9DP
email: info@iconbooks.co.uk
www.iconbooks.co.uk

Sold in the UK, Europe, South Africa and Asia
by Faber & Faber Ltd, Bloomsbury House,
74–77 Great Russell Street, London WC1B 3DA or their agents

Distributed in the UK, Europe, South Africa and Asia
by TBS Ltd, TBS Distribution Centre, Colchester Road
Frating Green, Colchester CO7 7DW

Published in Australia in 2010
by Allen & Unwin Pty Ltd, PO Box 8500,
83 Alexander Street, Crows Nest, NSW 2065

Distributed in Canada by Penguin Books Canada,
90 Eglinton Avenue East, Suite 700,
Toronto, Ontario M4P 2YE

ISBN: 978-184831-124-4

Typeset in 12 on 16pt Bembo by Marie Doherty

Printed and bound in the UK
by Clays Ltd, St Ives plc

Contents

About the author

William Little is a freelance journalist for the Saturday *Telegraph* magazine, *Weekend Telegraph*, the *Guardian*, *The Times*, and the *Financial Times*. He has also worked for *Arena*, *Esquire* and *Cosmopolitan*, and contributed articles to the *Independent*, the *Daily Express* and the *Big Issue*, among many others.

www.psychictourist.com

Author's note

All the events described in this book actually took place, and all characters depicted really exist. I have used real names except for a few occasions when, out of respect for privacy, they have been changed.

For Nikki

Introduction

I'VE JUST RECEIVED the most disturbing news of my life. My sister and my nine-year-old niece believe they are going to die in a water accident and it's all my fault. I'm devastated.

My 38-year-old sister, Sarah, is sitting on the sofa opposite me, her legs curled under for extra protection against this vision of death. 'It's that bloody birth chart you gave us. It was in there,' she barks at me. It's Christmas at our parents' house but this doesn't feel like a very festive conversation.

Her explosion of pent-up emotion is unexpected. I'd simply asked her where she was thinking of taking my niece, Elly, on holiday.

'I was looking forward to taking her sailing in Greece, but then I remembered that bloody birth chart. I'm even terrified of going to France on a car ferry. I'm certainly not taking the night ferry – we'll probably get trapped in our cabin as the boat goes down.'

My sister, normally a hard-headed individual, is having a near panic attack because of something she read in a horoscope.

'It's a load of rubbish,' I say, trying to sound rational. 'How the hell can a bunch of stars determine anything?'

'Yeah, well, if it's such a load of nonsense why did you give it to me, then?'

Ah. Good point. What the hell was I thinking? Well, as it turns out, not a lot. When my sister first mentioned the birth chart I couldn't remember what she was talking about. Then with a jolt, it hit me. Some time in the not-too-distant past, just a few days after the birth of my niece in December 1999, I had decided it would be thoughtful to present my sister with Elly's horoscope. But not just any horoscope, a birth chart – a full and detailed stream of predictions about her future and her character based on the date, time and place of her birth. Somehow, I thought – not actually thinking too much about it at all, if I'm being honest – the positioning of the planets, the moon and the sun would all be able to reveal whether the future Elly would be a teenage delinquent or a pioneering physicist. And it would be great if her mum, rather than waiting to see what her daughter would become, knew all of this before it happened. Did I think it was mumbo jumbo or an ancient form of soothsaying handed down to us from the wise old men of ancient Greece? Well, between you and me, I just thought it was a nice present.

Just as I think my sister's anger has evaporated, another problem emerges – it appears I also had a birth chart written out for her too.

'It says it in both of them,' she says. 'Mine says that I will have an accident in water, which will lead to the death of a child. Elly's says that she will be involved in an accident in water and that will lead to the death of a parent. I think I might just fly to France instead.'

Shit.

'That's ridiculous,' I shout. But moments later I'm sitting in silence. What I've just told my sister about it being a load of bunkum is now suddenly at odds with how I feel. Pinned down for eight long years, my superstitious side has just escaped from a high-security enclosure in the murkiest reaches of my brain. It's leaking out everywhere and making a mess of my view of the situation. Surreptitiously I glance over at Sarah looking miserable on the sofa, and I hear my niece telling my mum off in the kitchen in one of her endearing 'I'm now an adult' fantasies, and I suddenly don't want them to travel across any stretch of open water either. I'm scared. I'm cut up about it. It's like it's already happened. But I don't want to say so because it will just reinforce what she believes already.

There's still a part of me that thinks this is nonsense, but I'm hedging my bets just in case it isn't. I can't prove it either way, of course – there's just this rational part of me that dismisses it out of hand. But what if *that* is irrational? What if people really can see into the future and we just haven't been able to prove it yet? Or are all these fortune-tellers just charlatans, preying on the weak and the vulnerable? But, and this is the thing that's getting to me, my sister isn't weak and vulnerable, and nor am I. My sister's a nurse of vast experience. Whereas I weep at fictional deaths on TV, she routinely deals with the reality of death in people's homes. More than anyone I know, she really understands the meaning of life, the end result, the real 'future' of us all. She isn't given to getting sentimental, but she does worry about her daughter a lot. For instance, she wouldn't visit me in London for a long time because she thought Elly might get hurt. By what, I don't know. Her fear of the city was irrational. So perhaps that's it – maybe each of us has a weakness that the fortune-tellers, the tea-leaf readers, the crystal ball-gazers and the mystic gypsies are channelling into.

The questions are endless, and I need to get to the bottom of them quickly. But before I do, I need to take a closer look at myself. I have a dirty secret. At different stages of my life, during relationship crises, job dissatisfaction and general boredom, I have dabbled with the future, wanting to find out what was out there for me. And the experience wasn't overwhelmingly positive. A few years ago, in a state of confusion that followed the dumping of a former girlfriend, I went to see a fortune-teller at London's Mysteries – a bookshop that calls itself the leading mystic resource centre in Europe. It was all a bit baffling. The female mystic reckoned I had issues with my sexuality – that I wasn't getting any was the main issue, I thought, until she mentioned that I might be gay. Hmm. So I uncrossed my legs. She was clearly trying to read my body language. Once I put her straight, she then took the opposite tack and said my animal signs were the snake and the hedgehog – I was all spiky and a seducer and in the next few months I would have a lot of fun in the nightclubs of London town. Right. So now I'm no longer gay, just a sex pest. Thanks.

I came out feeling none the wiser. Yet in the months following I still got myself a couple of tarot card readings, and I had my palm read by a friend's girlfriend. I also had an astrological birth chart drawn up, which has since been ceremoniously burnt as my present girlfriend was unimpressed when she realised I had one. She didn't like the idea that my decision-making might be influenced by what I read in a horoscope. Would I, for instance, dump her just because it said so? Since then, as I've got older and become more sure of myself, I haven't needed the fortune-telling business. I'm far too rational. I explain it away as mind games, guesswork, clever deductions, or people in a crisis just hearing what they want to hear. But now that I'm thinking about it again, it doesn't seem enough to dismiss it out of hand. The fortune-telling business is everywhere. A surprisingly large number of people I know believe in psychics and mediums. And they aren't alone. Thousands call up psychics on premium-rate numbers every day and millions of people read their daily horoscope in the press. Can so many people be wrong?

There's not a single person I know who hasn't at one time or another tried to find out about their future. There's my mum, for instance, who's visited enough mystics over the past 30 years to be able to read her future backwards. One mystic recently revealed that her windows were going to leak. Great. Another one told her I was going to live abroad. (Hmm, my girlfriend will be going to live abroad with her job and I'll probably go with her – it was probably just luck.) Then one Christmas my mum tells me something that sends me reeling.

'Another one said your sister was going to have a motorbike accident,' she says casually. She hasn't noticed that I've stopped breathing. My sister did have a motorbike accident and she didn't tell my mum and dad. She chose to tell me instead, as she knew I'd just say 'Wow' and walk off, while my parents would have hunted down and dismembered the boyfriend who had foolishly decided to take Sarah for a ride on his bike. I tell my mum this now, and she just shrugs. What? Yeah, just shrugs. My mum believes in it all. It doesn't even occur to her that it might not have happened.

But what I can't figure out is that if people can actually read the future, what's the point? If mystics are giving out gems like my mum's going to have leaky windows, what's the point of knowing that? What's my mum going to do with this piece of information about her windows – put a bucket out to catch the water whenever it rains? Did knowing the future prevent my sister from falling off a motorbike? And if I moved abroad, so what? I could have told my mum that – she didn't need a mystic to tell her for me.

So on one level it seems people want to know the future just so they can say that the future can be known. Are they just ticking boxes about their experiences, or is there some practical application to all this? If the future can be told, can it be changed? These are big metaphysical questions. Have our lives already been lived in the future? Is there such a thing as fate? After all, if someone can read the future, then our lives are predetermined, which means we don't have any free will or control over it. If your future has already happened, why bother getting up in the morning?

So I've got to get to the bottom of this. I need to find out the truth about my sister and niece's horoscope readings, and I need to discover whether the future has already happened or whether the mystics are just giving false information to people in a crisis who want to hear some good news. A friend of mine reckons it doesn't matter whether they can read the future or not – mystics offer people hope by mapping out a positive future. Yeah, right, tell that to my sister. If they can say things that can seriously affect someone's well-being, should the whole future-telling industry be closed down?

In order to find out the truth about the future, I'm going to take a perilous journey and go there. I'm going to seek out my future from the best mystics the country and the world have to offer. I'm going to try everything from crystal ball gazers to tarot cards, witches, palm-readers and mediums, to the oldest and wisest gypsy in the most run-down caravan I can find. I won't leave any stone unturned in order to find out the truth. But will they all agree? That's the test. By the end of this journey into my future, how many futures will I have? And will any of it come true? But more importantly, will I still be the same person? If it's just the power of suggestion, what if the things that I hear make me subconsciously take disastrous decisions about my life?

Along this journey into the future I also need to talk to the modern-day mystics – the Derren Browns, the quantum physicists who reckon that there are levels of reality of which we aren't consciously aware. Could quantum physics explain the existence of spirits? I need to speak to psychologists and scientists. And I need to understand what psychics and mystics really believe and what's really going on in their heads when they see the future or speak to the spirit world. Above all else I need to talk to the psychics who claim to have predicted big events, like earthquakes and famous deaths, and the people who keep going back to them time after time. I also need to find out whether astrologers and mediums are tapping into the same 'spiritual' energy source when they predict the future. Are the stars, the planets and mystics' brains all connected in one giant psychic communications web? And I'm going back in time to speak to the original fortune-tellers, the witches, who claim to control nature using spells. Could they put a spell on me to help me see my future more clearly?

But the ultimate test is that I'm going to become a mystic myself. Some psychics believe that only a few have the gift, while others believe everyone is born with psychic powers but we choose to ignore them. Well, I'm going to enrol myself at a psychic school where they reckon they can teach anyone to have mystical powers. So by the time I reach the end of this journey I will be able to answer the biggest question of all – do we have a future? No ifs, no buts, no annoying compromises or partial answers.

But before I put on my walking shoes and hit the road to my future, I have one final worry, and it might put all my plans in jeopardy … Do they already know I'm coming?

It's a mystery

I'M BACK AT MYSTERIES, Europe's finest mystical resource centre, the site of my first reading ten years ago, open-minded, my brain racing for answers because I want … no, I *need* to give it another try. There must be something more to this place, I figure, judging by the steady supply of customers seeking their fortune, and I have to get to the bottom of it.

Before the disturbing conversation with my sister, I would have said that mystics were the ham actors of the occult. But now I'm not so sure. With my sister on astrological death row, I've got to tread more carefully and question my previous assumptions. It's a matter of life or death.

And I have to remember that the smirk is like kryptonite to these people – they can't bear not to be taken seriously. Maybe this is because fortune-tellers are the priests of a new-age religion helping give people's lives structure and meaning. After all, more than 60 per cent of people in the UK believe in the power of psychics. While others self-medicate with alcohol or overwork, is it so bad that some people choose mysticism as their drug of choice?

I'm disappointed when I meet the mortal who owns this place. I was expecting Professor Dumbledore, an eccentric with a long beard and wise old eyes, but Matthew, the owner for more than 25 years, claims not to have mystical powers and doesn't give readings. He's clearly a good businessman who saw a gap in the market during the new-age revolution in the early 1980s and is reaping the rewards today. Mysteries has expanded massively since it first opened its doors in July 1982 and does a booming trade.

Matthew hands me a piece of paper outlining the powers of Mysteries psychics. My choice is crucial. Is one among the fifteen dedicated mystics performing today the real thing? Will just one reading here give me the answers I'm looking for? There's Marco, for instance, who's straight-talking and deals only in hard facts. He tells it as it is. While tarot astrologer Chris looks like he might do a Kenneth Williams impression and charm you with his dry wit.

Only Alice and Mary are free at the moment. Both claim they were born with psychic powers as well as having a direct line to the spirit world. Yet they have other weapons in their psychic armoury just in case these should fire blanks. Alice consults tarot, while Mary tunes in to her intuition. Alice is also a master at psychometry, which is reading someone's energy from holding an item of their jewellery. Mary, however, has the ultimate sell – she has gypsy roots and can use Wicca, i.e. witchcraft. She looks intense in her picture, while Alice appears friendly. I opt for Alice. I don't know why. Maybe Mary's intense stare has unnerved me.

As I climb the back stairs to the mystics' den above the shop, I remind myself that I'm not going to give any ground to Alice. It's a straight fight between me the psychic sleuth and her the mystic.

Compactly small with a blondish bob and an ambiguously arched eyebrow, she sits at a small table covered with a dark blue cloth. The table and room are so intimately small that they seem to exist only for the sharing of whispered secrets. The atmosphere is hypnotic, the intensity such that I can hear my pulse throb. Yet nothing has been said. Alice begins by taking my watch, which she clasps to her chest, closing her eyes and channelling into my energy. She keeps me tuned in with a deep, soothing voice. Throughout she shoots understanding and dreamy glances at me. She adds to the mood by tilting her head to one side and frowning when she speaks to her spirit guide. Her concentration is unnerving – it's as though she's having a long-distance conversation with someone on a crackly line to Australia.

Every now and then she gets me to shuffle and pick out cards from a pack of tarot. I don't know what it is about these cards that unnerves me. The ancient figures of death, kings and princes of fortune are like a ouija board of the soul. Thinking about a particular aspect of life, say a relationship, while shuffling the cards orders them in such a way that Alice is able to reveal what's in store for me. Handling them feels like playing poker with the occult – will I get a good spread or will I fold into an uncertain future? Weirdly, these ancient pagan kings push out cards towards my fingers. Spread out on the table, these picture postcards of the future are so weighed down with the myths of the past that anything seems possible. I'm so taken in and primed to hear my fortune that when Alice starts predicting my future, I have to ask her to repeat what she says. I think I haven't heard her right.

What the disembodied whispers and the pagan cards reveal is that I need to leave my current place of work because most of my colleagues are backstabbing egoists and I'm bursting at the seams with integrity. They are, I admit, complete bastards.

I can't stand them. But I left my job more than four years ago to work for myself. She then tells me to dump my girlfriend within the next three months, despite moments before wondering whether she was pregnant. It turns out I have to dump her because she wants to have a baby and we aren't talking about it. If we start talking and stay together, Nikki will fall pregnant within twelve months. She also reveals that I will go abroad three times on a mission. My ears prick up and I map out a future for myself performing daring antics across the globe. But my Indiana Jones fantasy world is a permanent feature of my professional time-wasting daydreams anyway.

Despite the tension and drama, I'm beginning to feel disappointed. The mystical view of Alice is being slowly replaced by the reality of my rational mind. Her acting is astonishing. I'm more or less open to being impressed in my quasi-scientific search for the truth, but almost everything she says fails painfully to leave a mark. We're like two ships that haven't even bothered to leave port, let alone pass in the middle of the night.

I'm on the verge of losing interest when the mood changes suddenly and Alice looks at me like she's been possessed. My skin prickles. I feel dizzy – am I hyperventilating, or has the air suddenly become heavier? She closes her eyes and rubs my watch and frowns. I've stopped breathing.

'I have your granddad in spirit here.'

Holy shit. I nearly jump out of my skin. She's caressing my granddad's watch when she says this. I was given it when he died a few years ago. It has his name inscribed on the back. I'm so frozen with anticipation that the air seems suddenly thick with soot. My eyes are burning and my head hurts.

'He's saying your dad's stubborn.'

I was expecting him to tell me to take better care of his watch, or thank the family for throwing his ashes into the River Severn, something that only he'd know. But I'm so on edge that the nagging question forming slowly in my head like an ice age in the tropics suddenly brings me around like a slap in the face. My dad? Slap. I'm confused. Stubborn? Backhanded slap. I was expecting some information about my mum, because it's *her* dad's watch that Alice is now grasping. I never think about this granddad, my father's dad, who has apparently just dialled the spirit-world blower. He drank too much, lost jobs because he was down the pub all the time, and he was cruel to my Nan, even when she was dying. I'm surprised Alice can understand him through all the alcohol-induced slurring. And another thing, my dad isn't stubborn. He is, in fact, the least stubborn person I know, unless you count that time when I was ten and he wouldn't take me to football practice because I'd set fire to the lounge carpet. But that seems pretty reasonable to me. And then that's it. He hangs up. There's not another peep from my granddad.

Drunken granddads and childbearing aside, it's my relationship that keeps Alice busy for the rest of the session. She tells me that I'm going backwards and forwards in my mind because Nikki, my partner of nearly seven years, is clingy and will try to stop me going abroad on one of my work-related missions.

The reality for me is that she's more likely to dump me for being a stay-at-home bore. And the suggestion that we don't talk enough is like suggesting shit never hits the fan. It just doesn't wash.

I have another surprise. The spirits are frankly a bit pissed off about being taken for granted. This is because I've told Alice I'm here to do research. I've got to believe in them without question, otherwise they won't play ball. Spirits getting shirty, I hadn't expected that. Nor the twist that I'm the charlatan for trying to catch them out. I'm the destroyer of the faith for daring to hold them up to the light.

I'm concerned that there's nothing on which to judge Alice's assessment of my life and my relationship. If you don't believe in psychics and mediums, then Alice getting so much wrong about Nikki and me makes sense. But what if you do believe that Alice was tuning in to the spirit world, my energy levels, my thoughts and feelings – then what? That I'm deluded about my relationship and my life, or that Alice was having a bad day? Well, that's what Matthew believes.

'Their powers vary from month to month. Sometimes they get it all right and that can be very reassuring to the customer, but they do have their off months. But all our readers are tried and tested. They all do a trial reading with a member of staff who is experienced at receiving readings,' he says.

We're sitting in his office at the top of Mysteries, which is surprisingly well lit and modern. He has a big desk with a TV screen to the left showing images from a number of hidden cameras.

'There they are.' He points at the screen, showing the mystics at work. 'It's like *The Truman Show*,' he jokes.

I ask about Alice's predictions, but Matthew cuts in and says that it isn't fortune-telling like fairground gypsies. 'What they know is what has already happened in the past and what is happening now in the present. The future hasn't happened yet, that is common sense.'

'Right. So we all have free will, then? Our futures aren't predetermined?'

'Of course we have free will, and no, the future hasn't happened yet. All that psychics and mediums are doing are tapping into something that is already known,' he tells me. Matthew believes that the universe is integrated and that there's some kind of collective consciousness. Psychics use this like a mystical grapevine, listening in to our past and our present and giving suggestions about our futures. It's a captivating idea and I want to buy it, but it comes a little too cheaply: you know when you get it home it will break down under close scrutiny. I'm all for believing it, but if all it takes for something to be real is a passionate interest, then me and my dad would have made Birmingham City Football Club win the league every year since 1976. If anything, it's had the opposite effect. My quest is for truth based on verifiable proof. So far all I have is an idea that, in the shape of Alice, has no corroborating evidence. If she was plugging into the grapevine it must have been one hell of a windy day.

So I seek out another opinion on Alice. Nisha, a regular punter, thinks Alice's the genuine article. Nisha is a pretty Asian woman in her late twenties. She looks startled, as though five people are talking to her at once and she can't quite make up her mind who to answer. My initial Sherlock Holmes deduction is that she's a bit weak-minded and ditzy, but I soon learn she's a lawyer. Shit.

Despite her initial nerves and embarrassment about having to open up, Nisha comes across as intelligent and articulate. The gist of it is that she can't cope with her friends' judgemental comments on her life any more and needs a spiritual stranger to guide her. She's been visiting Mysteries for more than four years and sees Alice six times a year minimum.

'My first reading was very powerful. It shed a lot of light on an intractable situation that I had been in for a long time,' she tells me. 'I was seeing a man at the time. My friends kept on saying the same things, but coming to see a stranger helped put an objective light on it. She said some things about him and his personality that I hadn't wanted to face up to. It was what I really needed to hear and no one else had done that for me before.'

But coming to Mysteries wasn't just about helping Nisha to make decisions, which she had never been good at. It was also about becoming more spiritual.

'I used to have a lot of highs and lows emotionally. Now I'm much calmer about life,' she says, holding my gaze for the first time. 'I have a deeper understanding of life.'

Nisha gives me an example of Alice's mystical ability. She came to see her again recently about a man at work who was interested in her but who she was unsure of. 'Alice said that I should go and have some fun with him. She also said that I might not think he's the one for me or my type, which I didn't, but I should give it a go anyway. Then she said it would hit me suddenly, and bang, it did about three months later,' she says.

This seems reasonable enough, but in my post-Alice mood I'm in rationalising overdrive. The thing about Nisha is that she reminds me of half a dozen of my female friends, but ten years younger. Although they never went to mystics, they were always worried about blokes and dreaded making decisions. The advice we gave was always, 'Go for it, have some fun and you might find that he's the one for you.' The problem with this was that sometimes we were right and sometimes we were wrong, just like Alice. Nisha, you see, is back to see Alice today because the relationship that was meant to be is now no longer working, and she wants some advice from the same person who told her it would be all right. To me, this sounds like giving a second chance to the surgeon who accidentally removed your leg instead of your tonsils just because you've always trusted doctors.

Like Nisha, I can chart my own rise from seeing a Mysteries mystic all those years ago to where I am today as a kind of spiritual journey. But for me, it was the voyage of growing up, becoming mature and having the confidence in my own ability to make judgements. Youthful insecurity and indecision go together like Tom and Jerry – they keep winding each other up, which leads inevitably to a circular neurotic kiss chase. It's the cat and mouse of life.

I wonder aloud why Nisha didn't see a life coach instead, but that, she admits, wouldn't be spiritual. For Nisha, it's this sense of being grounded in something bigger than yourself that's the key. The idea that when you look in, it's not just yourself you're asking, but also the universe. On those long, dark nights when you're struggling with your inner demons and life's travails, it's nicer not to feel so lonely.

To be fair to Nisha, she does believe that mystics get it wrong sometimes. 'I do think they can channel information, but sometimes maybe what they say is what they think rather than what they channel.' Advice from a spiritualist, for instance, not to take a part-time job during her MA in Law left her saddled with debt. 'It was the wrong thing to tell me. I should have worked then.'

Despite my rationalisation of Nisha's experience, there's no doubt in her mind that it has helped her. She has become happier, more in tune with herself and more confident. But she's provided no real proof that these people have supernatural powers. She's been given no more than the kind of advice my aunt would give.

I'm about to give up all hope of finding any evidence and head home disappointed, when I'm introduced to Mike. He greets me by slapping me on the back because he's seen me for who I really am.

'It's a load of old bollocks, isn't it?' he says, giving me a knowing wink. He's a 50-year-old plumber and he's got a tattoo on his arm. He sits down and folds his arms in a confident East End, hard-as-nails kind of way. I just mumble 'right' and laugh weakly. Then he straightens up and all his chummy friendliness drops away.

'I'd be dead if it wasn't for Alice.'

'Excuse me?'

'If it wasn't for that mystic I'd be talking to you in spirit, mate,' he says.

I want to ask a million questions but I just sit there dumb. Mike gives it to me straight.

'I thought it was a load of old guff, right. Bollocks is more precise. I came here for a laugh with some mates a year ago after a couple of Saturday afternoon pints. And she says she has my dad and my granddad in spirit. She tells me this right at the end, and says they've been badgering her the whole time, but she thought it was too big a deal to tell me.'

'Tell you what?'

'That if I didn't go see a doctor right away I'd be in trouble. I mean, straight away.'

'And did you?'

'Of course I fucking did. If you hear something like that plays on your mind. What have you got to lose – nothing more than half an hour down the doctors. But it wasn't half an hour, was it? No, it was a bunch of tests by a bunch of doctors up at the hospital. It turns out I had some kind of rare blood disorder and they were bloody surprised I was still walking.'

Mike's in no doubt that his life has been saved by the power of a fortune-teller. This leaves me with a conundrum. Until now, despite a paucity of evidence, the unshakeable belief at Mysteries is that its soothsayers are bona fide, despite negative real-world consequences. And here I am presented with what seems like irrefutable proof. I feel unsettled by the stark contradictions.

I catch up with Alice a few weeks later to talk about her own beliefs. She's sitting on a packed train and she doesn't care who can hear her. It's not just that she thinks that she's more intuitive or more sensitive than other people, but that she actually sees spirits all the time.

'I was about seven years old when I first became aware. I didn't know what they were at first. No one else saw what I saw around me. They were people but there was something different about what they were wearing. One woman was covered in water. Then they started communicating with me.'

'Why you, why not someone else?'

'Because imagine if you're a spirit and everyone is ignoring you and then there's someone who you can communicate with, wouldn't you try to talk to them?'

'I guess. But why can't everyone speak to them?'

'I think we are all born with the gift but some of us choose to use it and some of us don't. If you look at babies they can all see it, but when they start growing up they switch their eyes off from it.'

So far, so spiritual, but what about the inconsistency of her predictions? She is, surprisingly, just as frustrated as me, yet not with herself but with her spirit guides. 'Especially one that just gives me random words. When I asked him what those words meant, he replied: "I am not here to spoon-feed you, I am here to guide you." I have to filter information that comes through. I don't just say anything. I have to make sure it's right,' she says.

Reading the future seems to be a serious matter of interpretation, littered with ambiguity and pitfalls. Spirits with attitude – maybe this is what affected my reading. Perhaps they only guide people who really need help, not some nosy journalist with an ulterior motive.

Alice also believes, unlike Matthew, that the future has already happened. 'It's not a big deal for spirits to see the future. What I feel is that we are all souls and we make a soul agreement before we are born about the choices we are going to make in our lives. You can change your decisions when you are born, but there is always a higher plan for yourself.'

I don't understand. Our future is predetermined but we can change it? Was me turning up to Mysteries to see Alice predetermined? I don't know, but something Matthew said about Alice has me wondering. When I said goodbye to him, he told me that he knew I was going to pick Alice.

'How's that?'

'Because she knew you were coming here when you got the commission three weeks ago,' he says.

I laugh, expecting Matthew to join me in the joke, but he looks back stony-faced.

This doesn't bother me at first. But later I think back to when I had the idea to investigate the fortune-telling business, back to that uncomfortable conversation with my sister at Christmas.

I'm in the kitchen when I'm thinking this. I rush back into my office. I pull the calendar from the wall and frantically count the days. I count them again and then once more. I have to admit it to myself, even though every fibre in my body is resisting. I met Alice exactly three weeks to the day after I decided to investigate fortune-telling – the very same day I learnt about the prediction of my sister's and my niece's death.

Spooky, huh? Or am I just playing with your marbles? Sure, it happened just like I say. But that's all I have. Apart from the trips, that is. Yeah, I unexpectedly went on a press trip to Guatemala, I'm doing a road trip around Belgium for a national newspaper, and I'm heading off to the US in a few months. So that's three out of three missions. Sounds promising? But there's still all the stuff she got wrong. You see, it's the pick and mix aspect of the mystics that does for them. They give you a whole load of blackjacks and aniseed balls that you spit out in disgust, then they throw in a strawberry mojo and you go giddy at the knees because it's your favourite and you think they knew it all along. We just forget about all the nasty sweets they passed us beforehand.

I once heard that Ken Dodd talked fast during gigs in order to tell as many jokes as possible in the hope that everyone would eventually find one funny. Aren't mystics doing the same thing with their predictions? But is this because they're charlatans or because their spirit guides are giving them a hard time? We expect them to be consistent and precise, but if they really are listening to a cryptic ghost talking down that crackly old telephone line, then it isn't surprising that sometimes things get a bit mixed up?

Yet it's this imprecise nature that's really bothering me. Maybe Matthew and Nisha were right – sometimes mystics channel what the spirits say, sometimes they get confused, give their own opinions and screw it up. And there's simply no accounting for Mike's good fortune. But perhaps it's because I'm aiming too low. It's early days yet and I'm still in the foothills of the mystic mountains. I've got bigger mystics to sieve. My planned trip to the US is to visit Sylvia Browne, one of the world's leading psychic phenomena. She has used her predictions to save lives and has predicted plane crashes and momentous world events. Could Sylvia be the real thing, and could she offer me a consistent, unquestionable reading?

FUTURE 1: ALICE AND ME

Predictions:
I'll go abroad three times
I'll leave my job
My girlfriend will become pregnant within the next twelve
  months
I have to decide in three months to dump her

Things I don't know but I should:
My girlfriend wants a baby
My girlfriend will prevent me from going abroad and this
  could cause the break-up of my relationship
My dad is stubborn
My girlfriend is clingy

2

Back to the past

I WAS EXPECTING the home of the Society for Psychical Research (SPR) to be a labyrinth of dusty corridors and experimentation rooms. I imagined shelves filled with cracked and battered books of the occult, concealing secrets of how to bring back an evil spirit or two from the underworld. Situated behind the neo-gothic Natural History Museum in Kensington – all turrets, looming towers and gargoyles – it seemed to be in the right part of town for paranormal activity.

Of course it was nothing like that, though the outside was promising enough, with an undertakers housed in the basement offices below. As I pressed the buzzer and was let in by Peter, the administrator of the SPR, I idly wondered whether they had succeeded in bringing people back from the grave. But inside I realised that the dead had already left for livelier places. It felt drab, cluttered and small. There was a small office with an old computer, a library and a scattering of odds and ends that didn't have any obvious function – if the SPR were a shop it would be Lidl.

After my unsettling experience at Mysteries, I headed over here to undertake some serious research. Having started on my quest for the truth about the future, I thought it wise to head straight back to the past and find out what I was up against.

I needed the help of the collected wisdom and knowledge of the Society's past psychic sleuths. This was essential before I headed off to the US to meet Sylvia Browne, one of the world's leading psychics. I had some burning questions and I needed help getting answers fast. Do psychics have off-days, like Alice? Are some psychics more powerful than others? There must be a history of psychics and fortune-tellers more reliable and convincing than Alice. I needed to find them urgently.

I figured that if these more powerful psychics had existed, then surely they would have been tested and the evidence would be lying somewhere in these dusty rooms. The SPR has been the home of scientists researching psychics and mystics for well over a century. It's also home to one of the best-stocked libraries on the supernatural in the country, if not the world, with thousands of books and journals on every aspect of the paranormal.

The SPR was set up in 1882 when Victorian Britain was breeding mediums and clairvoyants like rabbits on a spring bank holiday afternoon. The place was teeming with psychics and spiritualists claiming new powers every day. According to the official history of the SPR, a group of prominent scholars from some of the top universities wanted to get to the bottom of why the country was attracting so much psychic energy.

The first President of the SPR was Henry Sidgwick, a professor of moral philosophy at Cambridge University, who had 'enormous standing and moral authority in the intellectual circles of the day'. His chief colleagues were Frederic Myers, a classical scholar, and another intelligent fellow called Edmund Gurney. Early members included such 'prominent figures as the physicist William Barrett; the experimental physicist Lord Rayleigh; Arthur Balfour, philosopher and Prime Minister;

Gerald Balfour, classical scholar and philosopher; and Nora Sidgwick, one of the Balfour clan and wife of Henry Sidgwick, herself a mathematician and later Principal of Newnham College at Cambridge'. There was little chance, I thought, that a charlatan psychic could fool so much heavyweight IQ.

They took the investigation of the subject very seriously, applying strict scientific methods. Much of the early work involved investigating, exposing and in some cases duplicating fake phenomena. Yet occasionally they seemed to hit on cases that appeared genuine. The most famous of these was Leonora Piper, an American whose powers were brought to the attention of the SPR by William James, a pioneering psychologist and brother of novelist Henry James.

Leonora Piper, born in 1857, was considered the foremost trance medium in the history of psychical research. She was rigorously tested over more than fifteen years and holds the honour of converting Dr Richard Hodgson, the foremost psychic detective of his time, to believe that she was really speaking to spirits. He was renowned for exposing fake psychics and mediums, but with Leonora he couldn't do it. This was despite him and William James going to extraordinary lengths to ensure that she wasn't using any tomfoolery to hoodwink them.

James was first alerted to her powers by his mother-in-law Eliza Gibbens, who'd had family secrets revealed by the medium. Still unconvinced, Eliza asked Leonora to disclose the contents of a sealed letter. Mediums often used alcohol-soaked sponges to make envelopes briefly transparent (the alcohol quickly evaporated), but Leonora gave a convincing explanation while simply holding the letter in front of her. Even more baffling, it was written in Italian, a language she didn't speak. At first

James was amused that she had become a victim of a medium's trickery. He gave Eliza an explanation as to how mediums accomplished their fraud, but this did little to persuade her that Leonora was anything but genuine. The only way to sort this out was for James to uncover the fraud himself.

According to historian Troy Taylor in his book *Ghost by Gaslight*, 'When James arrived at Leonora's home, he was surprised to note the complete absence of spiritualist props – no cabinet, no red lights, no circles of chairs, no trumpets or bells.' James was intrigued. Leonora's spirit guide, it seemed, had given her the names of his father-in-law and his dead child. Yet throughout, James had sat there like a brick wall, not uttering a word or allowing her to fish for information. He was astounded.

The extra appeal of Leonora's story is that she didn't attract attention to herself. If anything she was a bit put off by being notorious for hanging out with dead people. Yet once she'd become well known for giving accurate readings, she became little more than a laboratory rat for the SPR.

Hodgson, the most disbelieving sceptic, took every precaution to bar the possibility of deception, keeping Leonora under house arrest and forbidding her to see a morning newspaper. He employed a detective to follow her around and watch possible attempts to obtain information. At one point he even shipped her all the way to Liverpool so that she was among strangers and kept under constant surveillance. But none of these precautions seemed to hinder Leonora's psychic abilities at all.

James was so taken by her powers that in 1890 he wrote in *SPR Proceedings*, Vol. VI: 'And I repeat again what I said before, that, taking everything that I know of Mrs Leonora Piper into account, the result is to make me feel as absolutely certain as

I am of any personal fact in the world that she knows things in her trances which she cannot possibly have heard in her waking state, and that the definite philosophy of her trances is yet to be found.'

When she went into a trance-like state, she could perform feats of telepathy that would make Derren Brown look like Tommy Cooper. A stranger would be led in, and told that the only communication he could have with the lady was a non-committal grunt. Leonora would then go into a long description of the stranger's life, including details known only to the person themselves. They would then leave, shaking and dumbfounded by her powers. Leonora supposedly used a number of spirit guides to help her uncover the facts, including an Indian girl called Chlorine as well as Commodore Vanderbilt, Longfellow, Lorette Penchini, J. Sebastian Bach and an actress called Mrs Siddons.

After years of research, Hodgson eventually reported in 1897 in *SPR Proceedings*, Vol. XIII: 'I cannot profess to have any doubt but that the "chief communicators" ... are veritably the personalities that they claim to be; that they have survived the change we call death, and that they have directly communicated with us whom we call living through Mrs Piper's entranced organism.'

Critics of the SPR's findings argue that Victorian Britain was still coming to terms with Darwin's theory of evolution. It was still a very religious society, even for such heavyweight thinkers. The need to investigate and find evidence for paranormal phenomena grew as the uncertainty produced by Darwin's studies on evolution intensified. If the natural world could not provide evidence that God existed, then mediums communicating with the spirit world would do so. Maybe Hodgson and James were just hearing what they wanted to hear.

There's much here to compare with Alice, such as Leonora's use of spirit guides and the suggestion that she was tuning in to people. There's also evidence to show that Leonora's powers were weakened and unreliable when she was feeling under the weather or had stresses in her life – for example, when she was looking after her dying mother she couldn't go into a trance or give readings.

Yet despite Leonora's communication with named spirits and Hodgson's belief in them, she gave a surprisingly rare insight into what was going on once all the experiments were over. It was all the more surprising because she suggested that maybe the spirits weren't real after all.

'The theory of telepathy strongly appeals to me as the most plausible and genuinely scientific solution of the problem … I do not believe that spirits of the dead have spoken through me when I have been in the trance state … It may be that they have, but I do not affirm it,' she said.

This apparently didn't surprise any of the scientists working with Leonora. They seemed to change their minds daily as to whether she was telepathic or communicating with spirits. They just couldn't decide most of the time. All the same, it was pretty impressive even if it wasn't telepathy. To the last, Leonora herself seemed to be uncertain what she was experiencing. 'Spirits of the departed may have controlled me and they may not,' she said, unhelpfully.

One thing is clear, though. Despite all the power Leonora had, she didn't predict the future once. Unlike Alice who said her spirit guides helped her to foretell events, Leonora, whether using spirits or telepathy, didn't do it. I don't understand why she wasn't tempted to use all that superhuman psychic energy at her disposal. If Matthew's right that psychics tune in to people, able only to read their past and present states because the future hasn't happened yet, then it becomes clear why Leonora didn't predict anything. Despite this, her powers of mediumship have definitely raised my expectations. If she can do all that, then I'm sure I can unearth something specific on predictions and prophecy.

Peter, the SPR administrator, seems to spend his time organising academic paranormal conferences. 'I'm not interested in the supernatural. I just, you know, work here,' he tells me flatly, with the look of an office worker earning less than his pay grade. For someone who's just filling in the hours before going home, he's a surprising fount of knowledge about modern-day academics working in the area of precognition – the scientific word for foreseeing the future. Some serious people with serious academic credentials are looking at this issue today. Peter clambers over my chair to get to an old filing cabinet which holds information on hundreds of study days. One of them last year was on the very subject of precognition, he tells me, flipping eagerly through the files. He pulls out a list of people with impressive credentials.

Physicist and Nobel Prize-winner Brian Josephson from Cambridge University heads the list, and I discover that he delivered a paper on matter/mind and the paranormal. Could this mean that science really might hold some of the answers? Maybe the future isn't a matter for spiritualism but for physics to decipher. He believes that we can 'sense' the future, which might explain paranormal experiences. Dr Edwin May from California University, who studied precognition during the Cold War, is also on the list, along with a Professor

John Smythes who looked at the neurological basis of fortune-telling. I write down their names on my notepad with a big asterisk next to them, and in big bold letters underlined four times I write the words 'CONTACT THEM'. Buoyed by the fact that I'm not on some lonely lunatic quest for the unknowable, I head back into the library more determined than before to uncover prophecies and predictions.

In a book called the *Door to the Future* from the 1960s, fellow journalist Jess Stearn claimed to have found the modern-day Nostradamus – a woman called Jeane Dixon who gave predictions from the 1930s to the 1970s. She read for politicians and celebrities and in one famous instance she told Winston Churchill that he would lose the 1947 election to Labour but would then regain power. What's disturbing about the accounts is that her predictions often appeared in newspapers dated before the events happened. So in the 1956 issue of *Parade* magazine she predicted the assassination of John F. Kennedy. Her actual prediction was that a Democrat president elected in 1960, a tall young man with blue eyes and brown hair, would die in office. She was a devout Roman Catholic and claimed her powers came from God.

Yet there are always two sides to any story. Dixon also clearly predicted that JFK wouldn't win that election and that Nixon might instead. Due to this unreliability, John Allen Paulos, a mathematician at Temple University in the US, coined what he called the 'Jeane Dixon effect', in which people loudly tout a few correct predictions and overlook the false ones. And boy did she predict some howlers. She thought that World War III would begin in 1958 over the offshore Chinese islands of Quemoy and Matsu, that labour leader Walter Reuther would run for president in 1964 and that the Soviets would land the first man on the moon.

Edgar Cayce is also considered one of America's greatest psychics. His followers maintain that Cayce was able to tap in to some sort of higher consciousness, such as God or the akasthic record – an imagined spiritual realm supposedly holding a record of all events, actions, thoughts and feelings that have ever occurred or will ever occur. Theosophists believe that the akasha is an 'astral light' containing occult records that spiritual beings can perceive by their special 'astral senses' and 'astral bodies'. Clairvoyance, spiritual insight, prophecy and many other untestable metaphysical and religious notions are made possible by tapping into the akasha.

Cayce apparently foresaw the stock market crash of 1929 and World War II, and predicted El Niño as well as global warming. Sceptics of Cayce's purported powers point out that all of the evidence for Cayce comes in the form of anecdotes and testimonials from true believers, none of which is considered scientifically rigorous. Cayce is a pretty famous guy by all accounts, and there are Edgar Cayce centres in 25 countries promoting his teachings, but there's just no proof apart from hearsay. Not convinced, I move on.

As I head deeper into the stack of books and papers in front of me, I keep stumbling across accounts of ordinary people who don't claim to have psychic powers, but who have experienced premonitions or presentiments. Some are just bad feelings or momentary glimpses into the future, while others are vivid dreams. Often linked to some dramatic event like a death or an accident, they could suggest that destructive and powerful events ahead of us might be sending back messages or echoes.

The first story I come across is that of 19-year-old Sarah Hicks, who discussed funeral arrangements with her mother and told her she wasn't afraid of dying the day before she was killed in the Hillsborough football stadium disaster on 15 April 1989. Her mother revealed that her daughter had dreamed of dying the day before her death.

I then read that in 1975, the 8.37am London underground train from Drayton Park to Moorgate, packed with commuters going to work, overshot the platform and ploughed into a dead-end tunnel. Twenty-nine passengers were killed and more than 70 injured. Shortly after the event a story emerged that four regular passengers who always sat in the first carriage of the train had moved inexplicably to the last carriage because of a strong sense of foreboding. In the crash, the front three carriages were crushed together, leaving the last three intact at the platform.

Reading on, I discover the tragic tale of Helen Peters from New Jersey in the US. In October 1967, she called the offices of British European Airways with a feeling of dread that the plane her husband was travelling on thousands of miles away in Europe was about to crash. The BEA staff were puzzled and told her not to worry, there was nothing wrong with the aeroplane. Shortly afterwards the BEA Comet crashed into the Mediterranean, killing all 66 people on board.

I feel uncomfortable and slightly unnerved by these stories. They deal with real events and seem plausible. Sure, the idea that people can sense something wrong sounds a lot like Yoda feeling a disturbance in the Force, but it also chimes with the idea that animals can sense danger too.

These and other examples are explored by an SPR scientist, Danah Zohar, in a head-churning book called *Through the Time*

Barrier: A Study in Precognition and Modern Physics. Zohar, a physicist and graduate of the Massachusetts Institute of Technology (MIT), is a clear descendant of those SPR pioneers from the 1880s – she's brainy and scientific. The most startling example of premonition she finds is the story of Marian Warren. Marian dreamed that the flight to Basel in Switzerland that she and women from her village were to take for a weekend away was destined to crash. In her dream she even saw the dead bodies of her friends littered about in the snow. She was so scared by this ghastly and vivid vision that she sold her ticket back for half price and told only one other person, afraid that she wouldn't be believed. The plane crashed, killing everyone on board. It's a horribly compelling story, yet I can't help but wonder, if Marian felt so sure the plane would crash, why she didn't tell anyone else. Danah Zohar suggests that many people who experience presentiments don't say anything because they fear ridicule. Not having experienced anything like it before, Marian may have felt that if she was wrong she'd have been responsible for ruining an expensive trip that everyone was looking forward to. Ordinary people not used to psychic powers aren't likely to start bragging about them, I guess.

Zohar then reveals that an American scientist called William Cox tried to discover whether people avoided travelling on trains that crashed. He collected information on the total number of people on each train at the time of an accident and compared these with the number of passengers who had travelled on the same train during each of the preceding seven days, and on the fourteenth, 21st and 28th day before the accident. His results show that people did in fact avoid accident-bound trains. The odds against it occurring by chance were over 100–1. Dr Jessica Utts, a statistician at the University of California, repeated the experiment recently and found exactly the same result.

Lots of examples, however, don't get us anywhere nearer an explanation. So Zohar tries to explain these phenomena using modern quantum physics. Being a scientist, she goes for the big guns: Einstein's theory of relativity and German physicist Werner Heisenberg's uncertainty principle. I make another big asterisk on my notepad to pay further attention to this area. Using Einstein's ideas, Zohar explains that time is not linear but circular. Human consciousness moves along the curve at a steady pace, but some people jump ahead in their perceptions and catch glimpses of the future. Heisenberg is then brought out of his box to explain how consciousness can leap ahead. What the theory suggests – not Heisenberg himself but an interpretation of his ideas – is that our brains, like everything else in the universe, are made up of sub-atoms. The theory suggests that sub-atoms behave unpredictably and can jump forwards and backwards over time, and that if enough of them jump forward then they might create a pattern of the future in our brains. Some scientists suggest that these sub-atoms act like waves and, like the ebb and flow of the tidal oceans, can move backwards and forwards to and from the future. Maybe premonitions are just the driftwood of tomorrow washing in on the waves of sub-atoms in our brains. Everyone knows, however, that what's washed up on a beach isn't always that useful and we can't always tell what it originally was – a possible reason why some predictions are so way out. Alice's predictions for me could have been floating about in the sub-atomic sea for so long that they'd eroded beyond all recognition before they'd arrived in her head.

Perhaps fortune-tellers are using these sub-atoms to read the future, but rather than just waiting for it to happen like ordinary people experiencing presentiments, they are somehow forcing or manipulating their sub-atoms to jump ahead.

Suddenly feeling that there might be a scientific explanation for fortune-telling, I then discover that the US government has been taking precognition and premonition seriously too. For many years the US military (and latterly the CIA) funded a secretive programme known as Stargate, which set out to investigate premonitions and the ability of mediums to predict the future. Apparently it was stopped under Clinton's defence budget cuts, but the programme had still found some statistically significant results. According to Dr Dean Radin, who worked on the project, five US government panels assessed the findings of psychic research during the 1980s and 90s and all five decided that something was going on.

Radin says that it was closed down because the effects they'd found had only limited practical applications. What he really means is that the psychics' powers under test functioned more like a carpet bomb than a precision missile. While the psychics might hit a few targets, there was also a lot of collateral damage and a hell of a lot of bombs off target. This made them too unreliable to be used by the military and the CIA.

Dr Radin became intrigued by a few fortunate soldiers' skill of glimpsing the future and using the information to ward off death in the fiercest of battles. He became sure that the hunches they were accessing were due to information moving backwards in time.

Radin tested these ideas by asking soldiers to take a lie detector test and measuring their response when they saw violent or erotic pictures. He found that they started to sense the photographs before they saw them. They weren't guessing either. The experiments showed that this was a reliable effect – they really were seeing the future.

Then I find that Dr Jessica Utts from California University, an independent auditor of the US government's paranormal research, believes that we are constantly sampling the future and using the knowledge to help us make better decisions. The data show this is happening, she says. My pen scribbles another asterisk even before I've stopped reading.

Finally, I come across some modern-day fortune-tellers who are giving sceptics a run for their money. Diane Lazarus, who recently won Channel Five's *Psychic Challenge*, can apparently see, hear and speak to spirits. She has been called on by the police, her accuracy in several murder investigations prompting senior officers to call for her psychic assistance in a number of high-profile crimes. Diane recently re-investigated the murder of twelve-year-old Muriel Drinkwater, a case that was closed 50 years ago. She was able to describe the child's final walk home from school, and her rape and shooting by a 'friend'. She identified the murderer as an old man living in Wales and the police re-opened the file.

Yet her predictive powers appear to be mainly used for professionals seeking guidance on career development, personal attainment and company growth rates, although I can find no concrete evidence of these predictions in the papers in front of me. Later at home I discover that Diane gives random celebrity predictions on her website. The one currently doing the rounds is that she has predicted that Welsh singer Charlotte Church and her rugby-playing boyfriend Gavin Henson will have a 'handsome son and a little baby "Gav"'. She goes on: 'I also see her being a brilliant mum! I see Charlotte doing a lot more on TV, even a show similar to *Blind Date*. Charlotte and Gav will also marry yet they don't feel the need to rush the wedding. I see Gav owning a rugby school in the future!'

Gosh. Well she's got a 50/50 chance of getting the baby's sex right, but all the rest of the stuff doesn't seem too impressive, considering Gav's a rugby player and Charlotte's a TV personality. I put another asterisk on my pad to remind myself to speak to Diane.

Diane's powers are matched by another TV psychic, Sally Morgan. She read for the late Princess Diana (who apparently talks to her from beyond the grave), Robert de Niro, George Michael and Bob Geldof. Her predictions are spot-on, according to *Daily Mail* journalist Danny Penman. He went for a reading and she told him that he would go on holiday to Greece – he'd already booked the trip. 'It was the beginning of a long list of insights that left me physically shaking and chilled to the core,' he says. During Danny's reading, Sally was accurate, detailed, and had a long list of dead relatives queuing up to speak to him. She told him about a family argument that only a member of the family could have known about, and revealed that his girlfriend was moving to Bristol, which she was.

In 2005 Sally's abilities were scientifically tested by Professor Gary Schwartz, who works as a professor of psychology and psychiatry at Yale University in the US. After a series of tests, Professor Schwartz commented that 'Sally is one of the most accurate mediums I have ever come across. I would rate her as one of the top five in the world.' Professor Schwartz was so confident in Sally's ability that he has even named a hypothesis after her.

I scribble yet another asterisk and then make a list of all my asterisks under one big asterisk. I suddenly have a long list of work to do, and still the future isn't any closer. I scratch my head, hoping to kick-start some of my sub-atoms to get a glimpse of where all this is taking me, but nothing comes. I sigh. Maybe we're all just gullible and being taken for one long cosmic ride, but on the other hand maybe something really odd is happening out there and we're all so damned sceptical and rational that we just can't accept it. My pendulum of doubt and belief is still swinging wildly back and forth and I don't know which side to come down on.

There's one person, however, who will help me make up my mind – Sylvia Browne, the world-famous Psychic Queen. I urgently need to get a reading from her if I'm going to start making any sense of this at all. Next stop USA.

3

The Psychic Queen

I'M HEADING TO CAMPBELL, California, heart of Silicon Valley and one of the richest areas in the US, with a collective IQ that would probably give Harvard an anxiety attack. In the middle of all this technological advancement, Sylvia Browne, one of the world's most controversial and well-known psychics, has based her headquarters. Sylvia's psychic abilities are in such demand that there's a four-to-five-year waiting list for a reading – and that's just over the phone. But there is one benefit – you'll have plenty of time to save up the $850 (£600) price tag for a half-hour's chat. It puts Alice's £35 fee into perspective. For that kind of money, you'd expect a prediction of life-changing potential.

But I haven't got four to five years to wait, and nor it seems do a lot of people. To meet the demand, every few months Sylvia runs a Spiritual Salon for 30 people so they can listen to her talk about spirituality and life after death, and, most importantly, get to ask three personal questions. The opportunity to see the Psychic Queen in action was too tempting, so I booked up straight away for a cool $1,000 (£700).

I had to find out the secret of Sylvia Browne's success and whether she really is the world's most powerful psychic. She's already made some pretty heady predictions, foretelling that in

2018 extraterrestrials will introduce themselves to us for the first time – although Sylvia herself has already lunched with an alien, telling her fans that he 'didn't know what to do with a comb and tried to drink his Jell-O. Bless his sweet heart.' Sylvia didn't manage to get the design for his spaceship, nor reveal what he was doing having dinner with her and not the US President.

So, is she the greatest psychic there has ever been? At last, I thought, as I boarded the plane at Heathrow, I'm about to start getting some serious answers.

Next morning, jet-lagged and bloated following an American-sized breakfast, I head for the courtesy minibus that the Prune Plaza Hotel in Campbell puts on to take Sylvia Browne's clients to her HQ. As it's the hotel recommended by the Browne Corporation, I expect it to be filled with the blue-rinse brigade of America's finest psychic addicts. But I have my first surprise.

Inside, applying the finishing touches to her make-up, is Sandra, a sales rep from the mid-west. She's pretty, young and funny. I've spent the morning making myself look as middle-American as possible: boring shoes, conservative shirt (with neatly fastened top button), straight Clark Kent hairstyle. Compared with Sandra, I look a little strange. On the ride over, she tells me that spending the money on Sylvia's salon has been a big decision for her and her husband.

'We've had trouble adopting a child from Vietnam, and I wanted to ask Sylvia whether we are doing the right thing. We have already spent $20,000 on the process. I also have chronic back and neck neuralgia that causes real painful migraines. I need some advice with that too.'

'And Sylvia can help with all that?' I ask.

'Oh sure.'

Arriving at Sylvia's HQ, a squat brick building off Winchester Boulevard, I discover that Sandra is not the exception. Near the front of the seminar room sit a couple of attractive twenty-something women, and behind them a 50-year-old woman from Denver, who's so excited to be here her face is on permanent full-beam. I notice near the front a tense-looking woman who glances sharply around the room and doesn't talk to anyone, which is odd because everyone else is chatting. This is possibly the friendliest bunch of strangers I've shared a room with since ... well, I can't remember when. I'm from England – we don't talk to strangers because they might do something embarrassing like talk back.

I start chatting to a woman called Justine and her dad, Bob, who are sitting in the row in front and have travelled all the way from Alaska. Bob's not supposed to be here. He's taken the place of his wife who's got a bad stomach. Justine wants advice from Sylvia about her daughter, Becky, who has a rare congenital disease that has slowed her development, affected her sense of balance and left her unable to walk. Becky's illness has taken over Justine's life. She spends most of her time and money seeking medical consultations, some from alternative practitioners, such as a man who claimed he could help Becky by firing bio-energy at her. Justine looks like she's at her wits' end and has loaded today with a lot of expectation.

A hush descends on the room and the 30 gathered disciples go still. I half expect some to stand as Sylvia appears from the back of the room and hobbles to the front, nursing a painful hip. She squeezes herself into a large comfy armchair on a raised platform.

Sylvia has blonde hair and a husky voice that gets into your pores like treacle. She starts talking and doesn't stop for three hours. She reels off her philosophy on life and life after death. It's based on what she's seen with her own eyes 'on the other side' and from her spirit guide Francine. The whole seminar room is in awe of her, and people laugh hysterically as she cracks jokes:

'When people tell me there's no devil, I say yes there is, I married him, he's in Chicago.'

In the flesh, Sylvia's down-to-earth with a well-developed sense of humour and liberal politics. She peppers us with pronouncements such as 'Bush is a monster', and 'Don't blame gays for Aids', and 'Stop picking on the immigrants'. She's sick of the Bible making women appear bad. She hates dogma and Christian fundamentalists throughout the USA. So far, so right on, but not quite what I was expecting. She tells everyone at one point that you should 'Be very careful about who you hate in this life because you just may come back as that'.

Then I get my second big surprise of the day. Until now, I've tended to agree with sceptics who criticise mystics for never revealing what it's like in heaven. Instead they tell us about domestic trivia, such as 'You're going to have new windows' or 'You're going to get married'. Despite their hotline to the other side, they never seem able to answer the big questions. Not Sylvia. If anything, she offers too much detail.

'When we die we go to the Orientation Centre. After that it's the Hall of Wisdom, which has a big scanner and 3-D TV so you can sit there and watch your whole life unfold.' She jokes that if she sees herself having sex, she'll act dumb and say it isn't her. This is followed by more howls of laughter.

Coming back down to earth, she gives us some life advice. She tells us to get away from dark entities in our lives. These are people who drain us and make us depressed, even if they are our 'flesh and blood', she says. 'You don't have to be mean or hateful. Just be busy. They suck the life out of you. Keep good things away from you. Everything they do is right, and you do is wrong. They are always right. If they stab you, it's your fault, you ran into it!'

People nod vigorously and a woman tells Sylvia that her parents are dark entities, to which Sylvia responds by telling her to keep away from them.

Then it suddenly stops being funny.

Justine sticks up her hand. Bob glances at her quickly. Her voice is near breaking. She's trying to contain herself, but she sounds all the more desperate for it. Justine's need for answers about her sick child is urgent.

'If negative people around us make us sick, I … I don't want to get too personal, but I have a sick child, and I am the main person in her life. Am I making her sick?'

The room is silent. Even a woman at the front who has giggled at everything manages to restrain her nervous laugh. Sylvia sounds tender, but seems a little thrown.

'Oh no, no, no. You can't start that. Don't do that. That's their theme. That is what they came in to perfect. But you, you could … you and the child could have picked that the child would be sick in order for you to learn patience to take care of her. I am talking about people with an onset. You see what I'm saying? No white entity causes illness. We're all white entities here. You don't think a dark entity is going to come to one of these [salons], do you?' Everyone laughs, thankful that Sylvia has managed to ease the tension.

She moves swiftly on. She reassures everyone that unless it's your time, you will not die. No one can make your passing happen more quickly. This is the reason for people walking away from plane crashes, she says. 'I had a husband who I told every night "Go to the light". He didn't go.' The room roars with laughter again.

According to Sylvia, everyone here has had 40 lives, including me. This will be our last. We aren't going to be reincarnated again, and frankly we shouldn't care because dying is like going home.

My head is spinning from this worldview that seems to mix and match Christian and Buddhist beliefs, but with a reassuringly American ingredient. It seems, according to Sylvia, that before we are reincarnated we sign a contract about what our next life is going to be like. It can only be in the US, the world capital of litigation, that you have to sign on the dotted line before you're even born. I wonder, absentmindedly, whether anyone's thought about suing God.

Then Sylvia begins to reveal her ideas about free will and prediction. I edge forward in my seat.

The only time we have free will is on the other side, before we are reincarnated and before we write out a new contract for our next life. She jokes that it's the worst possible time to be given free will because everyone is in such a state of utter bliss that they don't think through the consequences of their choices. It sounds like trying to cross the road while high on drugs.

'When they asked me what body I wanted, what in the world was that about? Sturdy. I don't know. Just give me something. I'm playing cards over here, don't bother me.'

Impulsively, I stick my hand up.

Sylvia looks at me and smiles. I've been given a green light.

'If the courses of our lives have already been charted and written down,' I ask, 'how can you change them through prediction?'

Expecting a simple answer, I get a shock. Everyone in the room, and I mean everyone, looks around at me as though I'm a simpleton. 'No, it can't be changed, it's in the contract!' they shout. Some smile at me as though I'm a bit slow, others roll their eyes. I'm taken aback by the response. I've clearly missed something. And that something is that everyone here already knows what Sylvia thinks. They're the reason why her numerous books that outline every detail of life after death are frequently on the *New York Times* bestsellers list. They already know that all life choices end before you're even born. D'oh! Every dumb-ass knows that!

When all the fuss has died down, Sylvia explains:

'You don't change them, you go through them.'

I'm still none the wiser, so she tries again.

'The more spiritual you get, the more the edge comes off. Say your chart reads accident. Okay, you could have a fender bender, rather than a full-scale head-on crash. It shaves off. It's one of the reasons to become more spiritual,' Sylvia tells me.

Act like a saint on earth and you can ease life's unexpected bumps. I don't get it. I thought being spiritual meant you'd have a better time on the other side.

I try again.

'When you're predicting someone's future, are you seeing it or talking to your spirit guide?'

'I open my mouth and it just flows out,' she says.

And then she moves on to deal with a woman who keeps dreaming of being burnt.

'You were burnt in a former life, honey, in one of those set-tler huts.'

The woman seems pleased, almost smug, as though she just got an A grade from the teacher.

After lunch everyone's excited and tense. It's time for our personal questions. This is our chance to ask Sylvia anything. This is the reason why everyone here has parted company with a small fortune.

The tense woman on the front row starts to speak. She's in her early fifties and looks miserable and crestfallen.

'I want to ask about a relationship. When will I see my granddaughters and my son ...' She doesn't finish the sentence, but it turns out she hasn't seen her granddaughters in four years. Sylvia asks, 'Who's the woman behind all this?'

The woman shrieks out 'My daughter-in-law' before burst-ing into tears.

But then Sylvia turns up the heat.

'Yeah, she's a bitch.'

Christ.

The woman agrees, but Sylvia's on a roll: 'Let me tell you this, your son is to blame and pardon the expression, but he's a pussy.'

'Absolutely,' shouts the woman, her voice suddenly shrill and hoarse at the same time.

But the woman shouldn't worry, as Sylvia says she'll be seeing her granddaughters again at Christmas. She then tells her to eat more protein, suggesting that her health problems aren't caused by her diabetes but because she eats too many carbohydrates.

It goes on.

Further along the row an attractive young woman in her late twenties tells Sylvia she came to see her a few years ago.

She'd spent her first $1,000 to find out which of the two guys she was interested in was the right one for her. 'The guy in the south,' Sylvia had responded. The girl is back to thank her for getting it right, but now wants to know why the boy in the south hasn't contacted her.

'Why don't you phone him?' croaks Sylvia.

'I don't have his phone number,' the girl reveals.

'Oh, you'll find it,' says Sylvia, not realising that the girl's worried because he hasn't called in two years.

The only relief Sylvia can give her is that the man has called, but he puts the phone down before speaking.

'So even though it's been so long, it doesn't matter? He's still got my number?' asks the girl.

'No, it doesn't matter,' Sylvia replies, then adds as a parting shot: 'Don't lose hope.'

Another young woman down the front is shrieking that she's scared of everything and she's convinced that tomorrow will be her last day because she'll fall off a cliff. Sylvia tells her she'll live until she's 89, so she should stop worrying. Sylvia's already on to the next person before I can catch my breath.

Another woman is told that her pit bull terrier will turn on her. She just wanted to know whether she should get another dog to keep this one company. The woman bursts into tears. Later, at the end of the salon, I watch her spend hundreds of dollars on various CD sets of Sylvia's.

Then it's Justine's turn, and I feel an urgent desire to leave. I look down at my lap, hoping it will be over quickly.

'My daughter Becky has global developmental delays. But we are seeing some progress with her,' says Justine.

'I do too,' shoots back Sylvia.

Justine latches on to this like a mother who's been on the receiving end of too much bad news. 'Do you?' she says, desperately. 'You see a lot more progress with her?'

Sylvia nods.

Justine starts crying. 'I'm not going to be able to talk. Are the doctors ...?'

'On the right track, yes,' says Sylvia, calmly.

'Therapeutically,' Justine says, taking a moment to recover. 'We've been bringing her to all kinds of therapies. I'd like someone to take her to Disneyland for fun instead of all this hard ...'

Sylvia: 'Just take her to Disneyland and stop all this other crap!'

Justine: 'Stop it ... let her body ...'

Sylvia: 'Her body will heal. It will wear her out and you out.'

Justine: 'Is she going to progress enough to have a life?'

Sylvia: 'Absolutely.'

Justine bursts into tears again and asks about her dad's health. Sylvia prescribes saw palmetto for his prostate and tells Justine that Becky's spirit guide is called Catherine.

Bob puts his arm around Justine. But the focus has already moved on to a woman who thinks she was Joan of Arc in a former life. Sylvia's having none of it, and explains that she was Jean, Joan's sister. The woman's not too happy about this.

'Why, cos you wanna be Joan of Arc,' Sylvia suggests sarcastically.

I stop listening. I'm next. The woman to my left, who seems like some tough businesswoman from Texas, smirks as I keep nervously checking my notes.

I take a large gulp and I'm off.

'My sister and her daughter have had predictions of their deaths in water by an astrologer. Is this true?' I say, to general murmurs around the room. Everyone, including Sylvia, is genuinely and visibly shocked by what my sister has been told.

'It's just wrong, they will live long lives,' says Sylvia.

'But how can they say that kind of thing?' I ask, sounding exasperated.

'I don't know why,' Sylvia tells me. 'That's just terrible.'

I really wasn't expecting so much sympathy.

'If they do say that kind of thing,' Sylvia continues, 'they should warn them about what boat not to get on and what not to do, you see what I'm saying? It's just like if you have ever seen me on TV that time when I told a girl that whatever you do, don't get in a red sports car. If they can tell you that, they can tell you how to avoid it,' she says.

Feeling Sylvia's given it her best shot, I ask my next question.

'When will my girlfriend become pregnant?' I'm sure Nikki would be shocked by this question, because it's not on the cards. I'm just intrigued what Sylvia will say. I'm not disappointed.

'God, what's the time!' she shouts out. Half the salon looks around at me with big cheesy grins, the other half sighs as though I've just wheeled the baby in with me. 'She could get pregnant right away,' she says, and tells me we'll be having a baby girl. There's a collective 'aaah' from everyone, and even Sandra looks around and gives me a cheeky smile.

I'm half smiling myself, but I've got to get in my next question before Sylvia, with her frenetic pace, decides to move on. I ask whether I should have a change in career, and she tells me that I'll go into electronics in two years.

'And my health?'

'You've got a bad back and weak left knee. Take 200mg of lecithin.'

And that's it. Before I've had the chance to wipe the perspiration from my brow, Sylvia's doling out business advice to the Texan.

I don't listen. I'm trying to think of a way to break it to Nikki that somehow we have conceived while I was more than 5,000 miles away.

Sandra is now asking Sylvia her questions, and I take a keen interest. Sylvia tells her to avoid eating dairy to get rid of her headaches, but Sandra, a sweet but feisty woman, answers back. She's the first person to do this, and the room bristles at her audacity.

'I pretty much don't,' she says.

'Nothing,' barks back Sylvia. Sandra tries a different tack.

'Is the spasm caused by a past life? Would I benefit from past life regression?'

'No,' Sylvia barks again, visibly irritated. 'It's just a body allergy to dairy. You can't have one drop.'

On the issue of adopting, Sylvia tells Sandra to try China, despite the fact that there are huge waiting lists and Sandra has already spent thousands of dollars on the project in Vietnam.

'What about the Philippines?' suggests Sandra.

'You can try but I think you'll have better luck with China,' she says curtly. One thing I've learnt is that you don't answer Sylvia back.

A brief meditation session follows, and then just when things can't get any more weird, Michael, one of Sylvia's helpers, walks up to her, puts his hands on her forehead and pushes her back into her chair. Sylvia kicks back her heels until she's lying prone. She has now, quite suddenly, morphed into her spirit guide Francine. Some people in the audience are so awed by the change in Sylvia that it's as though God himself has just arrived at the salon. Apart from the lack of wisecracks, the only difference I can see is that Sylvia's now holding a cushion over her stomach. To what purpose I have no idea, but it's intriguing all the same.

'Nice to see you and to be with you all. Sylvia doesn't have time to get into this but the book will be out next year, in your time, the end of the year,' Francine tells us.

Francine has arrived to inform us about the topic of Sylvia's next book – the mystical traveller. Becoming a mystical traveller is quite an honour, Francine tells us. Yet, and this is intriguing, to become one you have to give up your free will.

'This is where you will say to God that you will do anything. You could be sent to other planets and anywhere that needs your help. Your whole life will change ... The mantle will be dropped on you by the mother god, and once on you, you'll receive a sword yourself to cut through negativity and you will inherit the golden key of fortitude, psychic and healing ability,' she says.

It sounds like a spiritual division of NATO's rapid reaction force, a psychic James Bond being parachuted into troublesome hotspots around the world. I get the idea that you travel mystically in your head to these far-out places as a kind of spiritual superhero. Francine tells us that to fully understand the commitment of becoming a mystical traveller, you have to read Sylvia's book.

And then, quite suddenly, Francine is gone and Sylvia sits back up – our time at the salon is at an end. But before we're jettisoned back outside into the California sunshine, Sylvia gives us her final disclaimer:

'Take from today what you want. And leave the rest. If you don't agree that is fine. This isn't a cult,' she warns us.

We head back to the hotel and I arrange to have dinner with Sandra, Bob and Justine later that evening. They are genuinely lovely and caring individuals and I spend a fun night sharing stories. Getting to know them drives my fascination for what they think Sylvia's advice is giving them.

After dinner, and while walking past the café tables in the balmy evening along Santana Row Boulevard, California's very own slice of the Med, I begin to replay the stories I've heard about Sylvia Browne since I booked the salon. I've found well-documented evidence that she has got some predictions wrong on television shows, and I wonder why this hasn't dented her popularity.

Most dramatically, in 2002 Sylvia told the parents of Shawn Hornbeck, an eleven-year-old who went missing while riding his bike to his friend's house in Missouri, that he was buried beneath two jagged boulders in Nevada. The boy had already been missing for more than three years and his parents were desperate. Sylvia's advice was given live on *The Montel Williams Show*. His parents were devastated. Six months after Sylvia's advice, and four years after he went missing, Hornbeck was found alive in the suburban apartment of his abductor, Michael Devlin, in St Louis, Missouri. Despite this huge and very public error, her books are still bestsellers and ordinary people like Sandra, Justine and Bob still travel hundreds of miles across the States, paying $1,000 dollars each to spend a few hours in her company.

Shawn's family were clear about the impact of Sylvia's prediction. 'Hearing that was one of the hardest things we ever had to hear,' Greg Akers, Shawn's stepfather, told CNN's Anderson

Cooper during a special programme about the case. The Akers admitted that the search for Shawn was diverted based on the false information that Sylvia had provided.

Then there's the case of Opal Jo Jennings, who went missing in 1991. Sylvia told her grandmother on live TV that she'd been sold into slavery but was still alive in Japan. Yet four years later her body was found near Fort Worth, Texas. Her post-mortem revealed that she'd been killed soon after her abduction.

These stories aren't just exceptions. Former US computer technician Robert S. Lancaster became so incensed with the Opal Jo Jennings case, feeling that Sylvia was preying on the weak and vulnerable, that he set up a website, www.stopsylvia.com.

'It really offends me that she gives that kind of advice to the parents of murdered children,' he tells me when I call him up a few months after my visit to see Sylvia. His voice sounds oddly slurred, but forceful and passionate. 'This woman has to be stopped. She is not saying she is a fraud, she is saying she is a psychic. It is disgusting.'

Sylvia has threatened legal action to have his website closed down, but to no avail. 'If she wants to sue me for slander and libel, under US law she'd have to prove that the things that were said about her were false and that I knew them to be false. She can't prove any statements on my website are false because I have proof for all of them, and she does not want to be put in a position where she'd have to prove her psychic abilities in a court of law,' he tells me.

The website is still up and running and now Lancaster is receiving letters from former Sylvia fans, thanking him for opening their eyes about her. 'It's very gratifying to know that the information on my site has changed their minds,' he says.

Yet I've noticed that in the past few months he hasn't added any new information to the site.

'How's the website going?' I ask him, expecting to be told that he's even managed to convert Sylvia.

'I'm in hospital,' he tells me.

'What?'

'I had a stroke last August, and I've been in hospital ever since.'

'I'm so sorry, Robert,' I reply. 'I didn't know.' I'm shocked and moved at the effort to which Robert Lancaster will go to expose what he feels are Sylvia Browne's misguided acts, talking to me from his hospital bed.

'Thank you,' he says, with what I now realise is a huge effort to communicate.

Walking back along Santana Row with Justine in the warm night air after Sylvia's salon, I tell her about Shawn Hornbeck. I'm surprised that Justine hasn't heard the story before. She's visibly upset by it.

'Oh my God, I didn't know that. If I was told that Becky was dead, six months later there would be nothing left of me,' she says. Then she pauses, and looks like she's going to boil over.

'She'd better be damn right about Becky,' she says with real anger.

I've placed a doubt in Justine's mind. We walk on in silence. She's quiet, frowning. The mood has become brittle. I don't think she likes me any more.

Suddenly the frown lines flatten out and she excuses Sylvia's mistake with a vehemence that surprises me.

'Well Sylvia herself says that she's not perfect. She's only human. She's not God! She doesn't have "God" tattooed across her forehead,' she tells me, putting me in my place. 'I would say her accuracy rate has a high average.'

We come to the edge of the pavement and wait for the traffic to clear. Before we cross, she glances over.

'I would so not like to be that mum she told her kid was dead,' she says quietly.

But Justine still believes in Sylvia's powers. She tells me that she saw Sylvia at an event in her home town a few years ago, where the psychic revealed that Justine's cousin had died with a hole in his back. When Justine repeated this to the boy's father, his face dropped in shock and amazement.

'Only he knew that my cousin had been hit in the back by a car,' Justine says with a finality that dares me to contradict her. I don't. I don't know what to say.

We drive back to the hotel. I'm next to Bob up front in the SUV, and I lean back to tell Justine how when I get home I'm going to try to make her special mussels dish that she told me about over dinner. I like these two people a lot. I think that maybe the strength of their belief is only a reflection of how desperate their personal circumstances are. But most of the others who had attended the salon didn't seem that desperate. I still don't get it.

Outside the hotel, we all hug and say goodbye, and they wish me well. Then they remember that I'm going to have a little baby daughter. They're so happy for me and their goodwill is so infectious that, Christ, I nearly believe it. I'm also tempted, despite the eight-hour time difference, to call Nikki and break the good news to her.

But instead I head indoors with Sandra and arrange to meet her tomorrow before she goes home. There are still some things

Sylvia said that are bothering me, and I'm hoping she'll be able to straighten me out.

I'm concerned about the contract that we have to write before we're reincarnated. There was a suggestion in Sylvia's salon that we have asked for what happens to us in our lives, including tragic and unpleasant events. It's like when Sylvia said that Becky became ill so Justine could be a good mother. This means that the disappearance of Madeleine McCann would be justified as Kate McCann having agreed to this tragedy in her pre-life contract, just so she could experience suffering and her spirit could grow stronger.

I put these ideas to Sandra the following day as we wander along Los Gatos Creek near to the hotel. It's early morning but the sun is already intense. The locals are out enjoying the fine weather, but Sandra and I hardly notice it. We're too busy brooding about the day before.

Sandra doesn't get the idea that we write contracts before we're born. Yet she's religious and very spiritual and tries desperately to square a lot of stubborn circles.

'Why do we have to suffer so much pain in order to grow spiritually?' I ask her.

'Struggle makes people grow stronger. People in crisis are often stronger when they come out the other end,' she says.

'It can also ruin people's lives. You think Kate McCann is somehow spiritually stronger and more able to cope with life because her daughter has been abducted?' I ask.

Sandra frowns at this. 'I don't know,' is all she offers. Her infectious good humour has disappeared. I'm ruining her Sunday morning walk.

But then she hardens and tells me in an annoyed voice that 'We aren't going to figure it out on this walk,' which is a none-too-subtle hint for me to drop the subject. We carry on walking and I don't mention it again.

After saying goodbye to Sandra, I spend the rest of the day just walking around in the California sun. As I walk along the street next to my hotel, a long straight road that has no end in sight, I worry about Sylvia's salon and what it means for my quest. The people at the salon thought the advice they'd been given justified the huge expense. Most of them believed they were being helped, but it still feels as though these people have exchanged a certain amount of their free will for an unhealthy and dependent relationship with Sylvia.

I reach a crossroads and stand alongside a gigantic SUV pumping out aggressive R'n'B music, waiting for the green light. I look back down the road with no end, and worry whether my own journey has a finishing line. The green light flashes and I walk on, trying to decide whether there were any benefits to Sylvia's salon. Maybe Justine was given good advice to stop all the alternative treatments and spend her money on doing fun things with Becky instead, but she thought that anyway. She told me. She's just glad that Sylvia backed her up and gave her the confidence to do it. For Justine, Sylvia was positive reinforcement – is that what it means to be the world's most controversial living psychic?

I'm going to keep a close watch on my own predictions. If Nikki becomes pregnant in the next nine months, or I give up the last ten years of journalistic endeavour to become an electronics engineer, well, then I will personally write a full and glowing endorsement of Sylvia's psychic powers. Until then, I'll just keep on searching.

FUTURE 2: SYLVIA AND ME

~

Predictions:
Nikki will become pregnant while I'm in the US
I'll take up a career in electronics

Things I don't know but I should:
I have a bad back and a weak left knee

4

It's a psychic challenge

A WOMAN CALLED TINA is telling me a story of such accurate psychic power that I feel like falling over from the shock. Either that or I've been putting away too many beers in the fifteen-minute interval during the Diane Lazarus psychic show. I'm in a hotel function room in Swansea on Wales's south coast and I'm increasingly impressed with the locals' enthusiastic drinking at the bar. I've decided there's nothing else for it but to join in and drink my bodyweight in beer. Loosening up my inhibitions, I hope, might create a better connection to the spirit world. It's worth a try.

After my recent trip to the US to see Sylvia Browne and her adoring fans, I've been pining for some real Welsh bluntness, and Tina, a local woman who I've randomly sat next to, doesn't mince her words.

'Well, that was a pile of shit, wasn't it?' she tells me when the first half is over.

I actually thought it was quite good. I'm not too sure yet if anything that Lazarus said was psychic, but she spoke with such certainty to dead people that she deserved serious respect for pulling it off with such aplomb.

I've come to the show for a quick and dirty guerrilla operation to check out the potential of Channel Five's *Psychic*

Challenge winner. Apparently, against eight other psychics, and on TV, she was able to find a 'dead body' (well, okay, a boy called Sam who was very much alive) on a beach in ten minutes, and beat a professional tracker to locate another body in a wood in just seven minutes. Half an hour later the other psychics were still running around bumping into trees without a clue. Even Professor Chris French, a psychologist and sceptic from Goldsmith's College, London, who I called before I made my way to Swansea, told me that he has no idea how she found the body so quickly. He was a judge on the show – or rather the voice of reason.

'It's tricky being a sceptic on a programme like that. It's a hiding to nothing, as most of the audience are people who believe in psychic ability,' he tells me, adding that he believed in psychics when he was younger, and thinks the world would be a far more interesting place if they were real. He has yet to find any evidence, though.

He saw no deliberate cheating on the programme, but witnessed some pretty intriguing things. He was surprised by Diane's performance in beating the tracker to the body in the wood, saying on the programme that 'you've got to be impressed by that; and the question then is: could she actually do it again? If she could, then we might be on to something.'

And then she did by finding the boy on the beach.

He's a jolly chap, Professor French. Not at all like the bitter and twisted curmudgeons I expect all sceptics to be. He's very serious underneath it all, though, reminding me that TV challenges lack the rigour of real scientific experiments but seem to have more influence over people's beliefs. Lightweight TV as irrefutable scientific evidence – it just doesn't bear thinking about. But, in the name of rigorous lightweight journalistic investigation, I have to.

'I just commented on the performances of the psychics, I wasn't there to set the tasks. It would have made for a dull TV programme otherwise,' Professor French explained. 'It was a fun programme, but having a sceptic on the programme can do more harm than good in that it gives them an air of legitimacy.'

'So why are TV programmes so bad at doing science?' I ask.

'There were no proper experiment controls in place, and the crew or target could have been cueing her in unconsciously to the location of the boy,' he says.

I'm unsure what he means by unconscious cueing. Maybe Sam or the crew had left a trail of footprints in the sand, or a camera team was poised to capture the moment when he was found, hinting at his location. But that's all just speculation. There are no firm facts.

Despite his reservations, however, Professor French has got me thinking. If he, a worldly-wise and very clever man, can't work out how Lazarus was so effective in the find-the-body tests, then maybe she's got something. Coming to Swansea for the Diane Lazarus show is my chance to find out.

What's unnerving me most about Lazarus' performance so far is the unnecessary challenges she gives herself in front of so many people. The 300-strong crowd have left photos and pieces of jewellery on a tray for Lazarus to pick up during the show. Then she points to a member of the audience and just starts talking to a dead person associated with the item in her hand. When she does this, I feel like she's walking the plank blindfold. Yet just before she plunges off the edge, she pulls off

an impressive back flip to avoid the circling and snapping sceptics below. It's impressive and the audience love her for it.

'Please don't talk to me, don't give me any information. I
don't want it,' she tells the crowd.

I just don't understand how she can get up there and do it.
Her confidence is overwhelming, and once she has said the
name of a person in spirit she won't back down. I'm completely spellbound – heart in my throat one minute, brain in
my stomach the next.

She seems to come up with names that people can relate to.
One woman starts crying when Lazarus reveals that her son will
be okay, mouthing to her friend 'How did she know that?'

'I'm struggling with my breath,' she suddenly tells another
woman after she's picked up a photo, before revealing that
the man in the picture was her father and he has passed over.
Lazarus reveals that he died three years ago, had a dry sense
of humour, was energetic, and his death came as a shock. The
woman in the audience seems impressed.

'I feel he wants you to be happy. You were very close to your
dad. He'll be there for you every minute,' she adds.

Then Lazarus asks, 'Who's CA? Ca?'

'That's me!' says the woman.

'Rest in peace. I think he's done enough,' says Lazarus. Then
she goes on to tell us she would never have entered *Psychic
Challenge* unless her psychic powers had told her she would
win.

Later on she gets stuck when a group of people in the back
row refuse to acknowledge the dead person that Lazarus has
apparently spoken to on their behalf.

'You'll get home and you'll remember who Myra is,' she tells
them.

I feel like I'm back at school and the cool kids on the back row are getting a bollocking. It's embarrassing. I really wish they would just say that Myra was a dead aunt or a goldfish, rather than the old stony-faced routine. It's a bit tedious. Poor old Diane. At least she's trying to speak to dead people. They're just drinking beer, I think, as I take another pull of my pint of Guinness.

Lazarus also has a fascinating habit of talking out loud to the person in spirit, as though she's having a chat on a hands-free mobile. It's transfixing as she mumbles asides to her invisible friend.

'Yeah, okay, right,' she says suddenly over her left shoulder.

Yet despite positive reactions from members of the audience I chat to during the interval, Tina's having none of it.

'I've not convinced at all. She did seem to have one or two things. She was focused on the name Myra. It's not like she gives up. But it's a lot of guesswork. If you're good at reading people, psychology and body language, then that's how you do it.'

Fair enough. But I'm still wondering whether Lazarus can predict the future. Tina has an opinion on that too.

'I paid her £20 for a reading. She told me I had a wonky fridge, that I needed new clothes pegs, and that I would have an affair with a man I was involved in a car accident with. I went home and told my husband and he burst out laughing. He knows I would never do anything like that. She told me I'd also break my leg in the accident. Well, it's still alright, isn't it?' she says, pulling out her leg in front of her and chuckling.

Tina, in full stride, isn't done with Lazarus yet.

'She also told me that my maternal grandmother was watching over me, but she was a deeply unpleasant and bitterly jealous woman, so I doubt it.'

Her friend, Wendy, who is the reason why Tina's in the audience tonight, is shaking her head at Tina's outrageous scepticism.

'But I've heard her on the radio and she says some amazing things,' Wendy implores.

'Yeah, but I mean it's just general statements, isn't it?' shoots back Tina.

Tina seems the kind of woman who would give the arch-sceptic Richard Dawkins a bloody nose for not being hard enough on psychics.

I idly ask whether she's had any psychic readings that have been accurate, expecting her to roll her eyes and say that she just goes for the crack of it.

'I went to see this psychic down the Mumbles Road once. I went in sceptical. I wasn't going to give her any information. I was terrified of my daughter being hurt in an accident as she was always doing risky things. The woman picked up on it straight away and said she'd be fine. It freaked me out. I'd never told anyone about my fears. Not even my best friend,' Tina says, sounding deadly serious.

'Then she said my mother knows about the rose. I had no idea what she was talking about. But she didn't back off. She kept on saying "Your mother knows about the rose". Then suddenly I remembered. I was going to give my mum a rose before she died, and I didn't. I burst into tears.'

This is when I nearly fall over, sitting down. I'm genuinely intrigued and seriously don't know what to make of Tina's sudden about-face from ardent sceptic to full-on psychic believer.

Clearly, it's the accuracy of the psychic precisely naming the flower that moved Tina. She doesn't appear to be a woman who easily believes, so her sudden conviction that she found a real psychic leaves me feeling that my quest has been given a real boost.

The second half of Lazarus's show is a carbon copy of the first. She tells one woman that there will be two cakes at her daughter's birthday party – one from the local shop and the other from the cake stall in the sky, courtesy of her dead grand-dad. Someone else has a kitchen with a hard surface, while she tells another lady that her granddad liked dancing.

At the end of the show, Tina's off again, giving Diane's per-formance a roasting. She hasn't noticed Diane's lawyer husband right behind us, arms folded, looking unhappy at me sitting there with a notepad jotting down Tina's loud expletives at Diane's expense. She's proved herself on TV and you don't need a pesky journalist coming down and ruining the show. It's understandable.

But I want to ask Diane herself about her psychic powers, why she was so good at finding the bodies but didn't do well on some of the other tests on the programme. When she tried to tell whether a group of women were pregnant or not, she got only one out of ten, and she failed to match the right foot-ball boots to the right player.

Professor French also wanted to take it further and under-take a strict scientific test on Lazarus. But, of course, she wasn't interested. When you've accepted and won a TV challenge that anoints you the top psychic, why bother? Professor French says as much himself: 'She doesn't need to test her abilities again; they have been proven on a TV programme. I can see it from her point of view.'

But before I track down Lazarus, I've found some problems with the format of *Psychic Challenge*.

John Jackson, who set up the skeptics.org website, undertook a detailed analysis of the show. For him, being a sceptic is not about being mean and brutish. 'We adhere to the true sceptical approach, i.e. a scientific evidence-based approach to subjects and not the denialist/debunking type of approach that often gets mistaken for scepticism,' he explains to me.

In the pilot episode of the series, the psychics had to find a body in the boot of one car out of a choice of 50. It sounds impossible, yet three out of the six psychics got it right. This seems pretty impressive until you realise that the psychics could disqualify cars because some, according to Jackson, were 'in awkward places to get to, such as parked with their boot facing the wall. This would make it hard for anyone to get into them and, of course, difficult for the camera crew to film the opening of the boot.'

Some of the cars were also too small for a man to get into. And there could have been unintentional cueing as well, because the test wasn't blind, which means that everyone in the crew knew which car the chap had jumped into.

'This can lead to information leakage. The camera crew knew which car was the target, made evident by the fact that a nice full-on shot of the car was included as the psychics walked anywhere near it,' says Jackson.

Another obvious giveaway was that with a man in the boot, the back of the car sags. As Jackson claims, 'the test changes from a psychic challenge to one of deduction.'

What was also interesting, according to Jackson, is that it was the psychics who took the longest to choose who got it right, suggesting that they were thinking rather than being inspired by a higher power. Often they were hurried along by a 'sceptic' who was standing right next to the target car. And this kind of thing, apparently, happened in many of the tests.

Yet Diane Lazarus herself is more than sure that what she achieved on the programme was due to her psychic powers. So I try to track her down. This proves harder than expected. The first time I was due to meet her at her home in Wales, she cancelled the day before because she had to fly to South Korea. The second time, after her show, I was put off by an assistant because Diane was in pain as a garden gnome had fallen on her foot. But thanks to the trusty redial button on my telephone, I eventually hear her voice on the end of the line.

'Hello Diane, it's William Little,' I say.

'William Little,' she repeats in a light mocking tone. She's well aware how persistent I've been in tracking her down. But the conversation starts well and Diane comes across as a nice woman who wants to use her psychic powers to help people. I was surprised when I heard at the end of the show in Swansea that she'd given a large portion of the proceeds to charity. I scratched the back of my neck, took another sip of my Guinness, and looked around to see whether I had heard it right. Nobody else was shaking their head in wonder. She wasn't out to make vast wads of cash. In fact, everyone there had paid only £15 to hear her speak. That's a saving of £685 on Sylvia Browne.

'I've given money to charity from every show I do,' Diane tells me in her light Welsh accent. 'I've given thousands to cystic fibrosis charities. I've got a friend who has the disease. She's told me that I'm keeping her alive,' she says, sounding tired. 'At the moment I'm paying for DVD players for every hospital in the local area. I feel it's just something I have to do.'

Diane's not telling me this to sound worthy. I made a point of asking her about it. Part of the proceeds for the salon I attended went to the Joshua Foundation, a charity for children with terminal cancer, for which Diane's daughter Lisa is the ambassador in her role as Miss UK. It's a winning mix – a psychic mum and a beautiful daughter.

Diane also tells me that she pays her own way when she goes abroad to help families. She was recently in Dubai looking for a missing girl, and then in Switzerland, where she told the authorities that a man's body they were looking for would be found in water, which it was.

My phone call with Diane is proceeding amicably and I'm doing my best impression of being the biggest psychic fan ever. But at least I'm honest when I tell Diane that I enjoyed her show. I'm sure she doesn't believe me.

Then I move on to choppier terrain.

'So what about Myra, the woman who the people on the back row couldn't remember? It must be frustrating when that happens.'

'Yes, it was really frustrating,' Diane replies. 'The couple came up to me afterwards during the book signing and told me it was their aunt. Sometimes people say they can't remember then they call me or email me afterwards.'

I try again, but I just can't stop being bonny and positive. I think all the talk of her charity work has made me a bit soft. I should have predicted that.

'You were pretty effective on the find-the-body test on the psychic challenge TV show,' I say. 'I mean, the other psychics were just running around like Muppets, you know what I mean, Diane?'

'I was stuck in a room for four hours on my own before the test,' she replies. I was able to focus on where to go and what I was going to do. I just did it. And then when I did it again, the other psychics didn't speak to me, they were rude to me.'

'Really? That's horrible,' I say, realising that even psychics don't like winners.

But I'm determined to find out why she didn't do well on the other tests. Diane says it's linked to her concentration and motivation levels. Her psychic powers are strongest when she feels moved to do something.

'I just wasn't interested in some of the tests, and when they wanted us to look at something on the screen as well as tune into someone, well, it was just too much going on.'

And then I tell her all about my sister and her death sentence and how Sarah is paranoid that this will come true. Diane sounds genuinely shocked.

'I've been on *Kilroy* against psychics, did you know that?' she says.

I'm surprised that there's such inter-psychic rivalry.

'That's the problem with a lot of people calling themselves psychics,' says Diane firmly. 'It's wrong that these people are asking for lots of money for what they do.'

In fact she tells me she has turned down columns with a weighty pay cheque from national newspapers because she wouldn't agree to have premium rate psychic lines at the bottom of her page.

'I'm interested in helping Joe Bloggs. I'm not interested in making money, and I'm not interested in helping other people make money from just employing unemployed people to do the readings,' she tells me.

I've got one last question for Diane before I let her go and collapse on the sofa. She sounds exhausted.

'So, Diane, what about my future? See anything nice or positive?'

'Oh, William, I'm really tired, I can't see anything when I'm like this,' she says.

'Oh, no worries. Well, it was really nice talking to you, Diane. No, really,' I say, before putting the phone down and wondering just where my hard-nosed journalist routine evaporated to.

But then my brain jumps back to life and I remember that when I was at the Society for Psychical Research I discovered a prediction she made about Charlotte Church. She said that Church and her partner, Gavin Henson, were going to have a 'handsome son and a little baby "Gav"'. Having not read *Heat* magazine in, well, a lifetime, I'm unsure about the personal details of Church's life. In fact, so out of touch am I with the world of celebrities, I couldn't tell you when I read Lazarus' prediction whether Church had already given birth. But I'm ready to find out now. I stretch and limber up, knowing that I'm about to undertake some serious undercover research. Bracing myself, I lean over my keyboard and hit Google. Within seconds, I'm staring at a little baby girl called Ruby, Charlotte Church's daughter.

Oh dear. That pesky baby must have changed sex in the womb after Lazarus made her prediction. I'm gutted. Oh well, at least Diane Lazarus is a nice psychic, I think, as an email pops up from the lady herself as though she knew I was writing about her.

From: Diane Lazarus
To: William Little
Subject: FW: You were right!

***

Hi William

I just came across some feedback from a client. I have so many letters, emails. I thought you would find it interesting, what I see in the future. I have many more amazing letters.

Good luck with the book.

Kind regards

Diane

PS: And I see my own future and my family's.

I scroll down through Diane's message to an email from one of her clients.

From: Lee
To: Diane
Subject: You were right!

***

Hi Diane

I had a private reading from you previously (approx 11 years ago) it was shockingly accurate!

You had my lifestyle and my personality down to a T. The reading lasted 5 years and everything that you said came out over the years including the man I would marry. The reading said I was passing him all the time and he was like a statue but I didn't know him? The little girl with dark curls you could see in our future is my now 7-year-old daughter.

Turns out the statue like guy I was passing is my now hubby and at that time he was a bouncer [at the club] where I was partying every weekend. Wow! You got it! I am currently at a crossroads in my life and don't know if I should turn left or right, and in need of another reading.

Love and Light

Lee xxxx

On finishing reading the email, I heave an earth-shuddering sigh and realise that even after seeing two of the world's most powerful psychics, I'm still no further forward on my quest. I've heard people who are amazed by both Sylvia Browne and Diane Lazarus, yet I've also listened to stories from people who believe the opposite. They can't both be right, can they? All it proves is that either Sylvia and Diane's powers are not consistent, like Alice's, or some people are highly gullible and can be fooled into thinking they might be psychic, including me.

I turn off my computer and see Diane Lazarus' email disappear into the black hole of my screen. I realise that my perilous journey into the future is going to be a lot harder than I thought possible. I walk into the kitchen and put on the kettle to brew the strongest cup of tea this side of the Milky Way and wait for inspiration.

Nothing comes.

As the water hits the tea bag, with a waft of the brown stuff hitting my nostrils, I know what I need. I need a friend. I need to consult a guide to set me on the right path. I need to be the psychic grasshopper to a wise old master. I stir my tea with a steely glint in my eye. I know just who to consult.

5

The wise old master

So far, despite my best efforts at being genuinely open-minded, I haven't had a convincing psychic reading. Yet everyone I meet has. I'm not giving up, far from it, but I need to understand what happens when someone else believes they have a mystic experience when I don't. I need to know why their stories sound so convincing – are they real, or am I gullible? Or could it be that my questioning ways are blocking the psychic energy, as Alice suggested? Clearly, I'm still in desperate need of a consultation with a wise master.

If there's anyone who can make sense of this, it's Professor Richard Wiseman.

Working in the parapsychology unit at Hertford University, Professor Wiseman has been studying the paranormal and psychics for more than twenty years. A study he helped set up and supervise a few years ago with one of his PhD students, Ciarán O'Keeffe, the parapsychologist from *Most Haunted*, was one of the best-put-together studies of its kind. It makes Channel Five's *Psychic Challenge* look like an episode of *El Dorado*.

If you think setting up an experiment to test psychics is just a matter of turning up at Mysteries and having a bit of laugh, think again. Testing psychics is very serious scientific business. Over the years, experimenters have tried to develop a rigorous test, preventing the problems that occurred in previous studies. Many of these 'problems' were ironed out in Wiseman and O'Keeffe's work.

For instance, the study had to control potential 'sensory leakage', which is when mediums obtain information about the sitter (the person receiving the reading) via the internet, telephone directories, or eavesdropping on conversations.

Even a very limited amount of contact between the medium and sitter has the potential to provide useful information. Wiseman and O'Keeffe observed that the speed with which the sitter answered 'yes' or 'no' to a psychic's questions 'could unconsciously provide experienced mediums with useful feedback about the accuracy of their comments during a reading'.

To avoid this, the mediums were put in a soundproof room, while the sitter sat in another room. They never met. In fact, the experimenter who worked with the mediums and the experimenter who worked with the sitters never met either, just in case they unconsciously let information slip as well.

Then the mediums' readings were jumbled up and played back to the sitters in random order. The experiment found that the sitters picked out readings that the mediums had done for other people. The sitter, in other words, couldn't tell which reading was for them.

Interestingly, Wiseman and O'Keeffe were repeating a previous experiment undertaken at the University of Arizona that had suggested mediums could supply accurate information for people from deceased friends and relatives. They had detected flaws in the way the experiment was designed, leading to 'sensory leakage', and sought to repeat it, removing all leaky information in the process.

There have been many studies over the years claiming to have found the holy grail of psychic testing – the easily repeatable test. This is a test that can be repeated by other scientists using the same methods to achieve the same results. It's a benchmark of scientific standards. Without it we'd probably still think smoking was good for us. In fact, in 1929, statistician Frederick Hoffman in the *American Review of Tuberculosis* found that: 'There is no definite evidence that smoking habits are a direct contributory cause toward malignant growths in the lungs.' Frankly, I don't see why they bothered doing any more tests after that.

Yet while some scientists just need to improve the way they run their tests, others are so desperate to get positive results that they resort to out-and-out fraud. Testing psychics is a fertile area for sleight-of-hand experiments.

One classic example is the case of Samuel Soal, a mathematician based at London University in the 1930s, who tried to repeat the experiments of another researcher called J.B. Rhine. Rhine had famously produced 'evidence' for the existence of telepathy and precognition in his lab at Duke University in the US. Using Zener cards – five cards, each showing a different symbol such as a star, circle, square, cross or wavy lines – Rhine's subjects would either try to send a card to someone using telepathy or guess what card was coming up. Zener cards were also used in the opening scenes of *Ghostbusters*, with Bill Murray's character Dr Venkman testing college students for extra-sensory perception (ESP) in order to get dates with girls. Rhine, without the same interest in college girls, produced results that were so accurate they made hair stand up on the heads of bald men. Yet for all he tried, Samuel Soal couldn't repeat them. He tinkered and he toiled, but to no avail. Then he had a stroke of luck. He found that one of his subjects, Basil Shackleton, a professional photographer, was able to consistently guess the next card that would come up before it had even been looked at. It left everyone with a feeling that something very odd was going on. This was proof beyond all doubt that Shackleton had precognitive abilities. The world would never be the same again. Soal's experiments were also considered to be the best-controlled of their time. Sure, some grumpy and increasingly petulant sceptics and scientists shouted 'fraud', but they couldn't find any evidence. It was game, set and match to the psychics. Or that's what they thought.

The doubting and the denials rumbled on for another quarter of a century, until the quiet and unassuming Betty Markwick, a member of the Society for Psychical Research, entered the fray. Markwick, sick and tired of the 'yes he was', 'no he wasn't' tennis being played out between the sceptics and the psychics, wanted to clear Soal's name once and for all. More than 30 years after the original experiments, she set to work tenaciously going through every piece of data. Worryingly, she found that Soal had doctored his findings, adding extra hits for Shackleton when in fact he had failed to guess the right card. Without Soal's meddling, Shackleton's efforts were no better than chance – or, in normal speak, he was just guessing.

Though this doesn't beat Margery Crandon's ability to fool scientists with her spontaneous eruptions of ectoplasm. Throughout the 1920s, Crandon, from Boston in the US, was able to cover herself in a sticky-looking white substance that seemed to spurt out from nearby spirits and ghosts all over her head, neck and arms. The scientists, all very clever men used to dealing with fraud on a daily basis, scratched their collective heads in wonder. They frankly had no idea where it was coming from, or where, if Crandon was committing fraud, she'd been hiding it. Was this real physical evidence for the existence of ghosts? Again, it was nearly curtains for the sceptics, until one bright spark realised that she'd been hiding it and secretly removing it when the time was ripe from – there's really no delicate way of saying this – her vagina. Needless to say, any decent, or even half-decent man wasn't going to be check- ing any medium for fraud down there. And most worrying of all, the ectoplasmic substance she chose to stick in her sacred womanly space was taken from a sheep's lung. I know. It puts you off your dinner. I really hope she washed it first.

Wiseman and O'Keeffe, on the other hand, are so darn ethi- cal in the way they approach their study that even though their experiment should have been curtains for mediums every- where, they concluded in the following way: 'It is possible that genuine mediumistic abilities do exist, but that this study failed to find evidence of them because, for example, the mediums involved in the experiment do not possess such abilities or the setting in which the study was conducted did not elicit such abilities.'

After reading about their study, I'm certain that Professor Wiseman is the best person to help me find the world's great- est psychic. So in preparation for my meeting with him I've packed my best asterisk-making kit and a spare pen. I have a feeling it will be like going back to school.

I meet Wiseman in a bar overlooking London's Regent Street. He's precise with his language, slight, and wears geeky glasses. At my comprehensive in Birmingham, he wouldn't have made it home after the first day. He sips his sparkling water while I down my second coffee of the morning and start pouring out my problems. I've been worrying, almost to the point of losing sleep, why people spend so much money on psychic readings.

'I mean, how can paying $1,000 to be told that a dog will attack you be worth the money?' Wiseman listens like he's my family GP. 'Why do you think that, despite your work, all these people still believe that psychics are real?' I ask, shaking my head and looking out over the north London skyline for inspiration.

I expect Wiseman to guffaw loudly, slap his thigh merrily and say it's because they're all mad.

But he doesn't.

'They may be right,' he says.

I nearly choke on my coffee. Professor Wiseman believes, despite having conducted one of the most rigorous studies ever, that psychics might be real. This is the hope I was looking for, surely.

The professor continues calmly:'These people may well have this ability and until they are tested, you don't know.'

I'm lost for words. 'So accusations from sceptics that psychics are irrational is wrong?' I ask this, up to now, sceptical professor.

'But they are being rational. It's a matter of belief. If they believe that Sylvia has the answer, then they are behaving in an entirely rational way. Why wouldn't you spend $1,000 if you think she can see into the future and tell you something? It's $1,000 well spent.'

Well, I suppose, if Justine did take Becky to Disneyland and stopped all the other treatment, maybe her decision to spend the money on Sylvia Browne's salon was rational.

Wiseman, like the former magician he is, has another surprise up his sleeve that makes me think about psychics from a fresh perspective.

He reveals that many people see psychics for advice, and so in that respect psychics are acting like counsellors. It's more productive, says Wiseman, to judge them on whether they are good counsellors rather than on whether they have any psychic ability.

He takes another sip of his sparking water and explains: 'Good counselling is being given the tools to solve the problems in your life and be able to move on. Bad counselling is giving you the advice without the tools, so you have to keep going back to see the counsellor to get the next set of advice. Psychics fall into the second category. They are not telling you how best to look at the problem. It isn't great counselling,' he says.

That may be the case, I think, but not everyone becomes addicted to psychics, do they? Perhaps people don't need to keep going back over and over again if the psychic can use their special powers to get to the nub of the problem quickly. I'm beginning to sense that Professor Wiseman is more sceptical than he first let on.

He also thinks that most people don't actually think psychics are that psychic anyway. Now that really is confusing. It's not Professor Wiseman who's the sceptic, but, suddenly, all the people who actively seek them out. I take a sip of my coffee and let the professor explain.

'If you ask people why they go to see a psychic, few will say because they are psychic. They say it's because they appear to help. There is a sense of utility. Sylvia seems to help a woman find a partner ... it's as basic as that.'

'But the interesting thing,' he continues, getting animated and shifting forwards in his seat, 'is that when a real problem emerges, they won't go to see the psychic first. If your child is kidnapped, then you will go to the police first, and then, perhaps, you will go to see a psychic. That tells you a lot about what people think about the utility of the psychic. It's the same with medicine. Very few people who are ill will only go and see a psychic healer without also seeing a doctor.'

It sounds like those who visit psychics are using more of their brainpower than most people give them credit for. But I don't think it's as simple as Professor Wiseman suggests. Rather than proving that people don't believe in psychics, it could just show that people are aware that their powers, like Alice's, are unreliable, or that they think that a psychic's power – their sensitive intuition – is better suited to relationship and career problems. It could be that most people think that psychics are good counsellors because they *are* psychic, rather than because they're not.

Wiseman then tells me that psychics might serve a useful social function by being the poor person's counsellor. Clairvoyants may actually be helping to save the NHS money, he reveals.

'Most of the psychics I know are pleasant people and aren't after money. They charge £20 for a reading and you get 30 minutes with them. That's a lot more time than you have with your GP. And most people can't afford the private rates of good counsellors,' he says.

But what about all those sceptics who get twitchy and trigger-happy at the mention of the word 'psychic', those who suggest that all psychics should be banned with immediate effect? I guess the professor agrees with them?

'Not at all. It's a free country. I have a very liberal view of these things. People should be informed consumers. If people want to spend $1,000 on Sylvia then that's up to them. Providing that they are making that decision in an informed environment,' he says.

Right, so now we're on to something. Sceptics need to stop carpet-bombing and start educating. So let's educate. I've been researching something called cold reading, which is a technique that sceptics say psychics use to read someone's body language and fish for information. Basically, sceptics believe that psychics are just like Sherlock Holmes, right?

Wrong.

'Cold reading is just a myth,' Professor Wiseman explains. 'They don't pick up subtle body language. These people are not super-sensitive. Some psychics can be quite bullying and don't have good interpersonal skills at all. They just talk a lot and don't listen,' he says.

Cold reading is the technique that all sceptics use to undermine psychics, but Professor Wiseman, the ultimate sceptic, is out-doubting even them. Sceptics believe in cold reading, but not Professor Wiseman. I'm impressed.

'And the work is not being done by the medium, but by the sitter,' he adds.

Christ, they're lazy blighters too.

'They give some very slippery statements a lot of time. If someone says to you that you've had a trauma in the past, what do they mean by that? When the sitter says "Yes, that is accurate or that is amazing", you really want to know what their thought processes are. I think people who visit psychics are prepared to work quite hard for them. People are fitting the statements made by the medium into their lives,' he reveals.

This kind of thinking is best illustrated by a study undertaken by psychologist Dr Susan Blackmore. She surveyed more than 6,000 people, asking them whether specific statements were true. Over one third of people agreed with the statement 'I have a scar on my left knee', while over a quarter answered yes to the statement 'Someone in my family is called Jack'.

'Mediums can utilise this phenomenon to produce readings that may appear highly accurate but, in reality, simply contain very general statements that are endorsed by a large number of sitters,' says Wiseman.

This has also been called the Barnum Effect, after the famous American showman P.T. Barnum who said that a good circus 'had a little of something for everyone'.

But Professor Wiseman thinks it's more complicated. I really should have predicted that one.

'People's lives are complex and in normal everyday conversation you work hard to make sense of comments,' he says, sipping his water. 'That is what is happening when someone sees a psychic. They are not necessarily Barnum statements.'

Okay, so if it's all just people working hard to make sense of statements, which I'm not entirely convinced by, what about premonitions? They're not made by psychics out to make a fast buck. They're made by ordinary people with no motive to be dishonest. The fact that trains are more empty when there's a crash, or that people dream of their friend's death before it happens, makes sense.

'No it doesn't,' says Wiseman. 'My belief in premonition is zero. It doesn't make any sense. Think about it rationally.'

I thought I was.

'People who know that a train is going to crash could be assigning it to a psychic in order to get themselves off the hook or not get themselves in trouble because they know the wrong kind of people,' he says.

Right, but what about people who actually do have premonitions in dreams. It's well documented, surely?

'One-off experiences, yes, but do you know how many dreams don't come true? Think about it. If we all dream about three times a night and there are 56 million of us, that is a lot of dreams. So how many of them need to be about anxiety and loved ones travelling on a plane and how many plane crashes do you need to have in a year to get a back-up?'

Okay, so maybe we're just prone to dreaming about stuff that makes us anxious and every so often these anxiety-fuelled dreams come true by a random coincidence. And we ignore all the millions of dreams that aren't followed by a tragedy. But what about William Cox's statistical analysis that found lower numbers of people on trains on the day of a crash?

'That was confounded by the weather,' the professor says without a pause. 'Fewer people travel on days that have bad weather and that is when accidents tend to happen.'

It's time for him to go now. He gets up and walks quietly to the lift, leaving with me with my all-too-messy and confused thoughts. I order a sparkling water. Well, it certainly seemed to do the trick for him. I look out over the London skyline, cranes and construction works littering the view, and realise that Professor Wiseman's precise rationality is just what psychics and the people who believe in them are kicking against. It's not that he has to be rude or aggressive. He just slowly unpicks their beliefs.

The professor may not have intended to, but he has left me with hope. His belief that we can't rule out the power of psychics without testing them first matches my quest to test psychics by having my fortune told over and over. Maybe if I keep searching long enough, then I'll find that elusive thing: the psychic who really can read the future consistently.

I've also realised something about the power of belief. Despite Professor Wiseman undermining ordinary people's premonitions and presentiment, I'm not too sure that I believe him. I like the idea that we have some innate power, that we can sense the future, however briefly, like an animal sniffing out danger.

I head down to the street below, wondering where I'm going to find the evidence that I need to convince someone like Wiseman that it really is true. I'm also wondering how I will find a powerful and reliable psychic. Realising that I've still got a lot of ground to cover, I stride purposefully down the street towards Oxford Circus, wondering what that all-powerful psychic might be doing this very minute.

6

Life on another planet

No one realised that the ghost of Gianni Gandolfi had been hanging out at the G&C hair salon for more than two years, shouting at the top of his voice but being completely ignored. He was the owner and everyone acted as though he wasn't there. By all accounts, Gianni was a very loud and expressive man before he died. A typical Italian male, some people said. His larger-than-life character, it seems, had transcended the barrier between life and death. So it's no surprise that his frustration boiled over as the hairdressers carried on their daily trade, oblivious to his arm-waving and booming voice. He had a lot to shout about. He was sorry. So desperately sorry that he had left so suddenly, leaving his partner and co-owner of the business, Claudie, grief-stricken, up to her eyeballs in debt and with little clue about what to do with the business papers that he had left in such a mess.

Sometimes he stood right beside her, while she was cutting the hair of a regular customer, yelling about the special piece of paper that the lawyer needed to ensure the business was handed over to her in full. They hadn't married, so there were issues about the will to sort out too.

Gianni walked up and down the hair salon as though he was still alive, checking haircuts, trying to sweep up the fallen hair, making sure there was enough change in the till. Yet no matter what he tried to do, he couldn't make an impact.

One morning, the frustration almost causing a second coronary, he shouted that Claudie in all this time hadn't been to see a medium. If only she'd just have the initiative to get along to one of these people, use them as a channel, then he'd be able to communicate with the love of his life again and make everything okay.

On that very morning, a cool day in May, a medium, Angela Donovan, arrived outside the salon. She wasn't there to get in touch with Gianni; she'd just come along for a haircut. She'd undertaken none of the rituals and protections that mediums have to do before they get in touch with the dead – protecting themselves from spirit energy as though it's a dangerously strong electric current.

Angela Donovan walked innocently into the shop for a bit of much-needed pampering, only to be hit with the full force of Gianni's pent-up frustration and rage. To say that something unusual happened that day in the G&C hair salon would be an understatement. Everyone looked on in horror as Angela jolted to a halt, struck dumb, fending off Gianni's two-years'-worth of angst like a Jedi knight deflecting laser beams with a light sabre.

'Who's that man standing next to you, waving his arms about?' Angela asked Claudie.

Claudie didn't know. She couldn't see anyone. Yet whoever it was, it was terrifying. No one could remember the last time the salon had witnessed so much drama. Scissors clanked to the floor and the mouths of the hairdressers fell open in shock.

'He's so angry,' Angela told Claudie. 'He's been trying to get messages to you. Why haven't you been to see someone?!'

Claudie didn't know what to say, so to ease her flustered state she did what she knew best and helped Angela into the seat so she could start cutting her hair. It didn't help. Buffeted by the force-10 gale of Gianni's spirit energy, Angela ran out before her hair was even finished.

~

I'm sitting outside the G&C hair salon in the salubrious London borough of Knightsbridge, gripped as Claudie tells me the spellbinding story of that day in May. It's a sunny June afternoon and I thought I'd come to test out Professor Richard Wiseman's claim that psychics might be good counsellors. I didn't realise I'd also be confronted with a compelling ghost story that has the potential to leave all of the professor's hard science talk in tatters. Sure, anecdotes aren't scientific evidence and they can't be tested independently, but they are riveting and they seem more real than a piece of cold, hard research. It's difficult not to entertain the possibility that Claudie's story might be true.

Claudie's a no-nonsense businesswoman who looks like she might be working too many hours. Like other people I have met, she doesn't seem the type who buys into the psychic phenomenon. She's about 50, has bright blonde hair and wears more fashionable clothes than most of my female friends. They suit her. She also seems more than capable of dealing with life's knocks. Yet the arrival of Angela Donovan at the salon did more than scare most of her customers away. She suggests her future happiness depended on it.

'Everything was perfect in my life. Gianni and I were blissfully happy. Then he dropped down dead,' Claudie says with a steady gaze. We're still sitting outside the salon, trying to ignore a gusting wind.

'It wasn't expected. I was completely devastated in every way. I was left without the love of my life. I was in a really bad place,' she says.

Three years passed from when Gianni died and she met Angela Donovan, a psychic with a good word-of-mouth reputation. Claudie says she was a 'zombie' for most of those years, struggling to keep the business going, overwhelmed by the debts and not able to let go of the thought of Gianni.

'A close friend introduced me to Angela. I went to Angela's book launch and invited her to come to the salon for a haircut. I had never been to a medium before – this sort of thing had never been important in my life,' she says.

Claudie, the breeze blowing through her hair, thinks back to that spring day. She shudders. 'Angela described him exactly and, you know, he did shout a lot. He was Italian. It was such a shock. She told me that I had to go and see her,' she says.

After Angela had run out of the shop, Claudie tells me that she had felt like she was going to die. 'I nearly fainted. It was because the energy field wasn't closed,' she explains.

The salon that day was home to a dramatic scene. You can choose to believe it or not. That's not the issue here. Following the extraordinary moment she witnessed, Claudie decided to go to see Angela for a reading. What's important for Claudie is that she says it helped give her hope for the future, and allowed her to move on for the first time since Gianni died.

And, significantly, there's no evidence that Claudie formed a dependent relationship with Angela, desperately demanding more readings. It was quite the opposite, in fact. Angela gave Claudie only one reading, and that was relevant for the next eight to ten years. Afterwards, Claudie slowly began to rebuild her life.

Angela's reading for Claudie seems to have been very much of the extraordinary rather than the ordinary counselling variety. Claudie tells me that Angela revealed pieces of information that only she and Gianni would know, such as how they met seven years ago in Florence.

'She named my aunt Mary, calling her Marie. No one ever called her that, but that was her real name,' Claudie says. 'Even if she went on to the computer and found your whole life story she wouldn't be able to know these kind of things,' Claudie tells me firmly, sensing that my eyebrows are starting to rise into a big question mark.

Claudie says that Angela passed on information from Gianni. He was sorry about the state of the paperwork he had left behind, and told her he would show her signs that he was still around.

The wind picks up as a lorry rumbles into the street. When it's quiet again, I ask Claudie what the reading meant for her. What was it like being in touch with Gianni again?

'It was very emotional, but it made me feel much happier. And since then I have been able to ask questions when I have needed help with the business, and he has shown me a sign,' she says, telling me of the time when she was searching for an important legal document in his chaotic files. She called for help, and then found it at the top of the first drawer she opened.

Angela also gave her advice that eased her mind about some big decisions. She didn't know when to try to sell their big house in Norfolk, for instance. 'She told me people would come to buy it next year, describing them exactly,' she says emphatically.

It's a compelling tale, and Claudie believes, as do most of her customers, that Angela can help them get on with their lives, giving them confidence and a belief in, I suppose, a benign universe.

Claudie also tells me that Angela helps women whose husbands are having affairs and gives confidence to women with breast cancer. She's not offering a cure, or psychic healing, just a positive mindset.

'She puts your mind at rest, telling you it will be alright,' Claudie says. 'Angela doesn't make decisions for you, but she gives you the strength to make decisions for yourself. She makes you learn to trust in yourself. With your two feet firmly planted on the ground, she hopes you'll do the right thing. Gut instinct, we know, is such a powerful force.'

On my way home I try to figure out whether psychics are ultimately bad or good. Claudie, at least, seems satisfied, and it's hard to argue with her conclusions. Does it really matter whether her belief in the afterlife and the abilities of Angela is backed up by evidence, so long as she has been helped? Maybe, as Professor Wiseman suggested to me, Angela gets to feel important for pretending to speak to dead people, but she hasn't exactly harmed anyone. It may seem a bit churlish to mention that former Prime Minister Tony Blair believed he was more answerable to God than to the electorate and intelligent argument when he sent us to war in Iraq. Angela's success in helping Claudie to believe in herself again and take positive and constructive steps seems positively rational by comparison.

Yet it does seem, however, that Angela's skill as a counsellor is tied inextricably to her belief in her psychic powers. And Claudie's ability to move towards a brighter future is also linked to her perception of those powers.

But I know it isn't as simple as that. And tomorrow, I'm heading to north-east London to hear for myself the devastating impact that relying on an astrologer can have on people's lives when their words are taken too literally. Using the planets to predict the future might seem more scientific than listening to dead voices, but in essence there's no real difference. Both rely on all-powerful spiritual 'energies' to glimpse the future, and the outcome is often just the same. I'm not looking forward to it.

~

Anu Anand, a former BBC World Service journalist, is angry. Her parents have got under her skin. 'My mother had my birth chart done when I was young. The chart says I will die when I'm 83. My parents still make all their decisions based on advice from an astrologer. It makes me so angry more than anything else. They even objected to my marriage before finally giving in. Yet many of my close friends are fervent believers and seem to get some comfort from their horoscopes,' she says.

I'm sitting at Anu's kitchen table, the day after my meeting with Claudie, stroking her ancient tabby cat, while she lets off steam. She can't quite believe the impact that astrology has had on her mother and people she knows. 'It does my head in when people argue rationally in favour of astrology because to me it is not rational,' she says.

Anu and her mum are Hindus. While Anu is agnostic, her mum believes strongly. This is not the problem. The problem is the reliance her mum puts on astrology for important decisions in her life.

The importance of the stars for Hindus goes back thousands of years to the creation of the Vedas, a collection of writings that

Hindus believe were received by scholars direct from God and passed down the generations by word of mouth. As with many ancient civilisations, this had a lot to do with the importance of the seasons and looking for omens in the sky to help people make decisions in the absence of any other information.

This eventually developed into Indian sidereal astrology, based on charting the zodiac by fixed stars, in contrast to the astrology practised in the West, which uses a tropical zodiac based on the seasons of the solar year. So Indian astrology divines with reference to the fixed constellations in the sky, whereas we in the West use the path of the sun, divided into twelve houses or star signs – which don't align to the constellations any more.

This belief in the power of astrology is still a very powerful force in Indian society today, and many businessmen and women use astrologers to help them make decisions, while others use astrology to forecast events in people's lives.

Anu's story backs up this reliance on astrology. 'If you open an Indian paper today, all of the matrimonial ads are based on caste but astrology plays a big part. One whole column is reserved for people who are born under one astrological sign that is very, very inauspicious. They are mangliks and can only marry other mangliks,' she says.

'So if you're born under the wrong star sign in India you can't marry who you like because you'll be, what, cursed?'

'Something like that,' she says.

It isn't a funny story. It's taken very seriously in India, and it nearly brought the recent wedding of the son of the Indian screen legend Amitabh Bachchan to a stop. Bachchan junior, Abhishek, was set to marry Aishwarya Rai, a massive Bollywood star who took the lead in *Bride and Prejudice*, an adaptation of Jane Austen's novel, until rumours started that she was a manglik. Mangliks are born under a poorly-aspected Mars that can bring bad luck and even premature death to their husbands.

Even though the couple, described regularly as the Brad Pitt and Angelina Jolie of Bollywood, had the blessing of Bachchan senior, Aishwarya still had to perform a special ceremony to get rid of the bad luck.

'There were rumours that she had to marry a tree or a gold idol first. The idea is that you transfer the bad luck on to that, then you can go and marry whoever you want to,' explains Anu.

'Right. I see,' I say, but actually I don't.

Later I checked the story in *The Times* archive. 'Before getting married, manglik women are traditionally required to go through a symbolic wedding to an idol of the Hindu god Vishnu or to a peepal or banana tree. It is still unclear if Ms Rai has been through such a ritual,' the report in *The Times* stated. 'But the couple and their families have been spotted visiting Hindu temples, astrologers and priests in recent months, prompting a frenzy of speculation in the Indian media.'

As Anu grew up in the United States and wasn't part of the cultural experience that influenced her parents, she finds these beliefs difficult to deal with. 'My mum still goes to see her astrologer in the village in which she was born, in Jamur, Kashmir. She has gallstones and her answer after all these years was to go to India to see her astrologer for six months, who prescribed drinking raw cow's milk. Literally everything in their lives happens because of what their astrologer says. I exist because of it. It's an excuse not to think for one's self,' she says.

Anu has reason to be annoyed and upset. She wanted her mum to go to a five-star hospital and have keyhole surgery for her gallstones, but she wouldn't. 'It's because she's terrified of operations. It's abdicating responsibility for yourself,' she says.

Her parents also stopped speaking to her for a year when she married her husband against their and their astrologer's advice, who had warned her that they were incompatible. Eventually they welcomed Anu's husband into the family fold, but this was a difficult time for her. Her mother has also recently reminded Anu that she will be having a baby next year according, again, to her birth chart.

'She carries hers and her children's everywhere with her,' Anu tells me, looking exasperated.

But the thing that has made Anu most bitter is the poor business advice her parents have been given. 'Based on the advice of the astrologer they brought a motel business in Florida, despite the fact that their family were all warning them against it, advising them it was a bad financial move. They borrowed an enormous amount of money when they were in their 50s. We told them to put their money in a more shockproof investment, but they wouldn't listen,' she says.

It was a disaster. They lost a large amount of money, her father now works more hours than he's ever worked before, and they no longer have enough saved to pay for her younger brother's college fees. On top of this, rather than having the quick operation and helping out with the business, this was the time when her mother disappeared for six months to India. 'All their equity was tied up in the business. They've suffered a huge amount because of it,' Anu explains.

'It's a negative distorting influence. Rather than looking at the *FT* and reading about what the credit markets are doing, they completely ignore this set of information in favour of something mystical. It's reckless. If you are already in a place where you are looking for someone else to figure stuff out for you, then this is the perfect pseudo-science,' she says.

It's a distressing story and Anu is visibly angry. Clearly there are some spiritual counsellors who can do good, as in the case of Claudie and Angela Donovan, but there are also those who tear apart people's lives. Anu's mum has formed an unhealthy, dependent relationship on astrologers that has blinded her to the negative consequences. She has suspended her own judgement and goes by the judgement of someone who lives thousands of miles away in India, knowing little or nothing of her life in the US.

I leave Anu's house and head back down towards the train station. I know what I need to do next. I'm going to get myself a reading from one of the toughest kind of psychics there is. Someone who believes they were born to do this because they come from a long line of ancestors who have done nothing else. I've got to find myself a gypsy caravan and check out if the oldest form of fortune-telling can give me the one definitive reading I still need to find.

7

The gypsy

THE WIND IS BLOWING HARD, smacking the side of the old bow-top gypsy caravan and making it sway from side to side. The darkening sky closes in, and I sit in the shadows, lit only by the flickering light of a single candle. During a dip in the wind's rage, I reach over and slip my piece of silver into the palm of the wizened old gypsy fortune-teller. She thanks me with a silent nod, and removes the black cloth that has been shielding her crystal ball. A small flicker of light glows from its centre, reflecting back into her eyes. A cloudy haze fills the crystal ball, swirling slowly. The gypsy suddenly breathes in sharply and stares at me, as though she can see straight through me. The table starts to rattle and the wind beats against the side of the caravan once more.

'I can see a dark shadow cast over your life,' she says, her voice low like gravel.

I tell a lie. I'm sitting over a giant mug of steaming tea and daydreaming with a maniacal grin creasing my face. I'm so desperate for a powerful reading that I'm willing it on in my daydreams.

That's why, of course, I've picked on a gypsy fortune-teller for my next reading. Stereotypes they may be, but gypsies have a fearsome reputation. I also figure that if I'm really going to put to the test Professor Wiseman's idea that psychics are just counsellors, then there's no better place to experiment than with the toughest of the lot.

I've also grown up in the shadow of a gypsy curse. It's no laughing matter, I can assure you. In 1906 gypsies cursed St Andrew's, the Birmingham City Football Club stadium, for 100 years as revenge for the club kicking them off their land. And I've personally had to deal with the consequences. While my sister went off to Villa Park one Saturday morning in 1982 to have her picture taken with the European Cup that Aston Villa had just won, I had to deal with Birmingham City fighting to avoid relegation, again. The team's historic poor performance was all down to that gypsy curse, or so we liked to think, and I had to suffer the humiliation at home and school every day.

It's been blamed for a string of other disasters too. The team's first game on Boxing Day 1906 was delayed for an hour while directors shovelled snow from the pitch. The main stand was destroyed during the Second World War when a fireman threw a bucket of water over a fire. It turned out to contain petrol. And spookily, the team were relegated at the end of their first season at St Andrew's and were relegated in their last season under the curse.

The curse has also led to some highly entertaining attempts to reverse its power. The team's formidable manager from the 1982 season, Ron Saunders, put crucifixes on the floodlight pylons and painted the soles of the players' boots red. More than ten years later, manager Barry Fry urinated in all four corners of the ground. But none of it helped.

Before I go and see my fearsome gypsy, I've also got to find out just how accurate their reputation is. My life may depend on it. Writing in 1891 in *Gypsy Sorcery and Fortune Telling*, Charles

Godfrey Leland, an editor and folklorist, suggested that gypsies have done 'more than any race or class on the face of the earth to disseminate among the multitude a belief in fortune-telling, magical or sympathetic cures'. Leland really should know. He seemed to spend most of his time in the company of gypsies.

He goes on to say that 'their women have all pretended to possess occult power since prehistoric times. By the exercise of their wits they have actually acquired a certain art of reading character or even thought, which, however it be allied to deceit, is in a way true in itself, and well worth careful examination.'

Well, careful examination is just what I intend to do.

Records show that Romany gypsies originated in India, fleeing in about 800 AD during the clashes between invading Arab and Mongolian warriors, and bringing with them shaman traditions. These ancient beliefs and their reputation travelled with them through the years and across the continents until eventually they ended up in Britain in around 1500.

Their ancient mystical beliefs were clearly reinforced by their 'romantic' wandering lifestyle on the road. Playing on the superstition that gypsies had magical powers, fortune-telling was an easy way for female gypsies to make a living while their husbands were out trading horses or working seasonally in the fields. Yet their reputation has also resulted in a history of persecution which still goes on today. The 1530 anti-gypsy act attempted to get rid of them by either impounding their goods, deporting them, or, if that didn't work, killing them. They were mistreated under the brutal 16th-century vagrancy laws, and were specifically included in the 1597 Vagrants Act. By the 18th century, punishment for vagrancy included whipping. In that kind of climate, putting a curse on someone might get you into a whole lot of trouble, but it also might keep the trouble-makers away.

The gypsies' other great belief is inherited psychic power. Leland reveals that the last of several daughters born in succession, without a boy coming into the series, 'will enjoy second sight of many things invisible to men'. Such was the power of this belief that in 1883 the young leader of the Kukaya gypsy tribe offered an old gypsy woman, Pale Boshe, 100 ducats if she would persuade her seventh daughter to marry him. I think, wisely, she refused.

Their reputation as fortune-tellers was cemented by the Norwood gypsies, who set up camp just a few miles south of London in the 17th century. It was a dark, fearsome place, wild and dangerous. The woods provided fuel and shelter, and no doubt added to their reputation for being close to nature. As Steve Roud says in the *Penguin Guide to Superstition*: 'These are the Gypsies of the romantic imagination – wild and free, mysterious and enigmatic, possessing occult powers which house-dwellers could tap into; safe enough to visit but with just the right amount of danger to provide a frisson of fear.'

The Norwood gypsies became so renowned in the 18th and 19th centuries for fortune-telling that if you were seen travelling south of the river with a silver coin in your pocket, everyone knew where you were heading. And if you lived in the early 1700s you'd probably have had your fortune read by Margaret Finch, the original gypsy queen, who died when she was 109. Due to having sat in the same position telling fortunes all her life, her limbs were so set in place that she had to be buried in a deep, square box.

As well as checking out the gypsy powers of predicting the future, I also want to test their most potent symbol – the crystal ball. The technique called scrying is one of the oldest methods of divination because it can be done by looking at any pool of water or reflective surface. Some ancient cultures even practised onychomancy, which involved looking at the fingernails of a young boy to see the future.

The most entertaining scryer wasn't even a gypsy. John Dee, a 16th-century scientist with an unhealthy interest in the occult, experimented regularly by gazing into a crystal ball. When he wasn't doing that he was giving Queen Elizabeth I sound advice from his other hobby, drawing up horoscopes and telling her when to have her coronation or sort out the Spanish. But John Dee was convinced that he could use his crystal ball to contact angels. Unfortunately, he wasn't very good and didn't see any. Dee then found a perfect stooge in a man called Edward Kelly, who could produce spirits and angels at the flick of a switch and thus on whom he could conduct experiments. The fact that Kelly had already been caught by the authorities counterfeiting money, and that on a trip abroad he told Dee that the angels suggested they share each other's wives, didn't raise any suspicions as to his reliability. Kelly was eventually jailed for fraud in eastern Europe and fell to his death trying to escape from his cell using the old bedsheets-tied-together routine. And, yes, it's a wonder he didn't see it coming. But that's fortune-telling for you. Dee went home broke and rather disillusioned.

I don't intend to be like Dee. When I set out for my gypsy reading, I'm full of high hopes about seeing my very own genuine gypsy queen. I've arrived in Bristol to meet 55-year-old Betsy Lee in her caravan. The sun's shining through fluffy white clouds, and I'm standing in the middle of Bristol's International Balloon Fiesta in the grounds of Ashton Court. Not quite what I had in mind.

I'm having trouble locating Betsy in a sea of funfair rides, hot dog and candyfloss stands, and, oddly, recruitment tents for the army. I eventually discover Betsy's caravan opposite a simulator ride blasting out rave music, and my heart sinks – the old wooden bow-top has been replaced by a standard white caravan. Instead of being in a *Hammer House of Horror* episode, I've somehow ended up in *Carry On Camping*.

I head up the small steps and greet Betsy, who's sitting on one side of a foldaway table. Her crystal ball looks like something out of a pound shop, with large air bubbles splattered over its surface. I glumly sit opposite her, expecting to have the worst 30 minutes of my life, but my depression lifts immediately when Betsy begins to speak. She sounds like a character out of a BBC Christmas adaptation of Charles Dickens. She has a soft East End accent, the exact one that a Dickens gypsy would have; and what's more, she keeps calling me 'sir'. Betsy Lee's spiel is compelling and I love it. Her voice rises and falls, running on with a melodic old-world rhythm. Suddenly I'm in the middle of the most enjoyable reading I've had so far.

'I cross the life-line of your hand, sir, with love and appreciation. I cross the life-line of your hand, sir, with strength and courage and love. I feel that you are a very, very happy-go-lucky gentleman. In your life you're a giver, not a taker. You're a leader, not a driver. And you're a sentimental old stick. But I feel that you work, work, work, and work but you don't keep enough back for yourself.

'Sometimes you can be very abrupt, sir, very demanding, very dominating, but you do that when you want to make things good for people. But a good heart never wants and those who give to other people receive things back in many ways,' she says, her voice still rising and falling like a ship on a night-time crossing to somewhere exotic.

What I'm hearing so far is wonderful. I really don't think Betsy Lee has a sore bone in her body. And then she proves it.

'But you have grown together, not apart,' she says, talking about my relationship. I was under the impression that relationships, for psychics, were an opportunity to do the most harm. It's quite the opposite for warm-hearted old Betsy.

The only odd thing that happens is that she repeats herself, telling me again and again that I'll 'stand on my own two feet', and that 'health is good, wealth is good, intuition is there. Strength is there, courage is there, trust is there.'

I'm unsure why she does this. Either I really am the most amazing person she's ever met, or she's on a loop like an old-fashioned tape recorder and every so often gets stuck.

She's also given her crystal ball only the odd cursory glance. She doesn't peer into its depths, and there's no misty glow or images appearing on the inside. It's all a bit mundane, but frankly it doesn't matter. Her voice is mesmerising.

'I see marriage later and you'll be a father of three lovely children,' she says. 'One will make a fine business gentleman, one will be a teacher and one will be a carer. They'll have minds of their own and ways of their own, but they won't get ought for nought, they will be like you, sir, and have to work for what they get.'

She hasn't said anything that I couldn't say, but it's all rather encouraging. If you want to feel good, there are probably worse ways to spend half an hour than in the company of Betsy Lee.

When she tells me that a distant relative will leave me money, I almost get up and give her a big hug. I've always wanted a relative to leave me loads of money, especially one that lives far away. But, what's more, I've always wanted a gypsy to tell me this, and she has. I'm in psychic heaven. But then her East End wisdom comes to the fore: 'But when you get ya money don't let anyone wheel and deal it out of ya. Put it into a way that you can get a good income,' she says, nodding wisely.

I give her a firm nod so she understands that no one's going to be wheeling and dealing me out of my inheritance.

Winding up her spiel, I can tell she's going to end with a flourish. Her voice undulating like a satin sheet riding on a field of corn, she tells me my life will be full of 'happiness and contentment'. But she's not finished yet. The satin sheet is now blowing wildly in a sudden summer storm. She shifts into a higher gear and proclaims: 'You'll live to the great old age of 88. When you die, you'll die in your sleep with all your marbles, sir.'

I nearly laugh out loud. 'Thank fuck!' I think, 'I'm not going to go mad!' But Betsy's smiling pleasantly at me and I come to my senses.

I think she wants to usher me out quickly as there's already a queue forming, but I'm desperate to know more about this woman. She's the first real gypsy fortune-teller I've met and I've got loads of burning questions. I mean, does fortune-telling really run in the family? It's got to be a myth, right?

'My mum tells fortunes and her mother, and her mother before that,' she says. 'I inherited my ability, I'm not a book-reader. When I read people I read for what I see. It's a gift of giving. I have been coming here many years. If I don't come we let people down. We do a lot of good,' she says.

'Do you really help people?' I ask. 'Psychics and gypsies have such a bad reputation. I mean, you curse people, right?'

'I look to their futures. I try to remove their distress. I'm positive. I try to help them a lot. I see a lot of care workers and people working with children, they are so good and I talk to them. I tell them a good heart never wants,' she says, repeating part of her spiel.

In her spare time, Betsy's a housewife. She's no longer on the road, if she ever really was. I get the impression that travelling died out with her mum and grandparents, although her grandmother told her the other day how they used to go to London and sing and sell lavender. 'My dad's a Londoner through and through. He was born within Bow Bells,' she says.

And the bow-top caravan has been left at home because she thought it would make it difficult for people to see her. 'People hurt themselves trying to get up the stairs, they're so steep,' she says.

I don't feel annoyed any more that there was no bow-top caravan. Betsy Lee, like her reading, has put other people first. It's a strange experience to visit a gypsy fortune-teller and have a good time.

But despite my enjoyment, again, I haven't been truly convinced by a psychic's mystic ability, although she has certainly affected me, and possibly all those that go and see her. Sometimes it's important to sit in front of someone who is willing for a full 30 minutes to say healthy, positive and encouraging things to you.

I leave Ashton Court in a much better mood, and it's all down to this Dickensian gypsy. But I'm going to need all her powers of positive thinking, because I've already planned my next line of inquiry.

It's about death and murder. I'm about to investigate how psychics can change the course of justice and put murderers behind bars. It could be dangerous, and I'm half-tempted to ask Betsy whether she'd mind coming along.

FUTURE 3:
GYPSY BETSY LEE AND ME

~

Predictions:
I'll stand on my own two feet
I'll get married
I'll have three children: one will be a fine business gentleman,
 one will be a teacher, another will be a carer
I won't go backwards, I'll go forwards
A distant relative living overseas will leave me money
I'll die when I'm 88 and I'll go with all my marbles fully
 intact

Things I don't know but I should:
I'm a very happy-go-lucky gentleman
I'm a sentimental old stick

8

Psychic murder

THE FOG HAD SET IN THICK on Saturday, 14 December 1991 when eighteen-year-old Nicola Payne left her boyfriend's house for the six-minute walk back to her parents' home near Woodway Park in Coventry. She took, as always, the short cut across a local park called the Black Pad. The journey, a little over half a mile in length, was straightforward. It was a route that she took most days, so she thought it was safe. But she didn't arrive home and hasn't been seen since. There have been no confirmed sightings of Nicola since she left her boyfriend's house that foggy morning, yet the police and her family believe that she was killed and her body dumped. Her family feel the loss every single day and still work with the police, trying to locate her, attempting to bring someone to justice.

Desperate and struggling to make sense of the disappearance of Nicola and the overwhelming loss it has caused, Marilyn Payne, Nicola's mum, turned to psychics for help and support. Could they alter the course of reality and the future by tuning in to the spirit world to help find her daughter?

It made sense, especially as the psychic she sought, Christine Holohan, had helped the police solve another murder inquiry. Her involvement in that inquiry had been 'proven effective beyond all reasonable doubt' in a report published in the *Journal of the Society for Psychical Research* by two of the Society's most respected paranormal investigators – Montague Keen and Guy Lyon Playfair.

What is so striking about their report is the testimony they gathered from a police detective working on the case. Detective Constable Tony Batters, supported by Detective Sergeant Andy Smith, confirmed to them Christine Holohan's key role.

Both Keen and Playfair, after weighing up all the facts in their report, concluded that Christine Holohan had provided 'key information that helped lead to the conviction of a murderer and is highly suggestive of discarnate survival' – in other words, life after death.

Reading the report myself, it's difficult not to be swayed completely by the evidence.

It reveals that on Friday, 11 February 1983, 25-year-old Jacqui Poole, a part-time barmaid, was murdered in her council flat in Ruislip, a suburb of west London. First on the scene was DC Tony Batters, who, Keen and Playfair say, 'entered the premises on Sunday 13th and remained there for five hours, during which time he took notes on every detail of the murder scene and the victim'.

Little did Batters know at the time that an angry Jacqui Poole was trying to get in touch with a medium, livid that she had been killed and wanting justice to be done. In fact, according to Christine Holohan's own account in her book *A Voice from the Grave*, Jacqui appeared to her in full, late at night, waking her up from a deep sleep. Christine describes her as 'a woman; young and beautiful, with blonde hair down to her shoulders'.

So clear was the apparition that Christine could see her fidgeting nervously. 'She looked upset and confused as I heard her ask me to help her,' the medium writes, before dramatically revealing that the ghost of Jacqui Poole made a shocking request: '"Will you help me? I have been murdered."'

At which point Jacqui's ghost held her hand and took her to the flat to witness the murder.

'My body was her body. Her thoughts became my thoughts and everything became clear to me,' Christine reveals.

Christine Holohan says she learnt that Jacqui was off work sick. She saw the layout of the flat, noting two cups – one washed, one unwashed – and other details including a black address book, a letter and a doctor's prescription. And then Jacqui relived the scene of the murder for Christine to experience in its full horror.

'It was utterly terrifying,' Christine describes watching through Jacqui's eyes as a man strangled her. 'I saw his hands go round her throat and pull the cord tight. The vision haunted me for years. I suffered depression for a long time afterwards.'

This experience was crucial in ensuring that Christine Holohan was able to convince the police she was genuine. In taped evidence to Playfair and Keen, DC Batters reveals that when they turned up at Christine's house and she told them she was psychic, he was initially unsure.

'I was at the time completely sceptical and did not wish to pursue the interview, but as a courtesy we sat down in her lounge and she started saying things which immediately shook me,' Batters told the paranormal investigators.

Christine then entered a trance and described Jacqui Poole's flat to him as she had first seen it, mentioning the cups, the prescription and the attack, noting that only two of Jacqui's many rings remained on her fingers.

Christine then told the detectives that she could get the murderer's nickname through 'automatic writing', a technique in
which the psychic holds a pen and the spirit apparently guides
it across a piece of paper.

'Holohan made some squiggles and marks on a sheet of her
notepad, and wrote the number 221, an illegible word, and the
words "Ickeham" [sic], "garden" and "Pokie".' Pokie was immediately recognised by one of the detectives as the nickname of
Anthony Ruark, a suspect who thus far had a watertight alibi.

DC Batters says that the new information made sure the
police moved in a second time on Ruark, interviewing him
again and securing more evidence, including a jumper they
suspected he had worn during the attack. Yet with an alibi that
couldn't be broken, and no firm evidence either way, the case
was eventually dropped.

The Jacqui Poole murder case was reopened by the new
'cold case' unit in 2000, who were solving unresolved murders
using LCN (low copy number) DNA technology. Critically,
the pullover that had belonged to Ruark had been kept, and
traces of body fluids that were found on it were used to convict
him.

DC Batters makes it clear that 'without Christine's information, we might have failed to procure the most conclusive evidence [i.e. the pullover]', and therefore they might never have
prosecuted Ruark.

Ruark was convicted at the Old Bailey in August 2001 and
jailed for life. Yet Holohan wasn't mentioned in the trial.

After reading Keen and Playfair's report and hearing about
the reputation of these two investigators in paranormal circles,
I want to check whether they still believe that Christine is the
real thing. I arrange to visit Guy Lyon Playfair's flat in London's

Earl's Court the following week (Montague Keen died a few years ago). Playfair speaks fluent Portuguese and is highly musical, playing the piano and a number of brass instruments. With his many talents, he seems to be a real-life Renaissance man, just one who also investigates ghosts.

He originally made his name investigating the Enfield poltergeist in the late 1970s with another legendary ghost-hunter, Maurice Grosse. The Enfield poltergeist resided at the semi-detached council house of the Hodgson family in the north London borough, and seemed to take a great interest in the family's eleven-year-old daughter, Janet. Odd things happened when she was about. Beds moved with her and her brother in them when they were asleep, and visitors, apparently, were levitated and thrown around the house. A police officer also swore on oath that she'd seen a chair move of its own accord in the Hodgson home. Most bizarrely, the poltergeist spoke through Janet in a thick, treacly old voice, saying that his name was Bill and he'd lived in the house 50 years before.

Both Playfair and Grosse were convinced that the phenomenon was ghost-related. The ghost-hunters witnessed moving furniture, flying toys, cool winds blowing through the house, even pools of water spontaneously appearing on the floor. Once they saw a fire ignite and extinguish by itself.

I cycle along the Thames towards Earl's Court on a bright morning in late June, wondering whether Playfair has had a change of heart. It's a big deal to suggest that a medium actually played a key role in a murder inquiry. I lock up my bike and walk past the large white Victorian mews houses that dominate this part of town. Playfair meets me at the door in his slippers and immediately confirms that he's still 100 per cent certain that Christine Holohan played a key role in the Jacqui Poole case.

'We saw Detective Batters' original notebook, and this is the only case that I know of where a medium specifically named the murderer right at the start before she knew anything about the case at all,' he affirms. 'That is beyond question and cannot be denied. The usual sceptics and the police have been busting themselves to try and debunk this story,' he adds, looking at me suspiciously. 'But she made a very profound impression on the two detectives who went to see her.'

'So do you think the finding of the jumper was significant in providing DNA?' I ask, double-checking what I read in the report.

'Yes, that was the evidence. It was the only evidence. Well, the only evidence you could bring into court because there's no doubt that it was his pullover and they retrieved it from his flat, and it had both his DNA on it and Jacqui Poole's DNA on it, so go figure,' he says.

Then he tells me something that startles me.

'Of course the jury were never told about Christine. I think if they had been, it would have been completely conclusive. Certainly if I had been on the jury I would have said, "Well, that's it." That was it. I mean, there was no doubt that he did it,' he says.

Christ, Playfair really is certain.

The story sounds plausible, yet I still want to check it out. I want to see how a psychic detective works in action. So a few weeks after reading about the imprisonment of Ruark and visiting Playfair, I find myself sitting on the sofa of Marilyn Payne, the mother of missing schoolgirl Nicola Payne. I'm drinking endless cups of steaming tea and chatting with none other than Christine Holohan herself. I want to know more about how Christine is using her psychic abilities to help solve this mystery. I need to know how she's helping the Paynes find their missing child. With such a success on the Jacqui Poole case, she should be able to clear this one up quickly.

Christine has a strong Irish accent, is dressed in white linen trousers and sits on the sofa dangling her short legs over the side. She is, by any standard, exceptionally chatty.

She tells me that Nicola disappeared into thin air, but leaning forwards she adds: 'Well, let's just say that whoever was responsible for murdering her would have known her, and it would have been very ... very local.'

Right. I take a sip of my tea and look around the room. It's spotlessly clean, with white leather sofas and a family photo on the wall of Nicola and her four brothers. I haven't met Marilyn yet but I can tell she's a proud, hard-working woman who likes to keep things in order. Christine Holohan is sitting on her immaculate sofa, chatting warmly and laughing, and suddenly I really hope that she knows what she's doing. Did she think before she got involved with a bereaved mother desperate to know something – anything – about what happened to her only daughter?

'I did have reservations about getting involved,' Christine tells me. 'Marilyn phoned me and I was hesitant for a while. You see I never know what to do, because people depend so much on you and ... the little Jacqui Poole case, it doesn't work like that with every case, unfortunately,' she adds, looking thoughtful while sipping her tea.

'You can't just railroad in there,' she continues. 'You're dealing with somebody who's in a very vulnerable position. You've always got be careful of what you say and you can't lie either.'

Before arriving at Marilyn's house I'd headed down to the Black Pad myself. It's a small park at the back of some houses, well lit and bright. But these changes have been made since Nicola disappeared. Then it was a virtual wasteland that locals used as a short cut – it looked overgrown and unkempt but they'd considered it safe.

Christine has also been down to the Pad this week, feeling for signs. This, it seems, is at the heart of her investigations, as well as trying to get in touch with Nicola through normal medium channels. But there have been no solid facts, no visitation as strong and as clear as Jacqui Poole. There's no 'glowing maiden' talking in clear, crisp sentences.

I ask her what's she found.

'I was here two years ago. It was very much the same feeling. You see, the problem is, a person will show you a place, but you've got to remember that in seventeen years that place has changed. The place is not the same. But I just go with my energies. I just get the one area,' Christine says.

'As you walk away it gets cold, it gets that bit colder,' she tells me. 'The trail gets a bit colder and colder. And to communicate with someone that's been gone for sixteen, seventeen years, the trail has gone extremely cold by then.'

There's another problem communicating with spirits. Christine was worried because people in death, it seems, are just like people in life.

'You've got to remember it's the individual. You meet people in life and some are open and they'll even tell you what they had for breakfast. And this is what they are like in death. If they don't want to talk, they won't talk.'

Christine's back over again from Ireland trying to get more information, admitting she's now personally involved with the

Payne family and wants to see closure. 'I'm gonna try again, just give it one more crack, just see if there's something else I can do,' she assures me.

While the distance in time since Nicola disappeared makes it harder to get in touch, Christine has still managed to come up with some information. It seems that facts or bits of information pop into her mind, which she believes is Nicola trying to communicate.

Christine came up with the name Chloe, a dog called Barney and a scrapyard, and also revealed that the person involved has murdered two people before. She told Marilyn that Nicola died because she saw something she shouldn't have, 'involving drugs or something,' she said.

'Whatever the reasons are, what this is all about, I don't know, but I just know the police are working on it at the moment.' Christine pauses. 'I feel myself they'll get … they're gonna get results now,' she adds quickly.

And then she tells me something surprising.

'I was out with the police early in the week, and two years ago they drove with me and Marilyn out to tour scrapyards to see whether I could get any more information.'

'You went out with the police?'

'Yeah.'

I'm still taking in the extraordinary fact that the police themselves have been following up on her tip-offs when she abruptly changes the subject.

'Marilyn Monroe came and sat by me on my bed on and off for years.'

My thoughts are sidetracked by this sudden tangent and I look over at Christine with a new fascination. 'She did what?'

'Oh, she was a very beautiful girl, but she was very ... very ... very sad. Really sad, because she said ... she used to say to me a lot, like, you know like everybody loved ... everyone loved Marilyn, but nobody loved Norma Jean. She said, "I was still Norma Jean inside, you know." And it's like the two personalities used to clash. That's what caused a lot of insecurities. But there was definitely an affair there with the Kennedys, definitely, without a doubt, and Bobby in particular, you know.'

I don't really know what to do with this information, yet a slow realisation dawns on me. Marilyn Monroe has been dead since 1962, and yet back in the 1980s she was able to sit on Christine Holohan's bed and talk in full, unabridged sentences 25 years after she died, but Nicola Payne, who has been feared dead not half that time, comes back to Christine only as wisps of energy or odd, disconnected names. I don't get it.

'I don't know why they come to me,' Christine admits. Nor do I, I think, but I don't press the point.

Then Marilyn Payne enters the lounge. She sits down on the edge of the sofa, unlike Christine Holohan who sinks back and relaxes. Marilyn's the kind of woman who keeps busy, constantly running about finishing jobs and never giving herself a moment's rest. She's just finished hoovering upstairs, trying to keep her home spotless. She tells me she's turned her house into a registered care home where she looks after elderly residents. She talks quickly and intensely in a West Midlands accent with soft Birmingham tones. She's still confused by Nicola's disappearance and is still desperately looking for answers.

I don't really want to talk to Marilyn. I feel I'm intruding on her grief, no matter how long ago Nicola disappeared. She also reminds me of my mum – her Birmingham accent, her hard work, her nursing and caring, and the way she just never stops, ever. And she's real, with bereavement in her life that no one I know can come close to understanding. Hearing her talk about the day she realised Nicola had gone missing, you quickly realise that she's still feeling the pain intensely – it hasn't faded. It's a parent's worst nightmare. You know you just can't relate to what she's been through. It's unbearable.

I'm here to question Christine Holohan, not be a witness to Marilyn's pain, a leech on her memories and feelings. I just can't help wondering what Christine is doing here. If I'm feeling guilty about asking Marilyn a few questions, what's Christine feeling, and what's she getting out of this? Is she able to provide real comfort, able to change the future and help in the search for Nicola, or is there something else? Having Christine and Marilyn in the same room might provide some answers.

'I was catching up on a few jobs there,' Marilyn tells me, leaning forwards.

'How are you doing?'

'Not too bad ... not too bad,' she says, looking tired.

So how ... how are things going?

'Well, you know, I keep ... when Christine says she'll come over again I get a lot of ... I just feel that I get a lot of ... I don't know ... power, sort of, from her and ... and it gives me a bit more hope and that, you know. Just to see if there's anything else that she picks up,' she says, her speech hesitant.

'See, there's so much that I've seen over the years, but there's nothing concrete,' Marilyn tells me, remembering the long years that she's never once stopped looking for her daughter. 'My best friend died a few weeks ago and she came back to me the night after she died and she said to me, "You're looking in the wrong place. It's Wales, Cardigan Bay. They've put her in water." So I spoke with the police yesterday and asked what would it cost me to get some divers, just to go … just to make me feel … And then I don't know if … is it your mind playing tricks on you, because she'd just gone and I was thinking about her a lot and so you don't really know. And the policeman said, "Cardigan Bay is so big, it was …" I mean, I don't know, because I've never been there, see, so I says, "Oh well. Well just keep it in mind."'

In a further review of the Nicola Payne case last June, the cold case unit got involved and dug up someone's garden. But nothing came of it. The police had told her not to build her hopes up, but it left her reeling.

'I was so down, I just couldn't get back on. It's only perhaps in the last week I've just picked up a bit more. I wanna get back. Just keep working otherwise you just sit and you just get so depressed, you know,' she says.

'Yeah, I know,' I reply, but I don't. I don't know what Marilyn's going through, and nor, I imagine, does Christine Holohan.

Marilyn says that Nicola, still living at home at the time she went missing, was about to start a new life for herself, moving into her own home with her boyfriend Jason and her young son, Owen. The day she disappeared she was meant to come home and give the keys for her new flat to her dad so he could finish off some decorating. But, as we know, she didn't turn up.

'Her dad,' adds Marilyn, looking at the photograph of her family on the wall, 'it's killed her dad, hasn't it? I mean he never had blood pressure or nothing, but he suffers from high blood pressure now. He still works, he's a long-distance driver, but it's absolutely tore him to pieces.' Marilyn puts her hands up and looks lost.

In the middle of this, Christine suddenly joins in. 'She gives me certain amounts of information, doesn't she?'

'Yeah,' says Marilyn.

'I ring you up and you can fit the information in again,' Christine adds.

It seems that whenever something comes into Christine's head, she phones Marilyn and keeps her busy trying to make sense of these pieces of information, trying to make them relevant to that horrible day seventeen years ago.

There have been so many theories about what happened, from the police, and even from a neighbour who saw Nicola on her way to the park. First the suspect was young, then he was old. He may have had tattoos and then he didn't.

It's confusing. Yet Marilyn sounds convinced by (and is convincing about) each of the theories. Listening to her talk about the first of these, I can't believe how the police could have missed it – until another theory comes along, and another. It's not Marilyn's fault. She's still desperately trying to find answers which the police can't give her, and there have been suggestions and innuendoes all through the years which she's still grappling with – mistakes that the police made, people they didn't interview properly – and then, to top it all, there's Christine Holohan.

I've tried to observe Christine while Marilyn's been talking, watching what she says for any clues, and it seems she agrees with and reinforces every new theory.

'My energies end there, I cannot get my energies anywhere else,' she says at one point when Marilyn mentions a street where someone heard a scream and a car racing off. The suggestion is that Nicola was abducted before she even made it to the Black Pad. But Christine had already told me that she felt something in the park. Later still, she mentions 'a darkness outside a particular house' when Marilyn mentions that something could have happened there. At one point after Marilyn tells me her theory that someone local harmed Nicola, Christine chimes in with: 'Oh, yes, it happened at night, alright.'

So not in the day at noon, then, as Christine suggested before? And what about the scrapyard theory that she had told the police about two years ago, which encouraged them to spend time taking her round all the yards in the area to see if she could feel some kind of energy or presence?

'We'll get to the end of it,' Christine announces determinedly. 'I'm like a dog with a bone.'

'You don't let it drop, do you?' Marilyn agrees. 'She'll ring me up or she'll send me little things.'

Then, a moment later, when Marilyn tells me that the Black Pad was built over a former mine, Christine lights up with a new theory and an odd exchange takes place between the two women.

'Have they got any pictures of when it was a mine?' Christine asks.

'No, but they went down and had them all checked,' replies Marilyn.

'Did they?'

'Yes, that was all checked. They did ... they did it all,' Marilyn repeats.

'Because I get the strangest of pictures,' suggests Christine.

But Marilyn is firm about this and shuts Christine up. 'No, they did all of that, because it had been sealed up and done up for donkeys' years.' The last thing Marilyn needs now is yet another theory attempting to explain where her daughter might be, and I get the very strong impression that she knows it too.

Marilyn gets up quickly. 'Look, I must go and sort my little lady out,' she says.

Before leaving, she turns and looks at me. 'You've just got to try and carry on and just hope that something will come too.' Moments later I can hear her upstairs, keeping herself busy.

I look over at Christine, still chatty and friendly, and she starts telling me again about the patch of energy in the park, but I interrupt her to say that I have to go. I call a taxi, and when it arrives I walk to the door with Christine. She stands in the living room window and waves goodbye as the taxi pulls off and heads to the train station, back past Marilyn's neighbours and past the Black Pad once more.

I look at the passing houses and sink deep into my seat, ignoring the driver's attempts to make conversation. I feel uncomfortable. I'm unsure what just went on in the Paynes' house, and what role Christine is playing in Marilyn's life. But I can't stop thinking about something Marilyn said.

'All I pray for is to have her found,' Marilyn told me, her eyes wide open, her hands moving slowly against each other. 'All I keep asking for is where is she, where did they dispose of the body, just where is she so I can please have her found? I just need a closure, to have her found and it's ... I mean, I don't know, some people don't seem to understand that, but I just do. I need to have a closure and have her found.'

I do understand, Marilyn, I really do, I say to myself. You need to find your daughter and put her to rest.

9

Captain Realyvasquez goes hunting

CAPTAIN FERNANDO REALYVASQUEZ brakes and the car draws slowly to a stop on a winding dirt track through the San Pedro Valley Park, San Mateo County, California. He leans out the window and points up to a path that rises through the undergrowth to a ridge high above.

'That's where Dennis Prado died, and that's where Annette Martin said we'd find him,' he says, staring at me without blinking.

Captain Realyvasquez doesn't seem like a policeman to me. Sure, he's packing a sidearm that's large enough to break my foot, if he dropped it. But he's talkative, patient and respectful, apologising to walkers we pass for driving in the local country park and getting in their way. What's more, he's agreed to meet me to talk about Annette Martin, a local psychic detective who has worked intimately with the police for the past 25 years.

In the UK, the police draw down a heavy shutter when they're asked about the involvement of psychics. Even the Metropolitan Police Force gives a curt response: 'The Metropolitan Police Force does not include the use of psychics in its detective training. We do not actively seek the help of psychics during investigations of crime,' said Jonathan, the

Met's gatekeeper, protecting officers on the beat from disturbing inquiries like mine.

This is, of course, nonsense, as the police in Coventry searching scrapyards with Christine Holohan shows. So I try again.

'Can I speak to someone about this?'

'No,' came the police's reply.

'Not even to see how police weigh evidence from psychics as possible witness statements?'

'Definitely not!'

It's a pretty counterproductive approach, though, because people will just draw their own conclusions, and on past experience they will leap at the conspiracy theory first. That's the one that says that the police do use psychics but won't tell the public because they're scared of everyone laughing at them.

So thanks to the Met's desire for openness and transparency, I find myself back in the US, talking to Captain Realyvasquez from the Pacifica City Police Department. He was the officer in charge of finding 71-year-old veteran soldier Dennis Prado. I first came across the story on closure4you.com, the website for Annette Martin's psychic detective company, on which she claims she has helped solve tens if not hundreds of crimes, working exclusively alongside local police forces.

A statement on the site from Captain Realyvasquez, who was a detective sergeant at the time, made my own psychic detective antenna sit up to attention: 'The fact of the matter is that he had been missing for nearly three months. I am still a little bit sceptical, but on the other hand, in this particular case, we probably wouldn't have found him if it hadn't been for Annette Martin.'

It seems pretty conclusive then. A police officer has confirmed a psychic's successful involvement, and, what's more, it's been corroborated by its reconstruction on TV, which clearly makes its credentials bona fide. Sandra at the Sylvia Browne salon first brought the phenomenon that is Court TV to my attention, and its show *Psychic Detectives*. The episode about the missing Prado is a brilliant example of American TV, with a confused Realyvasquez scratching his head like Stan Laurel at the whereabouts of Prado, only to be saved by Annette Martin, who makes the screen go all wobbly and distorted when she enters a psychic trance. I love it. It's thoroughly entertaining for all the wrong reasons.

The Prado case is simple. He disappeared from his apartment and the Pacifica police detectives failed to find him, searching in vain for three long months. They eventually consulted Annette Martin at the request of Prado's family. Realyvasquez showed the psychic a photo of the veteran and a map of the San Pedro Valley Park, located right next to Prado's apartment. Martin quickly went into a trance, and saw that Prado had hiked into the park. During his walk he had suffered a stroke and dropped down dead, rolling into the undergrowth along the dirt path. Then Annette Martin marked the map with a circle, telling Realyvasquez that was where he'd find the body.

What's more impressive is that the San Pedro Valley Park is 2,000 acres in size and the circle that Annette drew covered only a very small area – a pinprick in a sea of trees.

In the Court TV programme, it's Roberta Hauser, a volunteer with the San Mateo County search and rescue team, who goes out to find the body, saying that she found him not just near Annette Martin's squiggle, but in the dead centre of the circle.

After my unsettling experience meeting Christine Holohan, watching her direct her psychic energies from a comfortable sofa in Coventry, I wanted to check out another verifiable case of psychic detection. I also desperately needed to have a case of psychic detection confirmed by a police officer to my face. If Captain Realyvasquez, a man expert at weighing up evidence, says Annette Martin helped him find Prado's body, well, that's all the proof we need, isn't it?

But first I want to get a handle on Annette Martin. I meet the psychic in her office in downtown San José, just a few minutes' drive from Sylvia Browne's world headquarters. She meets me at the door of her small office, one of a row of single-storey office units just off Winchester Boulevard. She's small, blonde and bright, showing me cuttings from local newspapers that she's had framed and stuck to her wall.

'This is where I let my clients wait,' she tells me, as we walk through a narrow vestibule into her office. Behind Annette's desk is a huge photograph of herself on the hunt for evidence. She and a group of people (I think one's a police detective) stand motionless looking at a field. It suggests that hard work and serious detection are taking place. In another world, they'd look as though they were trying to find a nice spot for a picnic.

'I saw him starting to walk on this dirt path and all of a sudden I see him fall, and he falls down and I said, "Oh my God! I think he's had a stroke or a heart attack",' she tells me. 'I knew he was dead, and I said to the officer, "He's right here on the map." So I drew this little tiny circle on the map and said, "He's right here, right in the middle of that circle." The detective just looked at me. You know, not believing a word I said.'

Annette Martin hadn't worked with Captain Realyvasquez before. Until then, Sergeant Richard Keaton from Marin County Sheriff's Office had been her main sidekick.

Unfortunately Sergeant Keaton was out of action due to a recent quadruple heart bypass operation. 'I had an immediate sense there was this connection with Keaton. And I knew that he would believe what I was going to tell him and it was going to be okay,' she says about the first case she worked on with Keaton more than twenty years ago.

After leaving the police force a few years ago, Keaton set up in business with Annette – he did the detective work, she used her psychic powers when the trail went cold.

'He's just an excellent detective. He could tell by my eyelash moving where I was. I mean he also became extremely intuitive,' she says. 'So when we're so intuitive, William, what happens is that we're sending out these waves, these electromagnetic waves that are very … very strong. So those of us who have the kind of mind like I do are able to pick up on that, it's like picking up a radio frequency, okay? And it's like, "Oh wait a minute. Tune that dial, what is that? What's going on, something's happening." And then as soon as I start focusing in on that, then I begin to see the pictures okay. And everything's in full colour. I hear, I smell, I taste and I see. So all of my five senses are working.'

Understanding that it's all down to electromagnetic radio waves, I head back to Pacifica to see how good Annette's reception really is.

After the drive through San Pedro Valley Park, I find myself back in Realyvasquez's office. I want to check his story. He's already admitted to me that he knows I'm interviewing him for 'entertainment purposes'. He's only showing me around, and only did the Court TV show, because he believes he owes it to Annette Martin for helping him find Dennis Prado.

'She's the one who gets kudos from being associated with the police,' he says. 'What do I get? I'm getting nothing from driving you around, showing you these things.'

Despite me wasting valuable police time, Realyvasquez is still exceptionally patient with being put under the spotlight. I want to know whether Annette really did help him find Prado's body, or just thinks she did. It's a big difference.

The captain sits himself down behind his large desk in his huge office. Every surface has a dark mahogany sheen. I grab a low chair and push it close to the desk and sit like a school child looking up at him.

The captain sits up straight-backed and seems to move only in short, sharp bursts. I imagine it's his gun preventing him from making graceful movements. He pulls open Prado's file, and a photograph of the dead veteran stares back at us.

'Let's see here, Mr Prado was reported missing on May 14th of 1997. Okay, and he had been missing for two to three weeks already from the time he was reported missing and, you know, I worked fairly closely with the family in an effort to follow up on any leads – on what his habits were, restaurants that he would attend,' he says in his deep American drawl, shifting the weight of his gun again.

'Once he was reported missing we went to the house, you know, there was no sign of foul play, and there was really nothing suspicious about anything, other than that he was just missing.'

Realyvasquez confirms that the Prado family suggested he use the services of Annette Martin – so he passed the request by his boss. 'You know, he rolled his eyes just like I did.'

The captain then went over to Annette's place, where she interviewed him for an hour and a half. Christ, for someone who told me she doesn't like being given that much information, that's a hell of a lot of time to spend shooting the breeze, as I imagine Realyvasquez might say if he was in a Raymond Chandler novel.

He confirms that Annette drew the circle on a map and said that Prado had been having breathing difficulties. She also thought he was still up there in the park. So far, so good. Everything checks out.

But then the captain tells me that when he went out looking for Prado the first time using the map with Annette Martin's circle outlining the area, he didn't find anything. I get the impression that Realyvasquez didn't have that many resources, that he and a fellow officer went out with a couple of sticks thwacking about for a bit. It's a big place and you really can't get far.

What I'm wondering is that if Realyvasquez had already been out with the circled map and didn't find anything, well, maybe the circle wasn't that accurate. Realyvasquez gets out a map – the type that Annette used – and also shows me the area on Google Earth at his computer. I'm shocked. There's only one path leading from Prado's home at the edge of the park, and so it would have been stupid to put the circle anywhere else. This small observation makes the area that Annette Martin was choosing from suddenly a hell of a lot smaller than 2,000 acres. It's not even a tenth of that size. Although, admittedly, the circle still had to go somewhere. I have only tracker Roberta Hauser's word that Prado was found inside the circle, but I find it pretty hard to believe that she'd have known exactly where the circle was in relation to his body, as the map isn't that clear. It's like one of those pirates' treasure maps, with an X marking the spot. It's not an Ordnance Survey map, it's a rough visitors' guide to the area.

Then, as Realyvasquez is telling me again how Hauser found Prado in the circle, he lets slip a revealing fact.

'The search and rescue worker went to San Pedro Valley Park with a friend of hers who has a rescue dog. It's a dog trained to find cadavers. So they walked into the park and the only way you can get a dog in there is in your official capacity, so they were in uniform,' he says.

'I'm sorry?' I interrupt. I ask him again just to be clear.

'Annette Martin circled the map, right?' repeats the captain. 'She circled the map and this search and rescue volunteer went up there based on that information. So, you know, whether it was luck or not, the reality of it is the reason we found him is because the search and rescue worker used that map to go look for him,' he says adamantly.

'You don't think,' I say, swallowing and glancing quickly at the captain's holster, 'that maybe Prado was found because they took a sniffer dog with them?'

'No.' He pauses. 'It's possible … it's possible, but when they called me and I went up there the reality of it is that he was about fifteen feet off the trail just like Annette Martin said he would be? So you can flip a coin and conclude what you want.'

So I do, I flip a coin. Heads, it's the dog trained to find dead bodies that found Prado; tails, it's the hound with a nose for cadavers that sniffed him out. If you're looking for a body that's been decaying and smelling pretty badly for three whole months, then a dog trained in finding dead bodies would, I imagine, find the goddamn body.

My only confusion is why they didn't think of taking a dog out before. Well, it turns out they don't have any. This is the great thing about the US police force. They work like separate agencies. The Pacifica Police Department is tiny, looking after just a few thousand citizens, while the Sheriff's Office, which has responsibility for county affairs, has all the resources and, importantly, the dogs.

'I recommended Roberta Hauser for a medal because she found the dead body but the Sheriff's department said no, she'd been acting in a voluntary capacity,' says Realyvasquez. In other words, she wasn't meant to be there with the dog.

To be fair to Realyvasquez, he's right. They wouldn't have found the dead body without Annette Martin, because without her they wouldn't have gone back out to look. And in answer to my question whether he's used psychics before or since, he's pretty clear:

'I can honestly tell you that I don't know if I'd go running back to Annette Martin to do this again, based on the way this happened. I don't know … If I felt that confident in the system, I mean I wouldn't even have detectives, I'd just go call her every time.'

The other interesting fact about this case is that the Court TV version of events left out the bit about the dog. It's a great big whopping hole to miss out. And it demonstrates exactly how public perception of the power of psychics is fuelled by popular accounts. I imagine Professor Wiseman wouldn't be impressed.

Yet I'm still unsure how the police use psychics in the US and the UK. Are they really useful, or do they just keep the victim's family happy?

In tricky psychic investigations like this there really is only one person to turn to. So I call the hotline to the parapsychologist for Living TV's *Most Haunted*, Dr Ciarán O'Keeffe. He also, it just so happens, wrote his PhD thesis on the very subject of psychic detectives.

I phone him in New York, where he tells me he's just finished filming for the latest episode of *Most Haunted*. Dr O'Keeffe first confirms that the police have to take evidence from psychics seriously, just like they have to take any witness statements seriously. It's not necessarily because the police are hedging their bets about the existence of the spirit world, but because the psychic may be fronting for someone more genuine, like a relative of the murderer who wants to protect their own identity.

'This is how psychics create their own press,' he says. 'They say they are helping the police with their inquiries. What it means is that they've just passed on some information to the police, that the police are obligated to take it down and respond.

'In the US it's a different state of affairs [to the UK] because of the number of police forces around the country. As you travel from small town to small town you find that each has its own police department, and members of the local police force will each have their own beliefs. They can therefore use a psychic without the knowledge of their superior officers.'

Dr O'Keeffe also reveals that psychics who have been associated with solving crimes usually give vague statements with a high probability of being correct. 'On the whole, psychics favour saying that the body will be found near water. In the UK, you're not going to be far from water no matter where you are standing,' he tells me.

Oh. I suddenly remember what Diane Lazarus told me in my conversation with her. She said she'd found a dead body in a river.

There's also something called post hoc interpretation. 'If a psychic says that the murderer will be driving a 1960s red Volkswagen and wearing a white T-shirt, and the police catch the murderer and discover he was driving a red car, that is seen as a hit. All the information that they didn't get right, the age of the vehicle, the make, will be ignored,' he says, slowly but surely dismantling my belief in the power of psychic detectives.

He quotes at me an article written in the magazine *Police Review* by Detective Inspector David Thompson and Detective Sergeant Michael Riley that assessed the impact of mediums on police investigations in the UK. As both officers are members of the CID branch, they're well trained at spotting fraud.

After a thorough search across most of the forces in the UK, and after looking in detail at the impact of the 600 letters of information from mediums received in the Sarah Jayne Harper murder in the 1980s, they conclude that the investigation was 'in danger of squandering police resources'. The police would have wasted valuable time interviewing mediums, following up with fruitless searches and distracting officers from more relevant lines of inquiry. As it is, they spent ten hours interviewing and following up on the speculations from a medium, which produced 'little information which corresponded with the reality of the situation'.

Overall, Thompson and Riley conclude that 'the consensus was that mediums supplied a great deal of irrelevant and inaccurate information'.

As Dr O'Keeffe points out, this is very different from the reports in the popular press. Journalists fell over each other in their desperation to print any claim from a medium that they helped the police.

Dr O'Keeffe sounds pretty unconvinced about the reliability of psychic detectives. But what about the Jacqui Poole case? It was ultimately solved using DNA, but, according to the officers involved, Christine Holohan provided key evidence that led to that DNA being found – i.e. the jumper that the police dug up.

It turns out that Dr O'Keeffe undertook a review of the report for the Society for Psychical Research journal. He was impressed with the level of detail that Playfair and Keen were able to amass, but he still has his doubts. If I want real answers, he tells me, I need to check out Tony Youens, the sceptic's sceptic, the nemesis for all psychic detectives everywhere. Youens is a health and safety training manager at the University of Leeds by day, but one seriously impressive sceptic in his spare time.

As a founding member of the Association for Skeptical Enquiry (ASKE), Youens began his investigations because he didn't like the idea of people being ripped off. He's almost hypersensitive to flaws of experimentation, and gives events a healthy critique in a way that people like Playfair and Keen do not.

'I have to emphasise that the explanation I have offered is not necessarily the right one,' Youens tells me. 'Montague Keen [Guy Lyon Playfair's co-investigator on the Christine Holohan case], a man seemingly willing to believe anything as long as it's paranormal, challenged sceptics to provide a possible non-supernatural explanation of what happened, and this I have done. The only person capable of revealing the real truth is Christine Holohan herself and I can guarantee that she will stick like new improved superglue to her ridiculous story.'

Youens goes on to express concern about an issue that no one else has mentioned so far. 'I am also bothered about another aspect of this case, one that is frequently ignored, and that is that the families of Jacqui Poole and Tony Ruark are still suffering from this awful murder,' he says, accusing both Keen and Holohan of raking over the cases with disregard to the families involved.

'That's not to say I am tarring you with the same brush,' he adds. 'You are, I assume, like me – simply trying to get to the bottom of the whole thing.'

I read through Youens' account of what happened in this case and have my first eye-opener. Tony Batters wasn't a detective as was stated in Playfair and Keen's report. He was a PC and wasn't even central to the investigation. He just helped out on the administrative side of things. If you don't believe Youens, ask Tony Lundy, who was the Detective Superintendent on the case. In a letter to Youens he stated very clearly that:

'Tony Batters was never a Detective. He was a beat constable and was the officer who attended the scene when the murder was discovered. Because of his local knowledge and keenness to help, I seconded him to the investigation team. He went to interview Christine Holohan with a Detective Constable and became somewhat obsessed with her views, and remains so!'

It's a huge mistake for Keen and Playfair to make, conferring on Batters an expertise and position that he didn't have. He wasn't an expert at sifting through evidence as I first thought. I also wonder why Playfair and Keen didn't talk to Lundy as Youens did. It seems pretty elementary.

'The basis of their claim,' says Youens, 'is that it was impossible for Christine Holohan to have obtained this information by normal means and therefore it must, by default, be paranormal. They believe it must have been either telepathy or mediumship.'

I read further on into Youens' own report and begin to feel the earth shifting underneath the account by Playfair and Keen.

With help from Detective Adrian Shaw, Youens sets about dismantling Christine Holohan's claims objectively, brilliantly and fairly, one by one. Rather than just asking the medium involved and the two police officers who were already convinced by her story, as Playfair and Keen did, Youens asked everyone, including Detective Chief Inspector Norman McKinlay who headed the cold case unit, as well as the detective who originally took Ruark in for questioning and also retrieved the pullover from his dustbin.

In fact, Youens takes issue with the idea that without the recovery of the pullover, Ruark would still be a free man. He's incredibly thorough, and his forensic investigations produce a series of eye-opening revelations. DCI McKinlay couldn't even remember the pullover, he reveals. Both McKinlay and Superintendent Lundy were in no doubt that Ruark's conviction was based on DNA evidence from semen and from skin found underneath the victim's fingernails. 'The pullover played no part and even if it did, it was not due to anything Christine Holohan had said,' Youens says.

Superintendent Lundy also assured Youens that at no time during the investigation did he take any action based on information supplied by Christine Holohan. He only ever followed normal police procedure.

Youens also thinks that Holohan had information passed to her by someone who wanted to alert the police to the identity of 'Pokie' Ruark and yet remain anonymous, as Dr Ciarán O'Keefe suggested.

In her book *A Voice From the Grave*, Christine acknowledges that she overheard two women discussing the murder on a Monday morning – three days before she contacted the police. Youens also found that much of the information about how Jacqui died was in the local paper before Christine went to the police. The two leading detectives on the case, Lundy and McKinlay, both told Youens separately that it was common knowledge that Ruark was a suspect. As Holohan lived only about three miles from the murder scene, and less than one and a half miles from the Windmill pub where Jacqui worked, it would have been entirely possible to discover much of this information from local gossip.

Superintendent Lundy also told Youens that Ruark was 'suspected immediately' and held in custody within the first 24 hours of the investigation, and it would have been during this time that Ruark's premises were searched and the 'vital' pullover discovered. This would have been at least three days before Christine Holohan was interviewed.

I think the last word on the case has to be with Lundy. In a letter he sent to Youens, the frustration boils over:

'Anthony Ruark was a local criminal and an associate of the victim and he was a suspect within a day of the murder. He was interviewed and kept in custody on more than one occasion and did not become a suspect because of Holohan. She did not supply anything that advanced the investigation. At the time I used to say to the officers dealing with her: "If she is so in touch with the case could she please tell us where the missing jewellery is." Of course, she could not do so. She did not supply

anything significant that advanced or assisted the investigation!!
That fact is beyond dispute.'

Youens' brilliant piece of detection makes me wonder about
the Nicola Payne case and why Christine has only been able to
get small pieces of information that haven't impressed anyone.
Marilyn has to do all the work, trying to make sense of these
brief spirit-world messages.

But Christine genuinely feels that she's helping people, and
if Marilyn thinks that too, then should we really worry? I don't
know, but there's something that Youens wasn't able to do. He
didn't interview Holohan, the central witness to this case.

But I did.

I sit back and relive the moment that Christine told me that
Marilyn Monroe came to sit on her bed. She worried that, in
retrospect, maybe she had been seeing things.

'I was open to all these things, I would have never questioned
that. Today, now, I would question a thing, if I had an experience. You're older and you get a bit more cynical at times. I
never questioned anything. Something happened, I'd think,
"That's okay, that's part of who I am," you know.'

'So when you question something that you've seen, what do
you do?' I asked her.

'You sort of say, "Well, was that my imagination, or why am
I doing that, or what's this about, or what am I supposed to do
with this?"' she said, becoming thoughtful.

And then she mentioned the Jacqui Poole case.

'It's like when Jacqui Poole appeared in my place and she
came through to me. Oh God, it was the weirdest feeling I ever
had. I could feel somebody coming up the hallway, but there
was no one in the hallway. And there was this white energy, it
was like an orb. It was flowing around my bedroom. It's like

you're somewhere else. You think, "Am I half-dreaming this here? Is this really happening, or what's going on?" You know, sometimes when you're dreaming, you're waking up and you're not able to wake up. You're going to open your eyes and they're not opening, and you're not waking up.'

Most of us would have just written it off as a dream. As Christine's doubts about that night more than 30 years ago seem to increase with age, perhaps one day she'll come to that conclusion too.

10

Deep in the witches' lair

I'VE GOT to get a grip.

I don't want to admit it, but I've got a sudden attack of the heebie-jeebies. I haven't been normal since I agreed to spend Hallowe'en with a coven of witches.

To fuel my fear, I've been reading stories about devil worship, about secret societies with cruel sacrificial rituals, and horses being mutilated in the north of England in bizarre ceremonies. Remains of sacrificial fires, bones and pentagrams have been found in Clapham Woods in Sussex. Charles Walker, an occult investigator and specialist on the area, has reported that dogs have wandered off in the woods never to be seen again. 'In other cases dogs appeared to go mad in certain parts of the wood, running round in circles and foaming at the mouth,' Walker reported.

He uncovered a secret society called the Friends of Hecate, devoted to the goddess of that name, who were sacrificing dogs in her honour. Walker was warned off many times by High Priests and Priestesses in other secret covens, while a friend of his was badly injured during an investigation into their activities.

I get nervous just reading this, because the coven I'm visiting is based near a haunted wood in Sussex.

To make matters worse, I've uncovered stories about Aleister Crowley, who has been called the most wicked man ever to have lived. For members of the Golden Dawn, the most influential occult group in Britain, he was beyond the pale. He experimented with magic rituals and told his followers that he was able to call up creatures from the underworld and encourage poltergeist mischief. It's been reported that he was able to summon demons and hold the most powerful dark ritual – the black mass.

I'm beginning to think that I might just stay at home. But then on Friday afternoon, the day I'm due to head to the coven, I get some of my old gung-ho attitude back and quickly pack my bag and head to the train station. I mean, really, what's the worst that could happen?

I arrive later that night, Hallowe'en, at an old stately home in the Sussex countryside. I'm directed to a banqueting suite. The big doors of the room are sealed shut. The witches are inside preparing a ceremony. Tonight is Samhain, the witches' New Year, when the veil between the spirit world and the living is at its thinnest. When the big doors open, I will be invited to take part in a ritual to welcome the waking dead back into the world.

I should be concerned, but also waiting for the huge doors to be pushed open is Debs. She's 29 years old, between jobs, and is fretting. She's been practising rituals and spells on her own, and reading as much as she can about witches, but last night she forgot to 'cast a circle'. She's terrified that she let in some harmful spirits that might ruin her life.

Compared with her, I've got nothing to worry about.

'I rang a bell to welcome in the spirits, chanting that they should do no harm. I left out burnt toast and cut open a lemon to feed the ghosts who are hungry on their journey between life and death, trapped in the in-between world that Hallowe'en has opened up,' she tells me, speaking as though she's reading from a prepared script, before taking a slug of a large drink she's poured.

She's down for the weekend from Birmingham to check out the coven. Until now she's been practising as a solitary hedge witch. But she wants to learn more. 'I used to tell everyone when I was a child that I was a witch. I just felt it was right,' she says, her skin losing colour as she begins to worry again about the dark spirit that might possess her at any moment.

The big doors open and Helen, a High Priestess in her early thirties, floats out, her witch's robes billowing behind her. She comes over, seeing from the state of Debs that something's wrong.

'I didn't know I had to cast a circle,' Debs says, looking to Helen, desperate for help and advice.

Before casting a spell, witches have to draw a circle with their wand while saying magic words to protect themselves from harmful spirits.

'But you had candles around you?' Helen asks firmly in a strong Dudley accent.

Debs nods.

'Oh, yaw'll be alright,' Helen replies.

I want to ask, 'So what could really happen to Debs? What's the worst possible thing – could she die?' But I don't have the opportunity because Helen is summoned back into the banqueting room to help cast the circle for tonight's ritual. Debs certainly doesn't need me piling on the anxiety, anyway. She looks like she's about to have a nervous breakdown.

A few minutes later we're invited inside. A long table with candelabras dominates the room. To the right, standing in front of the fireplace, are five witches, all decked out in robes, waiting for us, the initiates, to troop in. There's me, Debs, Helen's boyfriend Jeff, who reminds me of Dylan from *The Magic Roundabout*, and a witch called Brenda from Bradford.

The door is shut and we begin the ritual to welcome the dead.

Before we start I've got a burning question that I need answering. Leaning over, I manage to whisper to Helen:

'So, err, why's the veil so thin, then, you know, between our world and theirs?' It's an issue that's been bugging me for a long time and I can't wait to get to the bottom of it.

'It's because at this time of year thousands of years ago it was a time of death. Trees were dying, the leaves were falling off, and people were dying from the cold. It was a time of a lot of death,' she whispers back.

Right.

There's no more time for questions. The witches start chanting and honouring the gods of the east, south, west and north. A witch takes her wand and a black-handled knife called an athame and asks for protection from each of the corners of the room.

And then we ask the spirits to join us. Everyone has a part to play, including me. In fact, when Helen asks us initiates if we want to read out some of the ritual, I stick my hand in the air and almost shout 'Me, me, me', as though I'm back in primary school.

Each of those honoured to call the dead are passed a sacred candle. Eventually it's my turn and I call out:

The moon is bright, the crone is old
The body lifeless, the bones so cold
We all live and pay our dues
To die in ones and threes and twos.

I pass the candle to Jeff, and watch the seat at the table that has been left empty for the spirit to join us at dinner.

After the ceremony we are handed a glass of mead to drink, which tastes sweet like dessert wine, and we sit down to eat. The empty chair is still vacant. I'm next to Jeff. He doesn't seem like the kind of person that I expected to find at a witches' coven. Jeff shrugs.

'I'm just here, you know, to learn all about it cos Helen knows her stuff,' he tells me. 'You know, you might think it's coincidence but this stuff really works. Helen's done spells on me.'

'Really?'

'Yeah, yeah. I had this guy at work, he had connections, thought he was some kind of gangster, but he was really threatening and Helen did a spell and he went away.'

Helen, who I'm finding to be exceptionally friendly for a witch, overhears and glides over in her sweeping witch's robe to explain.

'It was a simple removal spell. It just removes the person from their life. Normally you just say a name, but for this I made a doll. The chap had put his photo on the internet, so I could use his picture.'

'Nutter!' I blurt out, shaking my head. For the moment, putting his picture on the internet seems far more ridiculous than Helen casting a spell. Helen's a witch who rights wrongs, this guy's a gangster who beats up harmless chaps like Jeff. It makes sense.

'I bumped into him later and all his animosity just disappeared,' Jeff says, giving me a meaningful nod.

Helen, a stickler for detail, corrects him. 'Well it was meant to remove him, but you were the one who went away. Sometimes when you do spells they just don't always work out the way you expect, but they still work.'

Helen tells me that to become a High Priestess you have to go through several initiation ceremonies. In fact, I'd already started reading up on these ceremonies and had also found out some interesting facts from the self-styled High Priest of the Coven of White Witches, Kevin Carlyon, whom I'd visited at his home in St Leonards, near the South Downs. 'I'm not a witch, I'm The Witch,' he'd told me. 'This place is renowned for witches.'

I was intrigued by Kevin because in photos he wears what looks like an orange terry towelling dressing gown for his witch's robes, he has an altar of skulls in his living room, and owns nineteen black cats. What's more, he told me how he'd put a curse on a devil-worshipping cult that was maiming horses. The attackers mutilated the hindquarters and genitals of four mares on farms around Bonnybridge, Stirlingshire.

Kevin, a kind-hearted white witch, was livid and cast one of his most powerful curses, saying that if the culprits struck again they would be made impotent and infertile.

'In the past, I have put a curse on people that are harming the horses – then suddenly they would stop,' he told me.

But he wouldn't take me to a haunted wood and show me a ceremony because he had no desire to be tested. As recompense for my long journey down he told me about his first initiation ceremony.

'I went to a coven in Portslade in 1978 and they were all naked. It was all bits and bums and they were looking each other up and down,' he recalled. 'There were a couple of women jumping over a cauldron that was in the middle of the floor and they knocked it over, and the carpet caught fire and the whole bloody place started going. The fire station was just up the road, so the fire brigade were down in five minutes and they saw all these naked people running out the front door,' he adds, shaking his head.

But, luckily, Kevin was in his dressing gown. Wise man. And he also thinks getting naked is farcical.

'Oh, I don't know,' I replied to his story. 'It sounds pretty reasonable to me, so long as you remember not to set fire to the house at the same time.'

Remembering this, I'm intrigued to see whether Helen got down with nature and went naked. She won't tell me what her initiation ceremony was. It's a secret. In fact, it's more than that. It's central to a witch's status that initiation ceremonies are hushed up. Jeff doesn't seem too bothered, though. I'm not sure whether that's because nothing untoward happened to Helen, or because nothing bothers Jeff.

Despite Helen's secrecy, I wouldn't be surprised if she was naked. Not to do anything dodgy, but because Wicca, the religion she believes in, is based in nature. They have the belief that getting naked makes the magic they perform more powerful.

Helen follows a school of witchcraft developed by Gerald Gardner, a British civil servant and witch, who attempted to stop Wicca dying out by publishing the *Book of Shadows*, a volume of spells and rituals, in the 1940s. While all witches are supposed to write down their spells in a book of shadows, Gardner claimed that his knowledge came from an ancient coven of witches in the New Forest, into which he'd been initiated.

It seems, however, that Gardner was mixing and matching his beliefs. He incorporated his interest in naturism into his ideas for witchcraft. Encouraged by the free love and sexual liberation movement of the 1960s, 'Gardnerian' witchcraft with its 'skyclad' (naked, clad only by the sky) rituals took off around the world.

There's certainly a lot of good feeling and love around the table tonight. In fact, I've got a soft spot for Helen. Not only has she got a great West Midlands accent, which reminds me of how I used to sound before it was beaten out of me at school, but she's already saved me a couple of times tonight from Brenda, the witch from Bradford. I've hardly said a word, but she already hates me.

She started immediately we sat down, pummelling me with a string of questions in an angry and aggressive voice. 'So why are you here?' What are going to do with your material? Who are you? Where are you from?'

She asks me the same questions over and over, forgetting that she's already asked them five minutes before. It becomes seriously unnerving.

Before long, Helen interrupts her: 'William's here doing research for his book and he is very welcome.'

That shut her up. Don't mess with the High Priestess.

We continue to eat dinner. I begin to find it a little too civilised and not quite what I was expecting. I think I've made a mistake in coming, until Kay, a first-year witch, reveals something that makes me swallow my next mouthful of food without chewing.

'I'm an inspector in a CID tactical unit. I kick down doors and arrest drug dealers.'

'You're kidding me?'

But she isn't. She really is a police inspector. 'It's more open in the police now, and I've told them that my religion is Wicca. If they give people Eid and Christmas off, well, they have to give me 31 October off if I book it. It's our New Year.'

Before she started kicking down doors, she worked in the missing persons unit, where she used her powerful crystal pendant to find a missing girl.

'She was a diabetic and had been missing for 24 hours. The team were out looking for her. I got out a map and swung my pendant over it,' she says. 'It pointed to a local farm. I rang up the boys and sent them there. They found her walking down the road from the farmhouse.'

Kay also reveals that being a witch has helped her career in other ways too. 'Being a witch has just made me more professional and calm. I used to get stressed and throw my weight around. Now I'm calmer and people have noticed.'

But there's something else about Kay that makes her being a witch far more interesting. She also sees dead people. In fact, she sees dead people all the time.

At the last witches' coven, held in a 13th-century building that used to be a prison and an 'institution for the insane', she saw the legs of a hanging man swaying as the coven were looking for ghosts in the dark and dingy upstairs rooms.

'I saw them knocking into the shoulders of Jane,' she says.

'I felt them too,' confirms Jane, the other High Priestess, from the far end of the table.

Apparently, some of the others saw him too. Jane's son Dan watched as they swung loose. Dan's twelve, attends a drama school full-time, and sees ghosts. It's a heady mix.

Debs comes over after hearing our conversation, looking glum. I think she's over her spirit possession ordeal, but now she's feeling down because everyone sees dead people but her.

'Kay told me earlier that she saw someone sitting behind me,' she mumbles, leaning in close. 'I just don't ever see them or feel them. I wish I did.'

I know how she feels. I want to see dead people too. Everyone here seems to, especially the police inspector. She's been praised a couple of times this evening already for being the weekend's best spirit-spotter. I'm feeling a bit annoyed about it. In fact, like Debs, I'm beginning to think there's something wrong with me. This is Hallowe'en, we've done a spell inviting dead people to dinner, and still they won't appear before our eyes.

Though I shouldn't worry. The following evening at midnight when the veil between this world and the next is still very thin indeed (as I've been assured many times this evening), we're going searching for ghosts in the haunted wood. A famous medium called Andrew West has told the gathered witches that there are a lot of elementals out there in the dark places between the trees. I know one thing for sure, I'm going to be sticking close to Inspector Kay all night.

I've also noticed in the middle of all this talk about ghosts that Jeff has casually wandered off to the window overlooking the wood. I know what he's up to. He's been spooked, and now on the very evening when spirits are wandering the earth he's trying to spot one. I watch him a little too closely.

If he says he's seen a ghost, I'm going to ignore him for the rest of the weekend.

A little later he wanders back looking as miserable as Debs and me. It cheers me up to know that he's just as useless as we are.

Then Helen, who had nipped outside for a quick cigarette, walks in and tells everyone she's heard hoofs outside.

'Maybe I didn't. Maybe I did. But it's a courtyard, so …'

'Yeah, they must have been hoofs,' says Jane, confirming the ghostly visitation.

Everyone looks on in silence.

I'm convinced I'm not going to see a ghost tomorrow.

Later, back in my room, I open my laptop and learn more about witchcraft before I hit the haunted wood tomorrow night.

I find immediately that I had nothing to fear from these dear, lovely witches. Rather than killing people, they've been the subject of victimisation and brutal persecution ever since the Christians wanted rid of them in the 7th century AD, when the Church stole their beliefs and symbols to drive out pagan worship. In 601 AD, Pope Gregory I issued an edict to his missionaries urging them to adapt the rituals of the old pagan festivals into new Christian celebrations that would cut out the pagan gods. So Samhain was changed to Hallowmas or All Saints' Day, commemorating the souls of those who had been canonised that year.

Then came the order to vilify them. To create a subservient and law-abiding Christian nation of pliant sinners, the Christian authorities corrupted the most sacred symbol of Wicca, the pagan god Pan. Witches call him the horned one. He was little more than a symbol of fertility until the Christians got their hands on him and decided he should be renamed the Devil. In fact, before Christianity there was no Devil. According to Anthony Aveni, Professor of Anthropology at Colgate University in the US, who wrote the book *Behind the Crystal Ball*, in the 15th century witches were linked with all sorts of evil deeds such as making men sterile, sacrificing unbaptised children to the Devil, making horses go mad, making rivers run backwards, and waking the dead. It was the Church that first suggested that witches got their magical powers from the

Devil. Before that they just wanted a quiet life of fertility rituals and a few harmless herbal potions.

Aveni also points out that the 'flight of the black witch silhouetted against a full moon can be traced to a 9th-century document that condemns wicked women who ride wildly at night across the sky with Diana, goddess of the moon, striking down anyone they encountered'.

All this woman-hating is very unsettling, especially as Wicca is a matriarchal system of worship based on a three-headed goddess – the maiden, the mother, and the wise old woman or crone. This goddess symbolised the seasons of the year, from the rebirth of spring to death in the autumn. Clearly, to the male-dominated world of the Christian era with its misogynistic God, backed up by the woman-hating Bible, a rival system of worship that gave women a voice just wasn't on at all.

Aveni himself has theories for this rapid dislike of the opposite sex. 'Ecclesiastical writing of the prophets suggested that women were the "weaker sex" and more susceptible to evil,' he says. He also reveals that female herbalists 'who dared ease women's pain in childbirth were interfering with God's plan, for He had considered this just punishment for Eve's sin'.

Reading this makes me far more sympathetic to the members of the coven, and I understand why some people might turn to Wicca. They are worshipping nature, and they have a strict code of ethics, as Jane told me after the ritual.

'Anything that you wish for people is returned to you threefold; but if it's negative, then that is returned six-fold.' Other important ethical Wicca teachings are that people should strive to live in harmony with others and with themselves, and with the planet as a whole.

In fact, around the dinner table before I'd gone to bed, some of the witches told me that they'd turned to Wicca as a reaction to a Catholic upbringing. 'I was made to feel guilty all the time,' Jane told me. For her, Wicca was about improving her self-confidence and getting in touch with her spiritual side, as well as doing loads of spells, of course.

The persecution of witches was finally legally abolished in 1951 with the introduction of the Fraudulent Mediums Act, which basically took witchcraft off the statute book. The primary cause for the new law was the controversial conviction of medium Helen Duncan of witchcraft in 1944, the last person to be tried for this crime in the UK. Yet it wasn't only the case of Duncan that propelled this new law. Popular astrology columns had started to appear in the papers, and it was ridiculous that they should be outside the law. This new law introduced a distinction between a fraudulent medium and a real one. The Spiritualist movement has been levitating with joy ever since.

We spend all of the following day on divination spells to change our futures. Helen tells me that the Celts thought the presence of otherworldly spirits made it easier for the Druids (or Celtic priests) to make predictions about the future. For a people entirely dependent on the unpredictable natural world, these prophecies were an important source of comfort and direction during the long, dark winter. And because we're in the middle of a financial crisis, Jane has decided that we're going to do four prosperity spells. Witches are out to beat the credit crunch.

Helen reminds us that there's no better time than now to ask the spirit world for something. Yet, says Jane, standing over a huge pile of packets of herbs, you can't ask for something and get it without giving something back. If I get rich after today, I'm told, I have to give most of it away to charity.

Firstly, we do a simple spell for Hallowe'en, to take advantage of the thinning of the veil between the spirit world and the terrestrial plane. What we're going to do, says Jane, ripping up what looks like expensive pieces of parchment, is write down our wishes on the pieces of paper and put them in her cauldron, to be burnt later in the haunted wood. We all scribble away, and then Helen uses her special bottle of dragon's blood to draw a pentagram on everyone's piece of paper.

'Dragon's blood makes spells more powerful,' she says. Though it's not real dragon's blood, but has been taken from some kind of cactus.

We then undertake a herb spell, filling a jar with sandalwood bark, comfrey and basil oil. We have to hold a silver coin to the full moon, though it isn't full and we can't see it – but it doesn't matter, says Helen, because magic works in mysterious ways. Then, when we get home, we have to drop a silver coin into the pot every day for seven days.

I ask how I'll know when the spell works. 'You'll know,' says Jean mysteriously. 'It could be a new job, an opportunity, anything.'

For the next spell we have to say an incantation to six coins. Jane hands Debs and me some money, as we have no loose change. Yet Debs is worried that if she borrows money from someone else for the spell it will cement her dependency on other people. She wants her own. She disappears to her room to get her money. After reading out more enchantments and sprinkling the money with yet more dragon's blood, we all pile out in the rain to bury the money in the wood.

11

The haunted wood

At DINNER LATER, Brenda is giving people impromptu psychic readings. She looks drunk. Swaying slightly from side to side, she tells me in a loud voice that makes everyone look at me: 'The number seventeen is very important for you.'

'Okay,' I say.

'You're from a very rich family.'

Jeff laughs. 'Not if he grew up in Birmingham, he isn't.'

Jeff's not psychic, but he doesn't miss much.

'Yes, your family is very rich. But very strange.'

'Thanks,' I mutter.

'And there's something about lions. You will have lions.'

I tell her, doing the old Richard Wiseman helping-the-medium-out trick, that I went to Gambia on holiday once for a week, and Jane suggests that's where Brenda gets lions from. Though I forget to say that Gambia doesn't have any lions.

Jane, for some reason competing with Brenda, is now telling me my fortune. Everyone looks at me in silence. Maybe they're resentful that I'm getting so much special treatment. 'You're going to write a bestseller that will be made into a movie, but it will take a long time because you're very lazy.'

I look down into my apple and rhubarb crumble and wish I wasn't attracting so much attention.

A few moments later, Brenda sweeps out of the room on her way to the bar for another top-up, shouting out, 'William's quite attractive but he's an intellectual and very posh.'

I dip my head even lower into my custard.

Margaret, a Scouse witch who hasn't said anything all night, suddenly leans over and tells me, 'I think she's drunk.'

'No shit,' shoots back Jeff.

'I hate it when they get drunk. It gives people the wrong idea,' says Margaret, ignoring Jeff. She then leans over to Andy, another initiate witch, to tell him, in case he hadn't noticed, that, yes, Brenda is very drunk.

Later, close to midnight, when I'm assured again that the veil is still wafer-thin, we take the heavy cast-iron cauldron into the haunted wood. It's carried by Jeff, who tries unsuccessfully to pass it to me.

It's dark, the rain is falling lightly, and everyone huddles together as we walk. The two boys with us, Jack and Dan, are staying in the middle of the adults. No one knows what's going to happen when we reach the wood, but as we walk on, the dark becomes an uncomfortable shade of black and visibility shrinks to nothing.

We walk deep into the wood and stop. I'm allowed to cradle the cauldron in the decaying shell of a tree. I light the parchment, enjoying the smouldering fire, but we're distracted. Inspector Kay has felt something.

'Oh, it was nothing, nothing,' she says.

Jane looks into the cauldron to ensure that all the wishes are now ash, and I scatter them on the floor of the wood, allowing the spells to work upwards into the night sky and, hopefully, the spirit world.

Feeling much happier than I've been in a long time because somehow I'm going to be four times richer than I was before, we head deeper into the wood in search of elementals and spirits.

Debs is in a good mood. Her earlier concerns about spirit possession have evaporated, and she giggles at everything, attempting to scare me by putting leaves on my head.

It's an interesting strategy, but one which is doomed to failure. I'm enjoying the walk, and also enjoying probably for the first time in my life a complete absence of being spooked in the middle of a wood at midnight. I try to liven things up by breathing heavily when suddenly we come to a halt. The mist rises in the distance and we wait around in the pitch black, just looking out. The boys are now getting bored, so I reach out in between them and point to something in the distance, shouting, 'What's that?'

They aren't impressed. They don't even bother looking where I'm pointing.

Then, quietly, like she's directing an oncoming funeral procession, Kay signals that she's seen something.

'Over to my left,' she says, sticking her hand in the air. 'Look. Over here in this tree, I can see the shadow of a man.'

Everyone turns around to look. Jack, a moment ago a cool teenager, is suddenly hyperventilating.

'It's a tree spirit,' whispers Kay.

In hushed voices, everyone agrees that the tree is very ancient and so it's no surprise that there's some kind of pre-Christian elemental spirit living in it.

Dan can now see it. He describes a shadow looking out, curious at what we're doing.

'He's just standing there, showing us he's here. He doesn't want anything from anyone,' confirms Inspector Kay.

Jack can see him now. So can Jane. I walk over and stand beside Inspector Kay. I twist my head to her eye level and stare hard, harder than I've ever stared at anything in my life. I try desperately to make out a shadow, a form of any kind. Anything would do. But I can't see a thing.

So I do something rash.

I walk past Inspector Kay and plunge straight into the foliage of the tree.

'William, what are you doing!' someone calls out in a scared voice.

'He won't hurt you,' Kay assures me.

I stand under the tree, twigs sticking into my head, kicking at a discarded training shoe on the floor. If there's a tree spirit in here I want to be the first journalist with an interview. I stand looking out at everyone looking in.

'He's gone,' Kay tells me, and turns around and walks deeper into the wood.

We walk on and stop at another clump of trees. We stand still for about five minutes, all looking at the same collection of branches. Then Jeff, standing a little bit away from the rest of us and looking in the opposite direction, whispers: 'I think I see something.' Everyone ignores him.

Then Kay signals that she's noticed something else.

She's staring hard at the space in front of a dark bush, and can see a shape.

'He's a shape-shifter,' she says.

'He's changing a lot,' says Jane.

Jack can see him; even Debs, who a few moments before was trying to put another leaf on top of my head, can just about see something. I can't. Jeff has wandered off on his own, hurt by the lack of enthusiasm for his own sighting.

I look away and check out where Jeff was looking. My heart skips a beat and my throat goes numb. I can see it too. It's a light hanging in the trees in the middle distance. It's shiny and bright and has the shape of a strange creature. I stare at it for a long time, trying to work out what it is. Then I realise it's the night sky, lit by the waning moon, shining through twisting tree limbs.

Sandra, another witch, is worried that we won't be able to find our way back and suggests turning round. But Jane and Inspector Kay ignore her and start walking further into the trees. We stop, and immediately Kay is signalling that she's seen something. But this time it isn't the shape of an elemental spirit but a man, or the ghost of a man.

'It's weird,' she says, 'but I feel myself being pushed back. There's pressure, tension, he's pushing me back. We shouldn't go any further.'

I look over at Kay and her body is visibly being forced back, as though a strong wind is pushing her torso out of line. Everyone's silent, looking hard at the empty space in which the man is standing and pushing Inspector Kay.

For the first time, there's a sense of real fear. Kay and the others can sense the presence of something unpleasant. Debs isn't giggling, and the boys have huddled in close to Jane, the High Priestess. I put down the cauldron which Jeff has finally managed to pass to me, and walk over and stand by Kay.

She looks at me as she's being pushed over. 'Can you feel the pressure?'

'No,' I say.

I look at where she's looking and then without really thinking about it I walk forwards and into the gloomy darkness.

'Don't!' Dan shouts out, his voice gripped by fear.

I stop. I don't feel anything. I don't see anything. I haven't been pushed out of the way or dragged down deep into the underworld.

'I think it was pulling me. It wasn't pushing me,' says Kay suddenly.

She turns to her right, away from where I'm standing. Everyone turns with her and leaves me looking at their backs. I go to the back of the huddle again, retrieving the cauldron, a dead weight in my hands, and peer into the dark.

'He's wearing a hood, like an old hat, and he's got tweed on,' says Inspector Kay.

'I can see him too,' says Dan.

'And here.' Kay draws a shape with her arms into the night. 'It looks like an animal. Maybe a deer.'

Debs bends down and moves forwards on her hands and knees. 'Can I talk to them?'

'Of course,' says Kay. 'They're only here out of curiosity.'

'Hello spirit, I just want to say, thank you for coming out to see us,' Debs says, looking into the empty night. Then she suddenly straightens up. 'I can't believe I did that with him here,' she says, referring to me. 'He's so going to write that I'm a knob.'

She gets up and walks over to me. 'You're so going to write that I'm a knob for doing that, aren't you?'

'No, I'm not.'

'Yes you are!' Debs walks off, and Kay joins her.

Small, terrified twelve-year-old Jack stays back and walks alongside me.

'Are you going to write that we're all fucking twats?'

'No, I'm not. I used to do this when I was a kid, and I'd get scared.'

'I'm scared.'

'It's okay,' I tell him.

Kay has stormed off ahead of us. I think she's gone off in a huff because I keep challenging the spirits – and her version of events. But I have nothing to fear. A few minutes later we've all stopped along the path, looking at a house.

'The man in the hood had something to do with this house,' she says.

'Yeah,' agrees Jack, looking over the fence.

'I feel it too,' says Jane.

'Look at the barn, it must be where he kept his horse,' suggests Jack.

'That's right,' says Kay.

We head back to the house. Realising that Kay isn't annoyed with me after all, I fall in alongside her and ask about elementals.

'They are ancient energies but we just don't have words to describe them today,' she says.

I'm glad that she's still speaking to me. For a moment there I thought she hated me. I try to be more encouraging, and suggest enthusiastically: 'What, like an Ent in the movie *Lord of the Rings*?'

I don't get a response.

Back inside, we sit around the banqueting table. It's nearly 1.00am now and suddenly communicating with the dead is about to get a lot more serious.

Jane, the High Priestess, suggests a seance. We sit in the dark around a large table.

The lights are turned off, and immediately Andy and Kay can see someone standing beside me. I take a look but there's no one there.

'I can see a person next to William. Right by him,' says Andy.

I look again. But I still can't see anything.

Then Sandra sees a strange red blob over the door. Dan stands up and turns on the light and the red blob transforms into the fire alarm. The lights go off again. Suddenly Jane screams.

'Will you two just piss off,' she shouts.

The tablecloth is bunched up and Jack is looking guilty. He's been pulling the cloth and freaking Jane out. Looking angry, Jane says it's time to take the seance down a level. We're about to get in deep.

We move around a small table and put our fingers lightly on top of an upturned wine glass.

'Are there any spirits with us? If yes, move the glass towards William; if no, move towards Sandra,' says Jane.

Debs bursts out laughing. 'Well, if the spirit says no, then we've got a lying spirit,' she says.

The glass starts moving towards me.

'Who is here? Move towards William if it's for Sandra, towards Kay if it's for Debs. If you are here for everyone, move towards Andy,' says Jane.

The glass moves, but not towards anyone. It moves in a circle.

'I think it's drawing a pentagram,' says Andy, sounding worried.

'Oh my god, it's drawing a pentagram,' says Jane. The glass moves quickly over the table, drawing the sign of the witches.

But then it stops.

'If the person is here for Debs, move towards her,' says Andy. The glass moves towards Debs.

'Okay, who's moving the glass?' asks Debs, fear edging into her voice.

We all show that we have hardly any pressure on the glass.

'Move towards Kay if it's my Nan,' says Debs.

The glass moves slowly towards Kay.

'Right, this is not funny. If anyone is moving the glass, stop.' Debs sounds tense.

Jack's eyes are bulging. Dan accuses me of moving the glass. I take my hand off, but it keeps moving.

Jane takes her fingers off, and then Kay, but the glass keeps moving.

'Right, everyone lift their fingers off now,' says Debs, sounding terrified.

We do. Well, sort of.

'Oh my god, the glass kept moving,' screams Debs.

We put our fingers back on.

'If I shouldn't be doing the degree course in September, then lift up the glass.' The glass shakes.

'Oh my god, the glass lifted,' shrieks Debs.

Debs now asks each of us to put our fingers on the glass separately — one by one. The glass keeps moving no matter who's touching it, until it's my turn to put my fingers on the glass. It stops moving.

'That's because William doesn't believe,' says Debs accusingly.

Inspector Kay suggests that it's because there's not enough energy, and puts her finger back on. The glass starts moving again.

Then the glass stops.

'Are there any spirits?' Kay asks. The glass doesn't move. She asks again. Nothing.

'Okay, I think we should try something else,' announces Jane. 'This is far more powerful. We all hold hands, and we don't, whatever happens, break the circle.'

Kay recites a protection charm and then asks the spirits to come talk to us. Immediately the room goes tense.

'I can feel a shadow behind me,' says Jane. 'He's standing behind Debs now.'

'What does he look like?' asks Debs, sounding worried.

'It's like he didn't expect to be here, as though he's just found himself in spirit. It's as though he was doing the crossword and didn't have time to finish,' says Andy.

'No, don't say that,' Debs shouts, scared. 'What does he look like?'

I'm surprised by the sudden intensity of the seance and how Debs is reacting.

'He looks like Amos from *Emmerdale*. A bald head, with a moustache,' says Andy.

'You're wrong,' Debs shouts, not sounding convinced.

'You mean he looks like Greengrass?' asks Jane.

Suddenly, Debs moans and then screams, pulling Dan's hand to hers. The table rocks, and everyone (even Inspector Kay) is looking scared. Dan jolts back and crashes sideways into my lap. His eyes are tight shut and he's moaning.

'Why did you say that?' Debs shouts at Jane. She's terrified. We can all feel her fear. Her face is white and she's shaking. 'Why did you say that?' She looks demented. Possessed, Jane would say later, out of Debs's earshot.

She starts tugging at her hands.

'This has to stop. We have to stop this now. I can't go on. Please.'

She pulls her hands apart from Jack and Dan and starts crying.

'What's wrong?' asks Jane.

'I don't want to talk about it.'

Suddenly something that I thought was fun has turned deadly serious. Everyone's looking worried. Andy leans in, concerned. I can feel my heart beating.

'Tell us what it is,' he says gently.

'It's my dad. He always does the crossword last thing at night and he looks just like you described him. Everyone, I mean everyone, says he looks like Greengrass. I can't believe you said that. I can't believe you said that.' She starts crying again. 'I've got to go, I've got to go and phone my mum to see if my dad's alright. I've always known that he would go doing his crossword.'

'Who's Greengrass?' asks Dan.

'He's the old guy with the dog in *Heartbeat*,' says Jane.

Debs gets up and rushes out.

Jack's looking terrified. 'I want to get out of this room. I want to go,' he says.

We get up and leave the room silently. Andy stays back and waits for Debs to return. I've had enough. I go to bed, wondering how all this will look in the dull light of another rainy morning.

Over breakfast, new developments emerge. Andy reveals that he stayed up with Debs, explaining that the ghost was just there because he was bored. Debs then went to bed and woke up laughing at four in the morning. Jack and Dan couldn't sleep, terrified that Debs was possessed, and went and slept in Dan's sister's room, barricading themselves in, terrified that Debs would knock down the door and attack them.

As we tuck into our beans and eggs, we learn that Debs's father hasn't died. But that doesn't matter, because Debs has a new theory. 'I think it was a premonition. You see, the universe has no concept of time,' she tells everyone. 'I've thought that my dad would die doing his crossword peacefully and last night was just showing that.'

It's the final day, and after breakfast we meet again in the banqueting room. By the time I arrive, Debs is being lectured.

'You're confused,' says Jane. 'I can see it.'

'I wasn't confused before I got here,' she snaps back.

'You may have thought that,' Helen butts in. 'You're confused. You don't know what you want. You think you were okay, but this weekend you've been opening up your chakras and all the confusion is suddenly coming out,' she says, not sounding all that friendly any more.

Debs sits at the end of the table, wide-eyed, taking it all in. 'Maybe what happened last night is because I didn't cast a circle,' she says, returning to her original fear of demon possession from the first night.

'You've got to learn this properly,' Helen snaps at her. 'People who play with magic and don't know what they are doing get into trouble. You've got a lot to learn. It's not just about reading a book, saying the spells and then realising you forgot to cast a circle. I've known lots of people doing spells, and not realising what spirits they're letting in, and then their lives have been ruined. They do a spell and suddenly their car breaks down or they find their boyfriend's having an affair. That's why it's important to be part of a coven.'

Debs's lecture slowly grinds to a halt, and Jane announces that we'll move on to working with pendants. I slip out and head to reception to call a taxi. By the time I'm back Helen is telling an anecdote about how you can't hide anything from the spirits.

'I'd finished work and had been moaning about one of my patients,' says Helen, who works with disabled children. 'Suddenly this leaf slaps me in the face. I knew then I shouldn't have been talking that way. They're always watching and listening to you.'

I look at Helen in silence. I realise, like the leaf hitting her in the face, that now is my time to go. I head out to the bar, where Dan and Jack are fooling around, already over the horror of last night. Jeff's there too, reading a magazine.

'Not going in today?' I ask.

'Nah, I'm going to leave it to Helen. I need a break,' he says, smiling.

I climb into my taxi. The driver grins and asks me about my weekend.

'Witches,' I say, 'but you really don't want to know.'

He nods and we drive to the station in silence.

When I get home, I pull out my prosperity bottle and add a silver coin. Well, I think, a bit of extra cash after a weekend like that wouldn't come amiss.

FUTURE 4:
THE WITCHES AND ME

~

Predictions:

I'll write a bestselling book but it will take me a long time
because I'm lazy

My campervan won't break down ever again

I'll become rich beyond belief due to undertaking three
credit crunch prosperity spells

However, I'll become poor soon after because I have to give it
all away

12

In the palm of my hand

I DON'T KNOW WHY I did it, but it's haunted my thoughts ever since. I was at a house party, just out of college and barely out of my teens, when I remembered my friend's ex-girlfriend was a witch and read palms. I was drunk, she was pretty, and it was a good opportunity to strike up a conversation. I've been looking over my shoulder ever since.

Tracing my life-line — I didn't have a clue which was which — she found a fork and a line that crossed it. She became uncomfortable, shifting uneasily, and told me that witches ran in her family. The idea that there was a special magical bloodline gave extra significance to the reading, as I'm sure did the shot of vodka I'd just downed.

'Something will happen to you and you will only just survive,' she told me.

What!

'The line that crosses your life-line is deep and it continues only for a short time. You might end up in a wheelchair but you won't last for much longer.'

Christ.

And that was that. That's all I can remember. I may have passed out and had to be stretchered from the room. Given that I had my legs and my health for only a short while longer, I think I handled the death sentence pretty well. But then I had an attractive girl holding my hand, albeit one who had just poisoned my life for good.

Despite occasional readings around the same time, I was probably like most people – not particularly well informed but with what I thought was a healthy, open mind. A psychic agnostic, I suppose. I don't need it, but that doesn't mean there isn't something in it. Yet I still looked twice before I crossed the road and always buckled up in the back seat. This gem of a reading, however, came just before some mystical fellow at an early 1990s road protest shook my hand, looked pained, and said I should take care of my heart.

I know. What is it with these people and me? Did I have a big sticker on my head saying 'Walking health disaster' or 'Sucker for psychic punishment'? I've always been laid-back about life, or so people tell me, but I remember beginning to wonder whether all this outward sangfroid was causing serious stress and tension on the inside. Maybe I was only just holding it together, perhaps I should shout and scream and have a few tantrums to let out all the steam before it built up and exploded within me, causing a fatal coronary or, Christ, a road traffic accident where I ended up having my legs removed.

Those readings, which were meant to be a bit of fun, were still getting to me. Even now, I'm constantly reminding myself to have my blood pressure taken and my cholesterol checked. If these readings can continue to do that to me, what on earth are they doing to everyone else?

So nearly fifteen years later, with a healthy heart and two working legs, I arrive back at Mysteries, near Covent Garden in London, to get freaked out all over again. I also want to remind myself about the 'lighter side' of psychic readings, after the depressing story of Nicola Payne and Jacqui Poole, and my 'scary' weekend with the witches. Although considering I've already been given a death sentence myself, I'm unsure just how much fun it's going to be.

I remember Matthew, the owner, telling me that Howard, a Mysteries palm-reader, is internationally renowned. Rather than being psychic, he gives a technical or 'scientific' reading of the palms. He also, Matthew told me, had scared the living daylights out of a few hard-nosed East End criminals because he was able to read their criminal underworld activities just by looking at their hands. Maybe they had blood all over them, I wonder as I saunter into the shop. Taking my free Mysteries tape from Matthew, on which Howard will record my palmist future, I head back up the stairs to the psychics' den.

Waiting on the small landing outside Howard's room while he finishes another reading, I have time to contemplate the research I've done on chiromancy, the art of palm-reading. Its great appeal, of course, is that it's tangible. It's not like Alice's powers, which rely on contacting a disembodied spirit guide in her head. Those mysterious lines on the palms must mean something. Sure, they could just be creases caused by opening and closing the hands, but they're there when you're born. Surely that means those lines must be divine? Cavemen drew pictures of hands on the walls of their underground homes, and even the Bible confirms the importance of palms. 'God sealeth up the hand of every man; that all men may know his work,' according to the Book of Job. Julius Caesar judged his men by palmistry, although I imagine Brutus kept his gloves on for that little treat. The practice of palmistry was enthusiastically forced underground by the Church, which believed it to be the work of Devil-worshippers, and anyone found to have an interest in the 'dark art' was quickly punished, sometimes by death.

Apparently, palmistry is a complex and skilled art, combining both intuition and an understanding of what the different contours and shapes on the hands mean. It's not only the dreaded life-line that's important, but the shape of the hands as well. According to the book *Palmistry for Beginners* by Sarah Fenton, a thumb that turns back at the tip suggests acting ability, while if 'the outside edge of the hand is thick and bows out sideways, the person will have a very short fuse and may be verbally or physically aggressive'. I, meanwhile, have small, oblong hands with a rotund nodule on the right phalange, which means I have a tendency to take the piss …

Howard, an Australian in his forties who looks like he has a beer belly, opens the door to his den and two women scurry out. I enter, sit down opposite him and rest my elbows on his table, holding my palms up as he instructs. On his table he has what can only be described as the most impressive collection of brass magnifying glasses I have ever seen, including one the size of my arm. I hope he gets to use all of them on me. He doesn't, of course; he only ever uses the small one.

Howard begins by telling me that my right hand is active and my left hand is passive. What he means by this is that the left hand shows the map of life, what we are born with, while the right hand is how we adapt and change, so it can alter what has been set when we were born. It's a nice idea – the gods have charted our lives and have provided a map in the shape of the crisscrossing paths on our palms, but we still have control of the rudder on this perilous life journey and can alter the course at will. It's free will meets destiny in full confrontation.

I like the reading immediately because, of course, Howard massages my ego. Peering closely into his small magnifying glass, he tells me that my head-line is strong – one of the longest he has seen. Clearly, I'm up there with Einstein and all these years have been quietly biding my time until I discover something of global importance.

Apparently I'm blocking 25 per cent of my communication skills. I'm also very streetwise 'by virtue of the fact that your finger curves'. I have a tip-top immune system, lovely nails and a nice personality. He says this while scrutinising my hand as though it's a bomb being defused.

I like Howard. I like him a lot. He makes me feel like I'm the best person alive, ever. Luckily, before my head explodes, he changes the subject. But it doesn't help. He just can't stop saying wonderful things about me.

He's back looking at my head-line, because this is what Howard finds very interesting.

'This is what really excites me about this hand. The head-line is extremely long and this means very exciting things for your career,' he says. He then mentions the Mount of Venus, which is the raised part of the palm at the end of the thumb, and tells me that I'm creative in the mornings and can be practical and abstract in the afternoons.

I also have a medical stigma, which makes me very empathetic and understanding. And there's a line that means a dead relative is now looking after me.

'I had a few close shaves in Australia, and I can tell you that there must have been someone looking out for me then,' he reassures me.

But then, like an iceberg heading for an unsinkable ship, my relationship comes into view. From the surface it looks stable, but peer just beneath and there's a whole lot of funny business going on.

'There's going to be a new influence coming into your life. You are either just coming out of a relationship or just going into one. Your life works in seven-year cycles,' he tells me.

He asks if I'm in a relationship and I confirm that I am. I don't know why my hands didn't reveal that small detail to him. He says that we're not bonding and that I'm too busy with work at the moment. There's not enough quality time.

'How long have you been in the relationship?' he asks.

'Seven years.'

I'm not too sure what Howard says, but it's something like 'Christ'. It's a dramatic moment. I've just handed him a gold-mine. My life works in seven-year cycles, a big change is coming, and there I am in a seven-year relationship. Bingo. Howard has uncovered a gemstone of information and he uses it to good theatrical effect, which I find riveting.

He looks at my palm again, wiping sweat from his forehead. 'There's nothing really bad on the hand, but the only problem I can see is this outside influence,' he says, peering even closer at my palm as though he's about to smell it. 'It's about you being in the right place at the right time. A contract could be coming your way. You could meet someone,' he continues.

He looks up at me and places his finger over a button on his tape recorder, forgetting that I'm recording it too, and pushes stop.

'Will your girlfriend ever hear this tape?' he asks intensely.

'No,' I assure him.

'It's bad news. You will meet someone else,' he says quietly.

He holds my gaze across the table. 'It's especially the case for the cocksure ones like you. You're cocksure about your relationship, but it's always the ones like that.'

Hang on, what's all this about being cocksure? I thought I had a nice personality. I look back at Howard through narrowing eyes. There's an uncomfortable silence until he changes the subject.

He quickly goes off at a tangent, saying that I'm going to have success in my career for the next four years. In fact, with so much going on, I could overdo it. He's not worried about the success, but the speed of it.

I'm not bothered about this. I'm far more interested in the news that I'm about to get myself a new lover, so much so that I forget to ask him about my impending death sentence that the witch — my friend's ex-girlfriend — gave me. Well, maybe it wasn't that important. He didn't mention it, and that suggests I'll live to a ripe old age. Anyway, he tells me, I have an immune system like his. If I do get ill, I shouldn't worry because my health is the equivalent of the SAS.

Our time together is over, but he suggests that if I have a difficult decision to make in the future, I should take a photograph of my hands and email it to him. He will then advise me what to do.

I thank him and rush home. Howard has just told me that my seven-year relationship is over and I'm keen to get Nikki's view on this.

We're in the kitchen and I relate every detail of Howard's performance to her. She doesn't seem too bothered at first. In fact, she laughs. Personally, I'm fascinated by Howard's attempt to create tension by turning the tape off when he had some bad news. What did he think, that we were co-conspirators hatching a daring plot to escape the imprisonment of my relationship? In Howard's world, Nikki's an evil prison guard preventing me from having the freedom to fulfil my deepest and darkest desires. It's Alice's view of Nikki repeated and exaggerated ten-fold. If they ever met her and compared their readings with the real person, they'd have a shock. I could imagine Howard meeting Nikki after giving his seven-year-itch advice. He'd swallow hard, look at me as though I was half-mad and whisper: 'Why the hell do you want to get rid of someone like her?' I, of course, would remind him that he was the one suggesting the change of relationship.

'Oh, no, no, William, don't do that,' he'd say, looking all innocent, our conspiring days already behind us. 'You can't blame me. I'm only the messenger, it's all in your palm.'

While we're mulling over Howard's words of wisdom, Rowan, a friend of mine and Nikki's, enters the kitchen. I tell her the story as well and expect her to laugh too. But Rowan's annoyed by Howard's performance and far from impressed by his destructive pronouncement on the relationship of two good friends.

'I thought palm-reading was harmless, but this guy sounds pretty irresponsible. I can't believe he seems to think it's okay to say whatever he likes, even if it could end up damaging some people's relationships,' says Rowan, shaking her head in disbelief and looking at Nikki.

'It's so manipulative,' Nikki agrees. 'I thought you said psychics were meant to say nice things to people,' she adds, reminding me how positive I was about good-hearted gypsy Betsy Lee a few weeks ago.

I'm fiddling with a packet of biscuits, looking sheepish. I haven't told them yet that he called me 'cocksure', somehow suggesting that no matter how confident I am in my relationship, it's doomed. The more confident I am, the less confident I should be.

An innocent piece of research has suddenly developed real-life consequences. I'm a journalist with an impartial and objective take on the world. The subjects of my investigations never impinge on my life, but this one's turning up the heat in the kitchen, and no one's left the oven door open.

The idea of me being called cocksure annoys Nikki. She has no concerns about our relationship, and I'd be exaggerating if I said that she thought it would make me look at other girls. Yet despite this, it's still got under her skin. 'I don't have any doubts. But it annoys me because it might make you think like that and think there's an alternative. I don't know,' she says, making me realise that even for someone as sceptical as her, Howard's words can be uncomfortable. Is she now going to dwell on the implications of what he said? Even after all our shared intimacy and time together, Howard's reading can still have an insidious influence, playing on the darker reaches of the mind.

'Yeah, but come on, you don't really think that affected me, do you?' I say, trying to reassure her. Though, come to think of it, calling me 'cocksure' isn't as funny as I first thought it was. It's not funny at all. It's actually quite unpleasant.

'Of course it's not going to bother me deeply,' she says, not sounding entirely convinced. 'It's just how dare somebody start suggesting those kind of things. What gives this person the right, knowing nothing about our relationship, knowing nothing about what makes us tick individually, to start making these statements?'

Rowan's been listening to Nikki and me work through Howard's prediction. Rowan's an intelligent and rational person, and I'm sure after the initial annoyance she won't think too much about it in the morning, and nor will I or Nikki. My girlfriend is far too level-headed to let it bother her for long.

171

But, worryingly, all three of us know people who would take Howard's reading far more seriously. We have friends who visit psychics to get reassurance about their love lives. They would be far more likely to believe that someone like him really can know something that they can't. It's ridiculous but deeply disturbing at the same time. If they were in the room now, instead of rational Rowan, they'd probably be advising me and Nikki to see a relationship counsellor, or worse, start telling me off for looking at other girls based on nothing more than Howard's weird and unsettling prediction.

Despite Matthew's claim that palm-reading is 'scientific', there really is no scientific proof for it. Yet, based on what Howard and psychics like him say, people could still make drastic decisions that will change their future. A suggestion of an affair, sanctioned by the great mystical palm-reader, is a planted seed that grows into a weed, throttling a beautiful flower. Sure, relationships end and people have affairs, but if palm-readers are giving out false information, then they should be careful in encouraging that course of action as a solution. They might like to think that it's up to us, people with free will, what we do with the information they give. But at the same time they're claiming to have special powers backed up by science. For some people, that's like Jesus Christ just whispered in their ear.

And what about me? Will I find someone new? Will I take the seed planted in my head and let it grow and fester? Will being cocksure make me destroy my relationship? Of course not, because I'm more than cocksure about my relationship, I'm so serious about it that Howard's words don't even register. But for Howard that attitude would just be evidence that I'm even more cocksure than he thought I was, and my relationship is therefore doomed to failure. Well, only time will tell.

FUTURE 5: HOWARD AND ME

~

Predictions:

In the next four years my career will race ahead

While my career is racing ahead, I'll be left behind suffering
health problems from overwork

. This is despite having an immune system like the SAS

I'll meet someone new

My seven-year relationship will end

Nothing untoward will happen to me, as a dead relative is on
standby for an emergency rescue

13

The Enlightenment under threat

I'M STANDING OUTSIDE a large, beautiful house in Oxford feeling nervous. This is the home of Darwin's rottweiler, otherwise known as Richard Dawkins, the evolutionary biologist and geneticist, and I'm worried that I'm about to get bitten.

Dawkins, formerly Professor for the Public Understanding of Science at Oxford University, writer of *The Selfish Gene* and *The God Delusion*, has been causing minor earthquakes wherever he goes in the name of Reason. If you believe in God, you're deluded, and if you believe in psychics, you're irrational. He'd probably think my recent visit to see Sylvia Browne was a sign that I was losing it. Yet I've come to see Professor Dawkins to find out if the rise of the psychic, and for that matter a belief in people like Sylvia Browne, is really putting reason and the whole edifice of science at stake. Is it actually the case that, because psychics have prime-time TV slots, then the Enlightenment, the movement that pulled us out of the dark ages and into the age of reason and science in the 18th century, is about to come crashing down at our feet?

Dawkins thinks so. A year or so ago, he set up the Richard Dawkins Foundation for Science and Reason to fight the growth in 'pseudo-science' and 'irrational' ideas. This came after he visited a bookshop in London and was horrified, although not surprised, to find the shop's shelves packed with books on fairies, crystals, and fortune-telling – pseudo-science outnumbering science books by at least three to one.

On coming out, he announced that the 'Enlightenment is under threat, so is reason, so is truth, so is science'.

To argue that the Enlightenment is at stake is a big claim, considering that modern science and society are constructed on its foundations. The 17th and 18th centuries were a time of major breakthroughs in thinking. Isaac Newton's theories, for instance, revealed that the movements of the planets were governed by natural laws rather than by God. John Locke pioneered the belief that human nature was characterised by reason and tolerance rather than by divine design, and David Hume believed that nothing about existence could be demonstrated – he was the world's first true sceptic.

The Enlightenment basically kicked us out of our superstitious medieval worldview into a place where all men, and sometimes women too, had rights. This led to the French Revolution and the wars of American Independence against the God-given hierarchy and the injustice of monarchic rule.

The main idea behind the Enlightenment that Dawkins is most concerned with promoting is that rational thinking leads to progress and civilisation. Or as Roy Porter in his book *The Enlightenment* puts it, the thinkers of the time were 'aiming to put human intelligence to use as an engine for understanding human nature, for analysing man as a sociable being, and the natural environment in which he lived. Upon such understanding would the foundations for a better world be laid.'

Discounting the odd war, genocidal purge, mass starvation and worldwide inequality, life has been pretty much plain sailing ever since.

What's fascinating about Dawkins' fight for reason and science is that it mirrors a similar struggle that happened almost 150 years ago following the publication of Charles Darwin's theory of evolution in his groundbreaking book, *The Origin of Species*, in 1859.

At that time, Dawkins' incarnation was the pioneering biologist T.H. Huxley, nicknamed Darwin's Bulldog for his ferocious debating skills in defending Darwin's theories. Famous exchanges ensued between Huxley and Samuel Wilberforce, Bishop of Oxford, the most famous of which in June 1860 saw the bishop ask Huxley whether he would prefer to be descended from an ape on his grandfather's or grandmother's side.

It was rumoured that Huxley, rising slowly like a bulldog on a full stomach, replied that he'd rather have an ape for an ancestor than a bishop. In fact, Huxley, far too erudite for such jokes, actually said: 'I am not ashamed to have a monkey for my ancestor. But I would be ashamed to be connected with a man who uses great gifts to obscure the truth.'

This was just the start. Out of this fight sprang Alfred Russel Wallace, the co-founder of the concept of natural selection. Wallace is famous for prompting the perfectionist Darwin to publish his theory of evolution. Darwin had been mulling it over for more than twenty years when Wallace sent him similar ideas which had occurred to him during a fit of malaria while specimen-collecting in Malaysia. Darwin must have choked on his toast when he read Wallace's mosquito-stained letter. He immediately set to work putting his own ideas on paper before he'd even wiped the melted butter from his beard. Thanks to Wallace giving Darwin the frights, the world was changed irrevocably for the better.

But Wallace, despite arguing wholeheartedly in favour of evolutionary theory until the day he died, didn't think that it accounted for the moral development of mankind. As Deborah Blum in the book *Ghost Hunters*, her excellent account of the rise of Victorian psychic sleuths, suggests: 'As he traversed England, Wallace gradually perceived dark spots in this polished progress. It seemed to him that the moral evolution of Western Society did not match its intellectual development.'

He looked at the slums, the brothels, and the poverty of London, the richest city in the world, and decided that what progress needed was not only evolution, but a good healthy dose of psychic energy. Wallace reckoned that there was a supernatural moral force in the universe, and that science risked undermining the belief in this, and so would tear apart the moral fibre of the world. To virtually every other scientist, including Darwin, Wallace had lost it.

Yet the ills of the world existed, and so they had to be dealt with. Instead of promoting social reform like the Fabian Society would a few years later, Wallace did something far more radical. He helped set up the Society for Psychical Research, complaining at the very first meeting that its President Henry Sidgwick was too sceptical by half. Wallace then set out to explore his idea that a supernatural force was underpinning our moral growth by visiting his first seance in 1865, as well as other table-tilting demonstrations that purported to show psychic energy at work.

Wallace was determined to use science as a way of exploring the supernatural, and he invited some of the leading scientists of the day to his home to investigate and explain bumps in the night. One of this motley crew was none other than T.H. Huxley, Darwin's still-growling bulldog. It so insulted Huxley's intelligence even to be invited to such an event that he took no time in telling Wallace where to get off.

'The only good argument I can see in a demonstration of the truth of "Spiritualism" is to furnish an additional argument against suicide. Better to live a crossing-sweeper than die and be made to talk twaddle by a medium hired at a guinea a seance,' he told Wallace. Touché.

By contrast, it seems that the modern-day Huxley, Richard Dawkins, may be willing to stand by his principles and conduct scientific experiments into the paranormal. In his recent Channel 4 programme *Enemies of Reason*, he joined the ubiquitous Dr Chris French in an experiment to test water-diviners. Reason and science should stand and fall by their own principles, and not just by opinion, he argued in the programme. Needless to say, the water-diviners were left scratching their heads when they didn't find any water; but despite the negative result, their beliefs remained firmly intact.

Back outside Dawkins' house, I'm ready to knock on his door and put his ideas under my own scrutiny. By all accounts his intellect is rather intimidating, and I'm beginning to regret not having made more effort in biology at school. My hand has hardly left the knocker when the door is opened by Rand, Dawkins' American assistant, who announces 'William Little' to my face.

I'm shown into Dawkins' living room, where Rand shoos away two white West Highland terriers. Sitting on his sofa, I have a few moments to look around. I'm amazed by the number of books Dawkins owns, but more seriously impressed by the size of his flat-screen TV. I bet he'd have a great time watching *Star Wars* on that, I think, before the door opens and the rottweiler walks in.

'William Little,' he says, with a warm smile and friendly handshake.

Dawkins is disarmingly courteous and puts me at my ease. The interview has started well, although I actually haven't said anything yet. I'm just hoping that when I do summon up the courage to speak, he finds in himself a deep well of patience.

I let him settle down in a small armchair opposite me, under the biggest bookcase I've ever seen, before I open with my first salvo. I want to see what he thinks about the reasons why people go to see psychics.

'Isn't it logical and reasonable for people to see a psychic if they think it helps them or because it makes them feel better? People are using their reason, so it's not irrational,' I say. Dawkins raises an eyebrow.

'It's a reason for going to see a psychic,' he says calmly. 'It's not a reason for believing that what psychics tell you is true. They might make you feel better, but so does the placebo effect. But that has nothing whatsoever to do with saying that what the psychic tells you is true.'

I nod probably a few too many times in agreement, but when Dawkins has finished and I've stopped nodding, my brain sends my mouth a message suggesting that Dawkins hasn't answered my question. What I want to know is whether using them as counsellors is rational. I suggest to him that psychics are poor people's counsellors, nothing more, nothing less. 'Do you think psychics can offer some benefit to them?'

'I just told you,' he barks. 'Yes, but it doesn't mean that it's true. And actually I suspect that you could just go and talk to a friend in the pub and it would probably do just as much good.'

I ponder Dawkins' remark and realise he might be on to something. I remember many years ago asking a friend some advice about a girl and he said, 'Go for it.' We weren't in a pub at the time. I think we might have been out walking some-where, maybe to a pub, but definitely not in one. I then asked another friend, in a pub with a pint, and he said the opposite. 'Nah, she's not your type, mate. It'll end messy, you know that,' he said, raising an eyebrow far too bushy for his seventeen years. Needless to say, the friend in the pub was right, every time.

Dawkins' suggestion is just a theory, but I like it, and frankly on the £30 you spend on a psychic at Mysteries or the £700 I spent seeing Sylvia Browne, I could have a good night, lots of advice and one hangover from hell. Actually, maybe not; hell doesn't exist, according to Dawkins. He wouldn't like that.

Suddenly a man, who I really hope is the gardener, starts up a chainsaw in Dawkins' front garden. The professor looks dis-tractedly out of the window at the racket, but resists putting a stop to it.

Next, I try on Dawkins my own evolutionary theory of why people might choose to be psychics. Maybe, I suggest, they aren't talented enough or intelligent enough. They are the weaker members of society, and in order to survive they become psychics. It's survival of the spiritualist rather than sur-vival of the fittest, I suggest. They just don't have enough pow-ers of reason.

I get a surprise.

'I wouldn't know. I don't know enough about it. It sounds plausible to me. Did you say unintelligent people?'

'Yes.'

'That sounds plausible to me. Plausible, but I cannot claim any expertise,' he warns.

Dawkins compares psychics to very good conjurors, hood-winking people into believing that what they do is accurate when it's just make-believe. But then I see a hole in his own reasoning. If psychics are just conjurors, then are they really putting the Enlightenment, science and reason at stake?

With the chainsaw humming menacingly in the background, I remind Dawkins about his trip to the bookshop and his idea that the achievements of the Enlightenment are under threat. He smiles and nods. Then I tell him that I think this is an overstatement.

I hold my breath and look over at him in his chair. He's been looking out of the window at the gardener while I've been asking my question. But now he turns his full gaze on me and answers swiftly, throwing my argument back at me.

'Oh, you mean it's not a serious threat because they are nuts. Well, I think you have answered it yourself when you say they get on prime-time television, haven't you? Or they sell best-selling books,' he says firmly.

I'd previously suggested to him that he was fighting a los-ing battle, because when he puts together a well-argued pro-gramme like *Enemies of Reason* on Channel 4, ITV counter it with *Sally Morgan: Star Psychic* in prime time, which is then repeated endlessly.

So I try again, warming to my role as the Jeremy Paxman of the psychic world. I still want some clarity over whether sci-ence and reason are on the way out.

'Do you think that spending time and energy believing in psychic power is a loss of potential when people could be doing something else?'

'Yes, I think it's a very sad loss. But it's also that there are a lot of people who aren't nuts, just ignorant,' he says.

Thinking back to my palm-reading, and the way that Howard and Matthew evoked science to justify its power, I ask Dawkins whether this use of science discredits it. But I also want to know this: if an experiment does show an effect proving psychic power, then isn't that science?

'If an effect is real, it's not ethereal. It just doesn't disappear when you try to grasp it. You can use the analogy of echo location in bats, where at one time the facility of bats to find their way around in total darkness would have seemed mysterious and one might have thought they had psychic or sixth sense,' he says, warming to his subject.

He tells me that when echo location was discovered, a lot of research was undertaken to figure out what was going on. Did bats have supernatural powers? Yet the evidence for echo location began piling up, and it became more and more solid and more and more convincing, until there was no possibility of doubting that bats use echoes to locate themselves. It was a real proven effect.

'The sort of abilities that people claim to have, such as a faint feeling about the future, are slippery and elusive. The evidence doesn't become consolidated by further evidence. I think that is a pretty good sign really that nothing is there,' he says, leaning back in his chair.

Richard Dawkins comes across in person as the very rational man he purports to be. He argues his case rigorously and empirically, with a zeal that demonstrates just how seriously he takes his quest against the pseudo-scientists. But I want to test how open-minded he is about science. Is he like Huxley, who wouldn't even attempt to use science to test psychic ability?

I ask him about the Asian tsunami of December 2004, when scientists struggled to explain reports that aboriginal tribesmen had somehow sensed the impending danger in time to join wild animals in a life-saving flight to higher ground. Doesn't this prove that humans have a sixth sense? I expect him to dismiss it out of hand.

'I would love to look into the evidence for that. It could be interesting, and if it's true, then we should do some more research until we can locate what caused it,' he says.

I'm surprised at Dawkins' openness to this idea. He just wants to ensure that the science is carried out properly. No one, I think, would disagree with that.

'If anybody found good evidence for a sixth sense, such as animals heading for the hills when a tsunami is on its way, it would make their career. It would be wonderful,' he says.

Did I hear that right? Richard Dawkins said it would be wonderful if we could find evidence for psychic power. That's quite a scoop.

In fact, as my own experiment comes to an end, I have to start weighing up the evidence. The hypothesis was that Dawkins would dismiss anything that wasn't rational and would grind down without a moment's thought any mention of mystical beliefs. My research hasn't borne that out. Dawkins is far more open-minded than I expected, and he's certainly not intimidating or aggressive. All he wants from psychics is proof that their powers exist. If they can provide that, then they can claim that to believe in the existence of an invisible force is rational. They could then argue that these special powers can be useful in guiding us on our life's journey. If they could do that, he would clearly be a convert.

Dawkins, however, has left me with a burning desire to find scientific evidence for the existence of extra-sensory power myself. If I can find it I'll be back in Oxford knocking on his door, expecting a full conversion right on his doorstep.

14

The psychics to the stars

SALLY MORGAN FREAKS PEOPLE OUT. Seriously. Or rather her TV programme, *Sally Morgan: Star Psychic* does. When I told a friend a year ago that I was writing a book about psychics, she turned green and said: 'So you'll be meeting Sally Morgan, then?'

'Err, who?' I replied, not recognising the name. Sally's series was showing on ITV2 at the time, just before its move over to the much more popular ITV1, and it had somehow escaped my attention.

'Oh my God,' she replied, looking at me as though I'd just admitted to not knowing who Jesus Christ was. 'She's the real thing. I have no idea how she does it, but she can do stuff on her show that I haven't seen before. It's weird, really weird.'

So I watched the show and was just as surprised as my friend. The programme makes compelling viewing, not only because Sally mentions dead relatives by name – 'Your dead aunt is called Anne', she tells one guest on the show – but also because she's the least likely psychic you can imagine. She's big, bubbly and so continually surprised by her own psychic successes that it makes her come across as endearing, rather than all-powerful and arrogant.

Sally Morgan is intriguing because not only has she convinced a lot of people that psychics are real, but, according to Richard Dawkins, she's a reason why the Enlightenment is under threat. That's a big responsibility for a former dental nurse from Merton, south London.

The programme itself, however, is controversial. TV programmes that include psychics are required by regulatory standards to also provide space for a sceptic to give a rational explanation. This is why every time you see a psychic on the sofa of *Good Morning*, Dr Chris French will be sitting alongside offering a secular viewpoint, or why *Most Haunted* employs Dr Ciarán O'Keeffe to suggest non-spirit-world explanations for the odd goings-on in the night. A way around this is to create- a programme that tests the psychic. *Sally Morgan: Star Psychic* is built around the idea that over a 30-day period she will have to undergo a series of difficult challenges.

One example of this is the phone booth challenge, where Sally calls up a public telephone box and lures in strangers from the street to give them a reading.

'First thing is, you shouldn't be in this country, you should be in Australia,' Sally tells one young man. The look on his face is one of complete shock.

'Oh my god,' he says slowly, as though an alien spacecraft had just landed outside the phone box.

'And there's just a real sense of what are you doing here in the UK?' Sally tells him.

'Oh my god,' the man says again, 'that is such a bizarre thing for you to come out with first off, because I lived there for a while. I lived there for just over a year and, yeah, it pained me to come back,' he reveals.

'That makes sense to me,' Sally replies, before moving on to the next phone booth occupant, telling her that she has lots of angst because she doesn't have enough work. The girl is amazed and agrees that, yes, she is having career issues.

Are these phone booth occupants working hard to make sense of Sally's general statements? I mean, don't most people have money and career worries? Yet there are other segments of the programme that make viewers' stomachs drop a few thousand feet, such as the professional mind-reader challenge, where Sally is pitted against sceptic and magician Matthew Wright. The voiceover suggests that Matthew is one of those disbelieving folk who think Sally's powers can be explained away by cold reading. Matthew says that 'if you need some psychic readings doing, you'd be as well to ask your auntie Betty as you would any psychic that was in the Yellow Pages'.

The challenge is for Sally and Matthew to reveal as many facts as possible about a young Polish girl called Anna, whom neither of them has met before. Matthew's performance is embarrassing. He waffles, tries to fish for information and gets only two facts right, one of which is that Anna is from Eastern Europe, which is so obvious that my neighbour's cat could have guessed it. Sally's performance, though, is far more assured. There's no waffle, no fishing for information, just a quick-fire series of statements, and Anna agrees with every one.

'You're not English,' says Sally. 'True,' responds Anna. 'You're Polish.' True. 'You're in the fashion industry.' True. 'You're a budding actress.' True. 'I think I can see France in your life as well,' says Sally, at which point Anna shouts out, 'You are amazing!' It goes on. 'Three days ago there was talk about a new agent.' Anna's eyes are virtually popping out of her head. It's specific and true.

'She managed to open my mind completely,' says Anna after the challenge. 'She knows everything about me.'

'What I do is not magic. It's come from somewhere else. I can't help that. I can't help that,' says Sally passionately, seemingly confused by her powers.

Matthew, on the other hand, now believes that Sally's powers come from the gods, or that's how I understand what he says to camera at the end of the challenge. It really appears for the first time that a psychic has convinced a sceptic and changed his mind. Would Sally's performance also convince Richard Dawkins that psychics are for real? Is it possible that this is the evidence I've been looking for all this time? I find Matthew's phone number and call him, feeling giddy that I might have found the one true psychic and that I'm about to have it independently verified. I ask Matthew whether he really has hung up his magician's top hat and sceptical braces.

'Not at all,' he tells me.

'But you were rubbish. And you said at the end of the programme that Sally's powers come from the gods,' I remind him. I mean, it's there in full colour, on TV, that Sally outperformed him.

'The editing on that show was awful,' he says.

'What?' How on earth can you edit Sally's performance in a way to show her performing better than Matthew?

'We read for four people each,' Matthew says. 'I did much better for one person than Sally did, we did about the same for two others, and then Sally did much better for another person than I did, and that's the one they showed on the programme. The final scores were 37 for Sally and 34 for me, not the 9 for Sally and 2 for me that was edited for the programme. I don't think she was impressive at all. They edited it to make her look good.'

Matthew tells me that they edited what he said as well, taking the bit about Sally's powers coming from the gods out of context. According to Matthew, this isn't a separate quote, and he said it before and not after the challenge had taken place. In fact, he says, it was part of the same sentence in which he joked that his auntie Betty would be a better psychic.

That would be shocking if it were true. But I'm trying to be impartial and so I need more evidence. I'll have to ask Sally herself. And Matthew is quick to point out that he wants to comment only on his section of the show. He knows nothing about the rest of the programme and doesn't want me to say that he's undermining it.

Something that's still bothering me is that at the beginning of the programme, a voiceover says that the show is an opportunity for the viewers to make up their own minds independently about whether psychics are real or not. According to what Matthew's told me, it seems that they actually have no independence or choice in the matter, because all of Sally's failures are edited out.

After Matthew's breathtaking claims, I call Sally. I'm still in two minds. I know that true fans of Sally Morgan won't take Matthew's comments as a reason for giving up hope in her, and at this point nor will I. Sure, the programme will have been edited to some degree, but Sally was still impressive, wasn't she? She still might have something.

When I speak to Sally on the phone, I'm pleasantly surprised to hear that her TV persona isn't contrived. She's as lovely and friendly in real life as she is on the programme, and she invites me round to her house for a cup of tea and a chat. I pop in on Sally a few weeks before she takes her live show to Fairfield Hall in Croydon. I have tickets, and I'm going with my friend who first mentioned Sally. The show is my scientific test. I want to see if Sally is just as impressive in real life as she is on TV. What's more, I want to see if my friend thinks so too. But first I want to find out whether Sally knows what causes her psychic powers. No psychic yet has managed to give me a satisfactory explanation. I'm hoping that Sally, with her unique psychic abilities, has a better idea.

I catch the train to Merton and walk through leafy suburban streets past Fulham FC's training ground and on to Sally's detached home. Her husband John, who's just as friendly as Sally, is out washing a Mercedes and a large SUV. Well, they aren't doing too badly then, I think. I walk in through the open door and meet Sally in the hallway.

She's ebullient and, just like on TV, appears constantly amazed at the information she's able to get from people. She recalls a recent reading where she saw a sitter's dead father lining up spoons on the table, one after the other. 'The woman told me that he had been ill for four years and had to take all these different medicines and was very particular about using a different spoon for each one. Some might say that I was telepathic, but that's only possible if one was talking about a living person. But I am talking about a person who is dead. I was as gobsmacked as the sitter,' she reveals, almost hyperventilating at the thought.

But today Sally is also excited about her new theatre show, and says that with two TV series under her belt, it was the demand from viewers that drove her to go on tour. 'After the last show of the last series we received 245,000 emails in just seven hours, and we got hundreds of thousands of emails last year,' she admits.

Face-to-face readings weren't keeping up with the demand. 'It became obvious that seeing five people a day five days a week wasn't satisfying people,' she says, bringing over a teapot from the kitchen and pouring me a nice hot brew.

Sally tells me that she has avoided doing a tour for the last twenty years, despite constant requests from promoters. She felt that with a thousand people in the audience there would be no way she could send a message to everyone there. 'It's not rocket science that you'd be only be able to give a message to a few people,' she says.

But she has come up with a way around it. At the end of last year, she had a eureka moment when she thought about trying to get into the audience in other ways without just standing in front and randomly speaking to people. 'What happens when a medium stands in front of a crowd is they tend to be pulled to a certain section because of the energy there, and others can miss out,' she explains. Instead, Sally will be reading messages pulled out of a tombola that people filled on the way in to the auditorium. Everyone now will have a chance to speak to Sally.

Sally tells me that scientist Gary E. Schwartz, based at the University of Arizona, has tested her and thinks he can prove that she can talk to dead people. He has called her one of the top five most accurate mediums in the world. The problem with Schwartz's experiments is that they were of the type that Richard Wiseman and Ciarán O'Keeffe repeated and found to be flawed.

Sally welcomes scientific experiments. 'I have no problem in being tested if the scientists are fair. If a true sceptic was looking into this it wouldn't matter what you did or what they found, because they have already made up their minds,' she says. 'I prove every day that there is an afterlife with my readings. What I say to the sceptics is that they have to prove to me that there isn't an afterlife.'

A fair point, I think. A sceptic like Richard Dawkins wouldn't have a problem with Sally if she could pass a test. I ask Sally whether she knew of any manipulation on the programme.

She disputes this, point-blank. 'All I can say on my grand-children's lives is there was no tinkering in the production. Of course there was editing. We filmed for four months, with one hundred hours of footage. I met the editors and they said the only problem wasn't in getting the good bits, but which bits to leave out. They had better bits on the cutting room floor,' she says, telling me that 'the TV format is very honest'.

Despite what Matthew has claimed about the editing, Sally's performance on the programme has still seeped into my pores. She starts giving me an explanation for her powers.

Sally thinks that spirits are balls of energy attracted by our loved ones. 'If I died, my soul would still be here, and I would still be attracted to my husband and my children,' she says. 'It's like a magnetic pull.'

'I feel that I'm interpreting energy pulses. I know at least half a dozen nuclear physicists looking into quantum physics who think that they can explain what I do. As far I'm concerned, one day a scientist will find an answer. I think what I do will be explained by quantum physics,' she says, looking at me squarely across the table before filling up my teacup again.

The reference to a scientific explanation surprises me. I have no real idea what quantum physics is, although I've certainly used it in arguments in the pub. I often resort to it when talking about time travel or why Manchester United always qualify for Europe.

Just as I'm left pondering this sudden turn into science, Sally turns on the charm once more. She wants to reassure me that she's still down-to-earth, despite talking to dead people. 'Watching other psychics on TV makes me want to retain my sense of normality,' she adds. 'If I came across like them on TV I would be worried,' she says, hinting at how success may have gone to the head of some other famous psychics. 'I really wish to remain very grounded and normal.'

Sally Morgan may be the most self-effacing and ordinary psychic there is, I think, as I finish my tea. John joins us, telling me how excited they are about the forthcoming stage show. They've spent a lot of money on it and want to give people a really entertaining evening. John tells me to say hello when I arrive at Fairfield Hall, before showing me to the door and waving me off. I head back through the suburban streets, walking fast, not having time to work through the insights that Sally has given me. I've just remembered that I've arranged a long-distance phone call to Australia to talk to another psychic before I see Sally in action, and I'm running behind schedule. It doesn't do to be late for a psychic – you never know what they've already got on you.

～

The reason I want to talk to Georgina Walker, probably the most famous psychic down under, is that she's the *doppelgänger* of Sally Morgan in virtually every way, bar the colour of her hair. Spooky. Georgina Walker is the Australian psychic to the stars. She's big, bubbly and has an infectious sense of fun. She could be the ultimate good-time psychic. Not only did she make her name hanging out and doing psychic stuff with a royal Sultan in the sun, but she has spooked John Travolta by revealing that someone close to him would have an illness that he would help find a cure for. Apparently he knew just what she was talking about.

But the thing that I find most intriguing about Georgina is not her star-studded background, but where she came from. Apparently she used her psychic powers and intuition to blow the whistle on corruption in the hospital where she was a manager, uncovering 33 allegations of mismanaged funds. The consequences were overwhelming. She lost her job, had to fight a lengthy court battle, and was left with only one Australian dollar in her pocket. In fact, the day she realised she had nothing was the day that the Sultan called her for a bit of advice about a wayward daughter, and that was the day she become Georgina Walker – psychic to the stars.

The other thing about Georgina that's interesting is how she interacts with the spirit world. It's unique to say the least.

'It was my own fault,' she tells me on the line from Australia, recalling a radio programme she was making at Maitland Gaol, the former home to Australia's hardened criminals and the spookiest prison in all of New South Wales. In all the excitement of the radio show, Georgina, like Angela Donovan at the G&C hair salon in Knightsbridge, didn't do her pre-spirit-world preparations, the charms that mediums believe are important to protect them from nasty spirits.

'I walked up the staircase with two DJs and as I walked into a prison cell, all of a sudden an entity or an energy of a spirit shot up my anus,' she says casually.

'Er, I think I misheard, you said it shot up your what?'

'My anus. I lost all colour.'

I bet you did, I think. It doesn't sound nice at all. Yet apart from the spirit with a peculiar interest in the human anatomy, something else happened. The DJs who'd been strutting around looking important and in control lost their heads completely.

'The two DJs started screaming,' Georgina says. 'They didn't know what was happening to me. I was mature, I shouldn't be acting like I've seen a ghost.'

What then?

'I ran outside and started vomiting,' Georgina says. But luckily she had some sage in her handbag, which apparently is to a ghost what salt is to a snail.

'When I pulled it out, one of the DJs went, "Oh my god, she's got the biggest reefer I've ever seen!"' Georgina tells me, chuckling. 'I had no idea what a reefer was!'

Once she'd smoked out the spirit, she asked the public relations officer from the jail to find out what had happened in the cell. If you're of a delicate disposition, I really think you should turn the page now.

'Charles Hines was the last person in there, for raping his stepdaughter. If you're in jail for raping a young child, then the other prisoners stick barbed wire up the offender's anus as punishment. When I went in there I felt either the pain that the girl went through or what Hines felt,' Georgina reveals.

I really think we need to change the subject now. All this talk of the tradesmen's entrance and barbed wire is making me feel a little queasy.

So we get on to my favourite subject of the moment – Richard Dawkins – and Georgina is refreshingly polite and thoughtful. This is odd for a psychic, very odd. Most psychics growl.

'We can get angry. But I think sceptics bring balance,' she tells me. 'If we are constantly in la-la land, then no one will strive to improve or ask questions of themselves. What purpose am I serving as a psychic? It puts us on a path that may encourage us to be better psychics.'

Her attitude is surprising but clever. She's appropriated Dawkins' criticism and turned it back on itself. For Georgina, Dawkins is their number one cheerleader, urging mediums on from the sidelines, encouraging them to be more, not less psychic. I don't think he'd like that. I don't think he'd like that one bit.

But talking of science, the real reason I called up Georgina is to see if she agrees with Sally Morgan about quantum physics. Georgina compares what happens when she communicates with the dead to speaking on a mobile phone.

'We have don't cords or wires, we push in a number and someone will pick up. We can't see the connection. It's like a satellite beaming to us. We don't see the atoms and molecules,' she says.

Atoms? That sounds like quantum physics to me, although Georgina also thinks that a psychic's ability is linked to left brain/right brain technology. 'The right brain is where the senses develop, and it was this intuition that saved people from sabre-tooth tigers. This is highly evolved in children, but society changes this and they become more left-brain as they grow up, more mechanical,' she says, suggesting that psychics keep on developing this right side of their brains throughout their lives.

Before I leave Georgina, she tells me about free will and seeing the future. It concerns a very unlikely spirit – Winston Churchill – and the Sultan.

'Back in 1988 when I was a farmer's wife, Winston appeared to me and said, "One day you will walk the paths of kings and queens." The reason I mention this is that some things are preordained, we can't stop the blueprint of the soul. We may get lost on the way, take a wrong turn, but if there's something we have a purpose for, or a lesson to learn, we will learn it,' she says.

Well, that could be describing my journey too. I just wonder how many more times I'm going to get lost, and what I'm destined to learn by the end of it.

I say goodbye to Georgina, who's so chatty it's like saying goodbye to an old friend – it takes ages. She certainly gives Sally Morgan some serious competition in the nice and friendly psychic stakes. But with Georgina also hinting at a scientific explanation for what psychics do, I've got a lot to think about before I arrive at Fairfield Hall, Croydon to test Sally Morgan in a few days' time.

～

Fairfield Hall is buzzing with excitement when I arrive with Sharon, my friend and scientific assistant. John's busy at the tombola stall, ramming it full of the audience's questions for Sally to refer to in the show. We've arrived late and in no time are marched into the auditorium. Everyone, and I mean everyone including me, is on the edge of their seats. I keep getting butterflies and I have no idea why.

The show is a mix of excerpts from the TV programme interspersed with Sally talking to the audience. At times I feel like I'm back in Sylvia Browne's salon. Not because Sally is anything like Sylvia, but because the audience is wearing its emotions on its shirtsleeves. Croydon feels very American tonight. The woman sitting next to us rocks back and forth in her chair, hyperventilating at Sally's performance.

Yet most people don't recognise the names that Sally starts to retrieve from the spirit world. John and Sally had warned me about this. They said that people in the audience wouldn't just shout out when they recognised a name – something I've heard psychics say before. Then an Asian man near the front sticks his hand in the air and claims the dead boy that Sally has connected with. I don't know what it is – the drama of the occasion, the big audience, or the professional air of the man now talking to Sally – but we're all suddenly feeling spooked. Sally's telling him that he recently had open-heart surgery. He agrees. The audience's pulse quickens. Sally says that his dead son was with him during the operation and that he died for a short while on the operating table. The star psychic then turns to his wife and reveals that she's recently had a stroke. The woman next to us almost faints when the man's wife confirms this. Sally's time with the man is over, but not before we've witnessed him bursting into tears at the thought of his son looking after him during his operation.

The show rumbles on, not really getting anywhere, but with a constant sense of anticipation. Then it happens again. Just when we're being lulled back into our sceptical selves and the woman next to us is calming down, Sally does something that makes us all wonder again whether she really is the real deal, as she likes to call herself.

She shouts out a name and no one responds. Then at the back of the auditorium a small voice calls out. Sally hears, and an odd exchange happens. Sally calls the woman by a name few people use, like calling her Beth when her name is Elizabeth. Then Sally tells her she can see a girl falling out of a window backwards. The woman knows who it is. It's a niece of hers. Then Sally says she can see horses, and the woman replies that she had an expensive statue of a horse, but it was stolen. Then Sally asks something like, 'Who's Dave?' The woman shouts, 'That's the bugger who stole it!' Everyone laughs. Sharon and I are now seriously considering calling an ambulance for the hyperventilating woman next to us.

Everyone in the audience is now primed, but Sally doesn't click with the next person, or the one after that. It's at these moments that Sally resorts to showing the audience a recording of her TV show on the screen, to keep people awed at her psychic powers. It's effective. The show drifts slowly to a close, and we all head out into the fresh Croydon night air.

Afterwards I have my first experience of scientific disagreement, because Sharon and I have different views about what happened tonight. Sharon believes that while the show wasn't as good as the TV programme, Sally still performed psychically on the two occasions I described.

Sure, the woman on the back row seemed to recognise the names, but she had to fill in a lot of the details. When I think about the show tonight, the majority of the time, people failed to recognise what Sally was referring to. It could quite easily have been luck that she told the Asian man he'd had a heart attack. He was also the one who stuck his hand up and pulled Sally towards him. I'm unsure, but I know what will make me certain. I've realised that I've been searching in the wrong place. I need to stop looking at psychics themselves and spend more time trying to discover what it is they think they're doing. Sally suggested some pretty complex science to back up her powers. If I can prove that this is a valid explanation, then I'll believe that she's psychic.

15

The Nobel-winning psychic

MY INTEREST PRICKED by Sally Morgan's suggestion that her supernatural powers can be explained by quantum physics, I try to track down the finest minds to put some meat on the bones of her idea. Physics, however, is a topic that gives me a cold shudder. I spent my entire physics GCSE sitting at the back of the class and doing what kids at the back of the class do best – a fat lot of nothing. Not knowing anything about the subject at all is not going to put me off on my search for the truth, however. I've committed to do whatever is necessary on my psychic journey, and so I've got myself an interview with a Nobel Prize-winning professor of physics. Why do I put myself through these ordeals?

Brian Josephson, Cambridge University Professor of Physics, has been causing waves ever since he found an effect in which pairs of electrons are able to undertake a bit of nifty quantum tunnelling across a barrier separating two superconductors. It's not easy to get your head around, but suffice it to say that the discovery was so important it was named the Josephson Effect and he bagged a Nobel Prize for it in 1973. Following that, you imagine, he could go off and do just about anything he wanted. And he did, by trying to explain *psi* (pronounced 'sigh'), the 'scientific' word for psychic energy, through physics. He set up the Mind–Matter Unification Project in Cambridge and hasn't looked back since. Except for the occasional run-in with other physicists, that is.

In the autumn of 2001, for instance, the Royal Mail caused a stir among normally restrained and well-behaved physicists when they realised that in honouring the 100th anniversary of the Nobel Prize, the Mail had published a pamphlet explaining how modern physics would one day lead to an understanding of telepathy and the paranormal. Part of a pretty presentation package containing six stamps, the pamphlet was part-authored by Josephson.

David Deutsch, a quantum physics expert at Oxford, was quoted in the *Observer* at the time as saying: 'Telepathy simply does not exist. The Royal Mail has let itself be hoodwinked into supporting ideas that are complete nonsense.'

But, come on, said the Royal Mail in their defence, the guy won a Nobel Prize. If that's not a good guideline for who to listen to, what is?

Quite.

Josephson went further, though, suggesting that the reason he was having such a hard time was that there was a conspiracy afoot. Lurking down the back corridors of the scientific establishment were to be found the editors of the most reputable scientific journals hatching a devilishly fiendish plot. In an act of collective skulduggery, they had decided to prevent the publication of scientific papers proving the existence of psi.

Josephson said: 'I think journals like *Nature* and *Science* are censoring such research. There is a lot of evidence to support telepathy, for example, but papers on the subject are being rejected – quite unfairly.'

Josephson was writing to redress this balance. He said in the pamphlet that the combination of quantum theory with theories of information and computation might lead 'to an explanation of processes still not understood within conventional science, such as telepathy – an area in which Britain is at the forefront of research'.

Deutsch, still giving the journalist from the *Observer* earache, went on: 'The evidence for the existence of telepathy is appalling. If engineers or doctors accepted the level of proof that is accepted by paranormal supporters, bridges would be falling down round the country, and new medicines would be killing more than they cure.'

But I just want to find out whether Sally Morgan's idea that quantum physics can explain what she does has any validity. If I can make sense of Josephson's thinking, and it's a big if, then Morgan might be on to something and her prime-time TV slot can't be dismissed as just another space-filler by unresourceful TV executives.

Like the psi he investigates, Josephson is hard to track down. It takes an age for him to get back in touch with my repeated requests for an interview and then he tells me to try some other parapsychologists at the University of Northampton. I rather get the feeling he doesn't want to talk to me. I eventually get an email from him agreeing to a telephone interview on the condition that I read up on his work and watch one of his lectures online.

Although the lecture leaves me none the wiser, I quickly click on Google and discover that Josephson's Mind–Matter Unification Project at Cambridge is an attempt to unify physics with the mind in some form of quantum brain. Simple. That's all I really needed to know.

Feeling confident, I take a look at his paper entitled 'Biological Utilisation of Quantum Non-Locality' to try to expand on this beautiful simplicity.

This is basically a theory suggesting that, because in quantum physics sub-atoms can interact with each other over a large distance, then so can our brains. It's a huge jump to make, but Josephson is working under the assumption that psi exists and that the evidence supports it, and so he's just coming up with a theory to explain it.

He reckons that psi functioning is a bit slippery – sometimes you see it and sometimes you don't – because, and I quote: 'Our assumption in relation to psi functioning is that … the relevant probability distributions are highly focussed in relation to goals, in a way that may become more effective over time as development through learning takes place.'

What I take this to mean is that if you're more motivated, i.e. goal-orientated, and have practised, like a tightrope-walker or a darts player, then your psychic ability should improve.

But Josephson continues, arguing that 'evolution through natural selection tends to give rise to adaptive elaborations of pre-existing phenotypes (manifest behaviour)'. What he means is that because we developed our sight due to being exposed to light over a long period of time, then surely psychic ability must have evolved in the nervous system and developed a way 'of interacting non-locally with other systems'.

Josephson is borrowing evolution theory to explain how we have adapted our senses to use psi. Considering Darwin's rapid dismissal of Wallace's view of psychic phenomena, you can well imagine the father of evolution turning in his grave at this.

Now that I'm clear, sort of, I put in the call to his office. He's a very quietly spoken man, so quiet in fact that I have trouble hearing what he's saying.

'I think the nervous system is a way we might reconcile physics and psi,' he says, explaining that 'we really don't understand at the moment mind and consciousness' and how it interacts with physics. Conventional science can't explain it. There are additional dimensions that we have yet to discover, suggests Josephson.

I thought I was the only one who didn't understand it. At least I'm in good company.

'What, like sub-atoms?' I ask, trying to sound like I know what I'm talking about, but Josephson puts me in my place.

'No, we don't understand it. I'm talking about something at another level beyond sub-atoms,' he says.

'Like what?'

'We don't know yet. We don't understand it,' he says. 'It's sub-atoms influencing sub-atoms at a level of physical reality that we don't understand very well at the moment.'

We go on like this for a bit, me asking what the new level of existence is, and him saying he doesn't know.

Then he tells me that he thinks precognition theory is a bit far-fetched. 'I don't think we can influence things back in time,' he says. 'We might be able to concentrate our energies and feel some kind of presence of an event before it becomes visible.'

I think I'm on to something. Here's a Nobel Prize-winner telling me that he thinks precognition is phoney, yet he believes in telepathy, which sounds, confusingly, a lot like precognition anyway. I ask him to clarify what he means.

'I don't have anything to add to what I've already said,' he tells me, sounding quieter than ever. 'You should speak to Dean

Radin,' he announces cryptically, his voice disappearing into some kind of vortex where sound is outlawed.

I try to get more out of him, but he doesn't budge. The only thing I'm clear about is that Josephson's got a theory but he doesn't really understand its full implications. I'm back at square one. Well, at least I'm as confused as a Nobel Laureate. My mum would be proud.

I feel like I've hit a dead-end. But still, I'm intrigued by Josephson's suggestion that I speak to Dean Radin. He's the scientist I read about at the Society for Psychical Research doing experiments on soldiers and precognition.

He's got to have the answer, I think, if he's actually been testing people and found positive results. I send him a quick email, not holding out any hope that he'll reply to my request to meet him. I'm not a soldier and I'm unsure whether I have any psychic power at all. But I have a pleasant surprise. He's agreed to meet me, and what's more, he's agreed to show me his precognition machine.

16

Testing for the future

I CAN'T QUITE CONTAIN my excitement. I'm in the heart of the cutting-edge centre of psi research at the Noetic Institute of Sciences in Petaluma, California, and I'm having electrodes fitted to my fingers. I'm about to undertake a precognition test. I'm sitting in front of a machine that will apparently tell me whether I'm one of the chosen few whose mind can leap ahead into the future. What's more, Dean Radin, senior researcher at the institute, has told me I'm juicy.

I was surprised too.

'You would probably do okay because your hand is warm, in which case your physiology is juicy. You are probably labile, as we say in physiological terms,' he adds, after seeing the look on my face.

The Noetic Institute of Science (NIS) was set up in 1973 by former Apollo 14 astronaut Edgar Mitchell following a revelatory moment in his space capsule, from which he observed the earth 'floating freely in the vastness of space'. Being struck by the image, he went on to say later that 'The presence of divinity became almost palpable, and I knew that life in the universe was not just an accident based on random processes. ... The knowledge came to me directly.' Ever since, the institute has been applying 'scientific rigour' to find evidence of extra-sensory perception. I'm here to discover what they've found out. I want to see whether the NIS can tell me what Nobel Prize-winner Brian Josephson couldn't. The problem is, I'm not even sure what it was that Josephson couldn't tell me.

On my drive up here from San Francisco, over the rusty-coloured Golden Gate Bridge, I'd been wondering about research into psi. If psychics can't consistently predict the future, then maybe the energy that they say they tap in to is unpredictable as well. Psi is a small effect that can only just be detected. Yet detected it has been, according to the NIS. Not by people claiming to be psychics, but by ordinary people. Joe the Plumber, Joe Sixpack, even, God forbid, Mondeo Man and Worcestershire Woman. This takes it out of the realm of show-business and back down to earth – ordinary people might be deluding themselves that they have premonitions, but surely they can't fool science, can they?

Within minutes of driving over the bridge, I begin heading up through the rolling hills of Marin County. Not far from here, a ten-minute drive away, is wine country – Napa Valley and Sonoma, which produce some of the best wines the US has to offer. It's fertile country. It's, as Dean Radin might say, juicy. I drive up more lush hills to the Noetic centre, which looks like a settlement of Swiss chalets, and I'm taken aback by the views over even more verdant, rolling countryside. This is surely a place, I think, where scientists can do their best think-ing. I walk down through the chalets, half expecting to hear the tinkling of cow-bells, ready to face my future once more.

Dean Radin is a small, slightly-built man who looks like he spends most of his time fixing machines. Actually, I think he does. While strapping me into the precognition testing machine, he explains about another contraption sitting next to it.

'It's a device which will measure the speed of light again to a ridiculously accurate degree. The clock and the device and electronics send out a laser pulse simultaneously to the two spools of fibre,' he says, which I think I understand, but I lose the thread when he says, 'the target and mediator on an SM2 slows their speed of light down in that tool.'

It's probably better if I just don't know.

The test that I'm about to take was designed by Dean to search for unconscious signs of presentiment, which is a sense of foreboding, a feeling of danger or an intuitive hunch that something's not right. Dean Radin believes that 'that we are constantly and unconsciously scanning our future, and preparing to respond to it'. The electrodes that have been put on my fingers are testing for signs of skin conductivity – the idea is that if our extra-sensory perceptive ability resides in our nervous system, then it can be captured as a emotional response in the skin. My skin conductivity is monitored continuously while I'm shown 40 images in random order on a computer screen. The images range from calm to exciting to dangerous, from an erotic photograph to a picture of a man-eating lion. The idea is that my skin conductivity will be raised before an emotional picture and stay the same before a calm image.

Dean Radin's tests have produced positive results, or, as he puts it, 'resulted in a strong presentiment effect', from 2,500 to 1 against chance and up to 125,000 to 1 against chance.

So I sit strapped in and wait for the images. Plugged in to Dean's laptop, I know that after a cross appears and then disappears on the screen, I have three to five seconds before a picture will appear. In that time, my normally none-too-responsive extra-sensory perception should leap forwards like the DeLorean at the end of *Back to the Future*.

Dean leaves the room and I'm left alone with only my precognitive skills and a load of bizarre images to keep me company. I'm not too sure what reaction I'm supposed to be having, but laughter isn't one of them. When a picture of three turtles lying on a rock appears, I start chuckling. I don't know why. It just looks funny — three dudes hanging out, shooting the breeze. When I tell Dean later that I laughed at this image, he looks at me as though I've got the weirdest sense of humour. I also see a water-skier and an erotic picture — well, a naked woman with so much soft focus that she may as well be fully clothed. There are also lots of photos that I can't really remember, so I'm not too sure which were meant to be frightening. All I know is that I had a difficult time keeping my mind on the job.

After the test, and while Dean analyses my results, he admits to not having a psychic bone in his body. Though, as it happens, I've arrived on a very auspicious day. Today, for the first time, Dean Radin had a moment of presentiment. I feel very privileged to be the first to hear this.

On his way to work this morning he was driving up the steep, twisting road that leads to the institute.

'Every time you go round a corner you get the sun right in your face. Normally I'd be driving up at about twenty miles an hour and figuring that at this time of day, everyone is going up and I don't need to worry about the trucks coming down,' he says.

But today is different. Today, the day that I arrive, he gets a hunch that something is going to go wrong.

'I'm mindful about driving in general, so I sort of keep open this hunch capability,' he says. 'I suddenly had a sense that something is not right.'

I'm on the edge of my seat. What could it be? A flash flood? A storm of African killer bees?

'So I slowed way down, I slowed down to probably five miles an hour, and I went round the next curve,' he says. Dean, come on, man, this is killing me! 'Around the next curve is a lady pushing a bicycle up the hill.'

Oh.

'But that is extremely rare,' he says quickly, seeing me staring open-mouthed. 'I do not remember ever in the last seven and a half years encountering somebody pushing a bicycle up the hill. Something alerted me that for some reason I needed to slow down. That is an example of a spontaneous type of hunch that people sometimes have,' he says, before telling me that the experiment that I've just undergone is 'basically the laboratory analogue of that kind of phenomenal U-turn'.

While Dean continues to whizz through graphs and spread-sheets, I try to do something useful. I think of all the times in my life when presentiment would have come in handy, like when I was four and my sister and her friends made a lean-to from an old bed sheet and some stones. They told me to walk under it, so I did and a stone fell on my head. Next thing I remember was my mum looking into the crack in my head, then being rushed off to hospital. Children are meant to be more intuitive, so you'd think I might have had a gut feeling. Or at least the smack on the head should have jolted some of those unstable and unpredictable sub-atoms into life. But no, so many things in my life could have done with a bit of presentiment that I begin to have a sinking feeling as Dean draws his analytical rummaging to a close.

'You've ended up with actually a highly significant result,' he says.

I can't believe it. I'm actually a precog.

'In the opposite direction,' he goes on.

Oh.

'This is a statistically significant anti-presentiment,' he says, pointing at the graph animatedly. I realise Dean really loves spreadsheets. He notices the look of profound disappointment on my face, and attempts to locate the ten trials, out of my 40, which produced the most emotional response. He looks at the chart for a while.

'No, it's basically the same. You have had some sort of peculiar anti-effect, and not a minor one but a pretty strong one,' he says.

'But I was making sure my mind was calm and I was breathing deeply,' I say, trying to avoid utter humiliation.

Then Dean notices something else. He pulls up the picture of the water-skier.

'This is the most emotional picture and you have no response at all,' he says looking at his graph. 'It's as though you're watching this picture as calm as a zombie.'

But Dean, always on the look-out for meaning and patterns in his statistics, finds something from which I can grab some precognitive pride.

'It seems that you suddenly became much calmer beforehand. I would recommend that if you are driving along and suddenly you become really quiet, that is the signal to pay attention to,' he suggests.

I tell him I'm terrified of crocodiles and that maybe if there had been a picture of one, I'd have had more significant results. He thinks this might be the case as well.

'So if I'm in Australia and I suddenly feel calm by a river, I should run away?' I ask.

I think he nods, but I'm not too sure. He's already using my statistically significant result as yet more evidence for another of his observations.

'That is why I like to work with the seventeen-year-old girls, because they are guaranteed to have a huge response towards the images,' he says. 'They are young enough not to have seen a lot of the world yet, and so they have a big range of emotional responses.'

This is compared with, say, a doctor on an emergency ward who'll 'look at accident scenes and will say "Okay, I know how to fix this" and they don't get that emotional rush, which is necessary for the experiment,' he explains.

As I'm here on a scientific as well as a precognitive quest, I ask Dean whether any of his tests have been repeated by other scientists with equally successful results. It's the benchmark of scientific inquiry, after all.

'Yes. There have been two experiments with pupil dilation and a colleague is now working on heart rate and brainwaves. I did a brainwave study too. Another colleague did it using earthworms,' he reveals.

'Worms? You means worms can see the future?'

'He would drape the worm over a stick and the stick would either vibrate or not, and worms don't like vibration. That was the equivalent of an emotional stimulus for them. Even with the worms he got a result that is quite similar to what we have seen in humans, so it's probably not a human-centric thing. It has something to do with the way perhaps that living systems perceive things.'

I ask Dean why he's no longer testing with Zener cards, like in the *Ghostbusters* movie. He says the experiments testing unconscious responses show 'much more robust effects'.

'It confirms the original suspicion that what is going on here is mostly unconscious and only very rarely reaches a level of awareness,' he says.

But the real problem with conscious experiments, Dean tells me, turning off his laptop and sitting down opposite me, is performance anxiety.

This is the reason why easily repeatable experiments for psi have eluded parapsychologists' best efforts. While for sceptics this means that psi doesn't exist, for Dean Radin and people like him it means that psi is elusive because people undergoing experiments get nervous or bored, and so are often pretty useless.

'For that matter, hardly anything involving skilled human performance is absolutely predictable, except perhaps stubbornness in the face of evidence one doesn't wish to see,' he says, sounding defensive and repeating something I'd read in his book on the topic, *Entangled Minds*. He sounds prickly because he's had to deal with a lot of scepticism, I guess.

But Dean has found a way of showing that many of the tests into psychic ability throughout history show consistent and significant results. While individual tests have been difficult to repeat, which raises questions about their reliability, Dean recruits meta-analysis to bring this doubting to a close. This is a study of all the studies ever done. It takes account of the quality of the methodology – so no ectoplasm-hiding stunts would sneak in – and the file-drawer problem, which is when scientists publish only their positive data and ignore the trifling inconvenience of the tests that showed nothing.

Interestingly, Dean used this approach to claim back the results of J.B. Rhine's experiments at Duke University in the 1930s. You may remember that Rhine produced results for precognition and telepathy using Zener cards that were breathtaking. One of his subjects, Adam Linzmayer, even achieved 100 per cent on two short (nine-card series) tests. The results were phenomenal. Yet since then Rhine's results have been dismissed as flawed because only the successful studies were published. The problem with Rhine's experiments is that no one has ever been able to repeat them, except London University fraudster Professor Soal. Rhine was also criticised for not disclosing the names of assistants he caught cheating. Yet Dean's meta-analysis of the 188 experiments described in Rhine's 1940 book, *Extrasensory Perception after Sixty Years*, suggests that the combined results are so far from chance 'that it would take 428,000 unreported studies averaging a chance effect to eliminate the results of the known 188 experiments'. 'The missing studies would have taken 137,000 years to produce,' he reveals dramatically. In the face of this meta-analysis, all the criticism has finally been answered, claims Dean.

Despite getting very defensive at times about sceptics, the thing I like about Dean Radin is that he tries really hard to convince us of his evidence. And, what's more, he has a well-thought-out theory to explain the existence of psi, or extrasensory perception. He's got the balls to stand up and say it, I suppose, even though he knows most other scientists will be giggling behind his back.

Like Professor Josephson, he uses quantum theory to explain it. But since speaking to the professor, I've been told that if a leading quantum physicist tells you they understand quantum physics, they're lying. That's how odd and difficult it is. In that case, what chance have I got?

Luckily, Dean Radin is the man who can explain it. Using an aspect of quantum mechanics called entanglement theory, in which sub-atoms become entangled with each other and communicate over vast distances, he thinks he may well have found the explanation for extra-sensory perception.

Of course, in reality it's a lot more complicated than that. In fact, I just read a quantum physicist's explanation of entanglement theory three times, and every time I felt tiny explosions going off in my head. For instance, this is the technical explanation:

'The analysis of entangled particles by means of Bell's theorem can lead to an impression of non-locality (that is, that there exists a connection between the members of such a pair that defies both classical and relativistic concepts of space and time). This is reasonable if it is assumed that each particle departs the scene of the pair's creation in an ambiguous state (as per a possible interpretation of Heisenberg). In such case, either dichotomous outcome of a given measurement remains a possibility; only measurement itself would precipitate a distinct value.'

Still with me? And that was Wikipedia.

Dean reckons that this sub-atomic interaction works between minds as well. In his book, Dean makes the story of entanglement riveting. Yet while I'm reading it, I can't help thinking about his constant complaint that sceptics use simple 'rhetorical devices' such as ridicule to undermine his and other believers' arguments. This is because Dean's got a pretty well-stocked armoury of his own rhetorical devices. He uses suspense, intrigue and shock, describing one physicist as being 'shaken to the bone' by his discoveries. After one lengthy explanation of Bell's theorem, which sort of proves non-locality in sub-atoms, he concludes:

'The concept of Bell's inequality is actually quite simple, but the first time you encounter the argument it's hard to grasp ... You'll know you've got it when your gut suddenly drops, like the feeling of freefall when a roller-coaster plunges off that first steep rise. Until you get it viscerally, the "most profound discovery" description seems like overkill. Afterwards "profound" isn't strong enough.'

And then there's metaphor, which Dean admits to using to explain quantum mechanics.

'Well, it's a bit tricky,' he tells me. 'I mean obviously nobody really knows the answers, so I'm struggling with the metaphors and analogies.' He gives it a go anyway.

'Aspects of the deep structure of the world are always connected to each other, and that includes us. Our minds presumably at some level are always connected to everything else. The vast majority of the time we are not aware of it because it's deep within us, it's part of the fabric of reality itself.'

And it's on this entangled fabric of reality that our minds float along and swirl around with everything else. 'Events may be thought of as ripples reverberating though an immense pool, and as an object bobbing along the surface like a cork,' he says.

In this huge swimming pool of reality, we can sense our own future and a loved one far away because entanglements happen both in space and time. Yet couldn't we become overwhelmed by the noise of all this rushing water pushing down on us? How would we know what to listen to? 'It's the same reason why at a cocktail party you can hear your name called across a room even though there's this huge din of noise. We pay attention to the things that are important to us and not what's happening on Pluto right now,' he says.

So on the huge sea of quantum reality our brains can somehow hear the tiny, distant distress bell of a loved one in peril, and that noise somehow feeds back into our minds. Josephson suggested that this might happen through the nervous system, but wouldn't say any more.

Dean suggests that we can view the information we receive based only on what we already know. So rather than entangled sub-atoms sending actual information to us like a newspaper headline, they just send us a feeling, and we use our data bank of past memories and experiences to create what that feeling might represent. In fact, he says that no information transfer actually takes place at all, because in the quantum universe we are always connected. 'It would appear to be a form of information transfer, but in fact it would be a pure correlation,' I read later in his book.

The idea that we can understand messages from the future based only on images already in our memory banks causes problems when a psychic sees something in 4,000 years' time. Our brains just wouldn't have the conceptual understanding of what we would be seeing. Leaping too far into the future would be 'like demonstrating a portable DVD player to Benjamin Franklin,' he explains.

Dean illustrates this by telling me that he has asked a psychic to leap ahead into the future and describe a device that he's currently trying to invent, and which he has already patented. He calls it a 'psi switch' – 'a technological way of detecting mental intention at a distance'. Basically, it seems, Dean has patented a design based on foretelling the future. He's convinced that it's useful, and that 'sometimes remarkably detailed technical information can be obtained with talented psychics'.

As I say goodbye to him, I can see a distant look in his eyes. He's already busily inventing his next machine. I close the door to his office and walk back through the tranquil chalets, looking down over the lush hills.

It feels good to be outside in this fine weather, especially as I know it's freezing and pouring with rain back home. It's a perfect opportunity to ponder my next move. What Dean has told me has raised the prospect that something might actually be going on. Dean's tests show a very small effect – a presentiment, a hunch. It hardly registers on the radar of his experiments, yet through painstaking meta-analysis he thinks he's found robust scientific proof that with the right motivation we can all sense the future. And what's more, it seems that Sally Morgan was right. Quantum physics may be able to explain what she thinks she's doing. But, and here's where I'm stuck, Dean also believes that 'talented' psychics can leap ahead to the future and come back with complex designs for devices that haven't been invented yet. That's not presentiment, that's full-blown clairvoyance – that's Nostradamus gone to town and come back with too many toys. That's, frankly, a bit weird.

But there's something far more troubling that I have to come to terms with. I know I had to face this eventually, but now I have the scientific proof. I'm about as psychic as a piece of toast. According to Dean, I'm little more than a dead man walking. Yet he has also left me the hope that with the right motivation, barring any performance anxiety, I too could train myself to become psychic.

As I walk up along the path, breathing in the warm air and enjoying the California sunshine for the last time, I've made a decision – well, it was more of a hunch, an intuitive feeling. As soon as I'm back in the UK, I'm going to enrol in psychic school.

I turn on the engine, floor the gas pedal and pull away from the Noetic Institute. I'm going to become so darn psychic, I tell myself, that I'll blow fuses in Dean Radin's machines next time.

17

Psychic school

Sᴛɪʟʟ ʀᴇᴇʟɪɴɢ ꜰʀᴏᴍ the discovery that I'm about as psychic as a zombie, I enrolled at psychic school a few moments after my plane touched down from California. Both Dean Radin and Professor Brian Josephson suggested that psychic power could be improved by practice, motivation and being goal orientated. So, high with positive thinking, I'm fully expecting to be at least marginally less dead by the end of my course. Unfortunately, I've been in the psychic classroom five minutes and things are already looking a bit ropey.

I've arrived at the College for Psychic Studies in Kensington, London, to join Lizzie Towers' twelve-week Developing Psychic Ability course, and I feel out of my depth. The college was set up in 1884 at the height of the Victorian surge of interest in psychic activity, and is the main training centre for the spiritualist movement in the UK. Yet even if I'd started studying from its inception, I feel I wouldn't be as psychic as some of the other students on my course. Compared with them, I've virtually got learning difficulties.

The problem started when Lizzie asked the twelve assembled students to give a reason for joining the course. I'm one of the first to go, and I say weakly that I just want to know what's out there and how we can use the information. She seems happy with this reason, and even gives a little story to back it up. A woman once rang her doorbell asking for money, but Lizzie, feeling an intuitive hunch, didn't open the door and spoke to her through the letterbox. When the woman finally left, Lizzie saw that two men had been hiding, ready to pounce. That's Lizzie's example of how psychic ability can help in tricky moments. It sounds a lot like Dean Radin's 'hunch capability'.

Lizzie's question creeps slowly around the room. Nearly all the female students say that they want to feel more confident. From how quietly and timidly they speak, I can't help agreeing with them. But then the question arrives at the other two men in the class. Suddenly everyone else's excuse for attending is blown apart by the sheer force of their experiences.

I'm sitting opposite Ian. He's smartly dressed. He looks like a lawyer or an accountant, and seems very normal. That is, until he speaks.

'I'm surrounded by spirits all the time and I need to learn to close off, shut down. They're driving me insane. They just won't stop. They touch me and I'm beginning to be worn out,' he says.

Lizzie nods in an understanding way, as though what Ian is describing is a usual complaint at the College for Psychic Studies.

Next to Ian is a big Irish man called Kieran, and he's raising the stakes.

'I've seen dead people since I was born and I've got to stop them trying to hurt other people,' he says.

I notice Ian shift uneasily in his seat. Kieran's bettered him and he's visibly peeved. Even in the world of psychics, men just can't stop being competitive. I try to think up something harder-hitting to say next time.

Compared with these two, I've got some serious catching-up to do. I think about suggesting to Lizzie that I should be put in the remedial class. But there's no time. She starts giving us a lecture about the spirit world, telling us how the universe started. These psychics don't like the easy topics, do they?

'If you imagine that at the beginning of time there was just one – and this is just a theory, but I like this theory – one huge circular mirror, and that's all that there was ... it was just this huge mirror,' she says. I frown and nod in an understanding way.

'And then people talk about the moment of the big bang, which I think starts off from one crazy thought, one crazy, unique thought from this energy consciousness, which I'm going to describe as a mirror. So this energy consciousness suddenly went, "What if there wasn't just me, what if I could experience myself?"'

She reveals that the mirror then shattered and created the universe, and in the centre of the mirror was God. The first ripples out from the exploding mirror made the angelic realm, which has a memory that we were all one, and then it's us, who sort of 'implode into ourselves'. I don't understand, but I'm not worried. There are lots of things that I've not understood on my journey, and I've learnt that sometimes it's safest to not even attempt an explanation.

What Lizzie's saying, I think, is similar to Dean Radin's entangled universe theory in which we are all connected. For Dean, we're all joined together by sub-atoms; for Lizzie, we're the shards of a shattered looking-glass. If we look hard enough into this universal mirror we can contact the spirit world.

I suddenly begin to feel anxious. I've realised, sitting in the middle of this group of people, that I'm going to have to produce some spirit energy from somewhere sooner or later and it's going to be embarrassing when it doesn't happen.

It doesn't take long before we get serious. Once Lizzie has finished telling us about the big mirror in the sky, we have to open up our chakra points, which are located throughout the body – there's one in my foot, another in my stomach, various others around my bodily organs, but the most important of all is the one on the top of my head. Through this hole will come the spirit-world messages. But before we open it, Lizzie tells us to ground ourselves. It's a serious business. Remembering Australian psychic Georgina Walker's experience with the ghost shooting up her back passage, I'm not taking any chances. We close our eyes and Lizzie tells us to think of our feet pushing through the floor like roots from a tree until they reach the ground. Once we're grounded, we rip open the chakra points in the tops of our heads by closing our eyes and by Lizzie telling the chakra point to, well, open. That's it.

Once these precautions are out of the way, Lizzie gives us a task. I have to swap places with the woman next to me and pick up psychic messages from the energy she has left on the chair. I then have to interpret this information and tell her something about her life. I'm worried. This is the only woman who didn't say she lacked confidence. In fact, she admitted to being swamped by psychic power. She was the only woman who matched the boys' psychic bragging and I now have to convince her I'm psychic. This is worse than my driving test.

I sit down in her chair and close my eyes. I immediately feel my upper legs becoming warm from the heat left over from her body, but that's it. Nothing comes. I open my right eye a crack and calculate the distance to the door. I think about feigning illness; better still, I might just faint instead. In the middle of trying to hatch my break-out plan, Lizzie announces that it's time to start sharing our psychic thoughts.

Sonya, my partner, is looking at me with a warm smile and starts talking straight away.

'I feel, I get a sense that you are very tired, completely exhausted. Is that right?' she asks, raising an eyebrow.

'Yes,' I say. 'Yesterday I drove back from my holiday all the way through France. I'm exhausted,' I tell her, yawning.

It's true. The day before, I had driven my old campervan back from the south coast of France through the driving rain. If I'd had more hours in bed, maybe I would have seen that she'd observed me yawning. But due to my sleepy lack of judgement, I'm impressed.

'I can also feel pain, here,' she says, rubbing her back.

'Oh yeah,' I say, 'I've got a bad back too,' forgetting that the pain disappeared five weeks ago and my back doesn't hurt any more. But, you know, maybe she was just remembering the pain. I'm getting really good, I realise, at just filling in the details and making whatever Sonya says relevant to my life.

She then looks at me and smiles.

I smile back, rubbing my eyes.

'Well,' she says.

'Well what?'

'Did you feel anything about me?'

'Oh. Well, I, er ...'

She smiles.

'I, mmmm ... thighs,' I say before I can stop myself.

'Thighs?' Her smile suddenly falters.

'Thighs. Yeah. I mean, I ... I feel warm thighs. Not yours. I mean, well, they are. But ... I don't want to touch them or anything, it's just I ...'

Oh Christ.

'Pain,' I say next, trying desperately to rescue the situation. 'Er, just warm thighs, maybe tingling.' I look at her, hoping for Professor Wiseman's theory to come to my rescue. This is the one where Sonya will start making the nonsense I'm coming out with somehow meaningful. I don't have to wait very long.

Sonya's thinking hard, trying to work out how my word 'thighs' fits into her life.

'Well, I did run here,' she says. 'I do a lot of exercise and I ran here in my shoes,' she tells me, rubbing her thighs. 'Hmm, that's it.'

She smiles at me again. 'So, anything else?'

I look at her blankly and say what I always do when I've run out of conversation: 'So, where are you from?'

'Belgium.'

'Oh, that's such a lovely country,' I say.

We spend the next five minutes swapping stories about Brussels, before Lizzie reels us back in. I'm relieved, though at the end of the session I notice Sonya ask Lizzie whether she can be moved up to the advanced class.

Later, at home in the kitchen, I replay the first day of the course to Nikki. I tell her I'm feeling anxious.

'I can't go back,' I say.

'Why?' She looks at me as though I'm joking, but I'm not. I'm deadly serious.

'I just can't. I was awful. I didn't know what to say to them. And I've got eleven more weeks of fretting and making stuff up. I'm going to be a nervous wreck by the end of it. I'm not psychic and I can't even lie to them convincingly.'

'So what did she look like?' Nikki asks.

I tell her that Sonya had black hair and was overweight, although she reckoned she did loads of exercise. In fact, she told

Lizzie that she couldn't understand why she was so large, and Lizzie replied that all mediums are fat because it helps ground them. We laugh.

'So why didn't you just say she gets indigestion problems and that she often feels bloated?' Nikki asks.

'What?'

'Well, she's overweight,' she says.

'Yeah, but I was trying to be psychic, not make stuff up. Come on, I mean, that's lying.'

Nikki doesn't say anything. She just looks at me.

I tell Nikki that I'll try harder next time, but I go off to look up the contact details of someone I know who can help. I'm in a tight spot. I've agreed to do a psychic reading for a friend of a friend in a few weeks, and I'm feeling faint just at the thought of it. I've been warned that I should call this number only in a real emergency, but I decide it's time to call Derren Brown.

On a recent TV special, Derren visited the States and convinced leading psychic practitioners that he was genuine. While he didn't give away any of his tricks in the programme, he says he wasn't being psychic. It was all psychology and showmanship. I put the call in, but I have to wait to speak with Derren because he's busy, very busy, so I bide my time reading his latest book, *Tricks of the Mind*.

It certainly does take my mind off my own impending psychic performance, because the book is hilarious. I knew Derren Brown was a good entertainer, but not this good.

I take particular interest in the section on cold reading. Professor Richard Wiseman didn't believe in this approach, but Derren Brown is a full-blown disciple. I read how, in one of his shows, he undertook a test called the Forers experiment in which he gave a written reading for three groups of five people in their twenties – one group from the UK, one from the US, and one from Spain. One person from each group was verging on being sceptical, while the others were open-minded. He asked them for their dates of birth, an outline of their hands and an everyday personal object, and then wrote a very specific character analysis for each of them. Once they'd read his 'psychic' reading they give him marks out of 100. The most sceptical in the groups gave him about 40, while one girl thought he was so accurate that she accused him of gaining access to her personal journal. Two more wouldn't speak to camera because they also found the information too personal. The rest were shocked because they were expecting vague statements, but what they got instead were detailed and highly personal readings. Most of the marks were in the 90s, with one girl giving him 99 out of 100. Afterwards, Derren mixed up the readings and handed them back and asked the group whether they could guess whose reading was whose. They all suddenly realised they'd been had. All of the fifteen readings were exactly the same. He'd basically made the assumption that we all share the same insecurities, especially in our twenties when we're still struggling to make sense of who we are.

Reading through the transcript of his 'psychic' reading, I also find it quite specific and I can easily see how he fooled so many people. He states that the person will be prone to self-examination, and suggests that they have nonetheless developed an ability to appear very socially engaged – 'the life and soul of the party' – even though they know deep down that it's a façade. He also mentions that they will replay conversations back to themselves, signalling their deep worry, and also that they are frustrated by the idea of mediocrity. He says that all this anxiety will have encouraged them to think about writing a novel. This mysterious everyperson will also have developed a dry sense of humour because they're an outsider.

I'm impressed with this technique and make some notes, but I don't have time to finish them. The phone goes, and I'm sure I can hear the *Thunderbirds* theme music, because it's Derren Brown – the emergency cold reading psychic fixer – on the line. He apologises for taking so long to get in touch.

I tell Derren that I'm at psychic school and it isn't going well. He understands. He'd undertaken some filming at the very school I'm at, but rejected the material because the psychic students were useless.

'They just massaged each other's ego,' he tells me, adding that 'they were so transparently unpsychic and vapid.'

They were brilliant at convincing each other they were psychic, by just wanting each other to succeed. But they had a harder job convincing a random person from the street. They weren't using any of the cold reading techniques that Derren uses. It sounded like they were just having a nice chat.

'They would say, I can see you getting on a bus going in the wrong direction, and they would work with a statement like that, but our control subject [the man from the street] wouldn't,' Derren tells me.

I admit that I'm pretty useless too. I'm worrying whether my lack of belief in my psychic abilities has undermined my confidence.

'Oh, no, no,' Derren replies, sounding like he doesn't want me to think bad things about myself. On the phone he's not projecting his famous controlled and all-powerful stage persona, he's just being Derren, and this version of himself sounds like an understanding and pleasant chap. When I tell him about my sister's prediction, he sighs like it's his own sister who's been given the bad news. He then reveals a similar story, but one which had horrible consequences.

'I heard the story of an African man who'd been told a curse had been put on his family. Either he or his son would die if they didn't pay $3,000. He couldn't find the money so the father killed himself to spare the son's life,' Derren tells me.

'Oh my God,' I say.

I assure him I won't be putting a curse on anyone, and I just need a little bit of advice to see me through this one reading. 'There are two approaches,' he tells me, providing me with a cold reading lifeline for when my psychic abilities let me down. 'You either make very general statements that can be applied to lots of people, or you can make very specific statements and the sitter will forget the misses and only remember the hit, thinking it was a miracle. The best thing is to meet somewhere in the middle of these two approaches.'

Helpfully, he gives me an example. 'You could say that you see a dog sleeping in a hallway, then if that doesn't work, it becomes a picture of a dog, then a picture, followed by a picture of a family. Eventually you'll get a hit,' he says.

He gives another example of a medium he made a recording of a few years ago, giving a young woman messages from her dead father. The medium said to the woman: 'He passed not so long ago – I feel like in the last couple of years, is that right? [*Disagreement*] He's telling me you've been saying it *feels* much more recent than it was. I know it was longer ago, but it feels closer to you.'

This medium seamlessly moved from a miss to a 'hit'. Very clever. And the woman thought he was spot on, too.

The most powerful weapon, Derren suggests, is convincing the sitter that I can use my magical powers to see straight to the heart of their problem and understand them completely. I also have to say that I can feel their energy, and then once I've got them on side, they'll bend over backwards to make what I say fit.

Before I let him go, I've got one last question for Derren, and it's something that's been bothering me for a few days. I was having a chat with a friend who believes in mystics, and he told me he believes that Derren Brown is psychic.

'There's no way he can do the stuff he does without being psychic,' he told me.

'But it's all tricks,' I said.

'Yeah, but you don't see that. You only see him being amazing. He may not know it, but Derren Brown is psychic,' my friend said adamantly.

I put this conversation to Derren and remind him that in his TV programme *Messiah* he performs a feat of telepathy that is highly unusual. He gets a woman to draw pictures in another room, and without having access to what she's doing, he tries to replicate the pictures using 'telepathy'. He gets it right every time. Even the people who claim to be psychic don't have such a high success rate. Yet Derren doesn't reveal how he did it. When I watched the programme, I racked my brains trying to figure out an explanation – hidden cameras, psychology, careful editing? My friend, however, took the lack of explanation as proof that Derren was descended from the gods.

'It's a tricky one,' Derren tells me, comparing the profile of his viewers to a bell curve with believers at one end and sceptics at the other. He reckons that even if he revealed his tricks, true believers wouldn't be swayed.

'Debunking is usually witless and bitter and ends up being rather bloodless and negative. I try to avoid doing that. I want to incorporate the magic of what psychics do, but leave people guessing how I do it. I think it's more entertaining. I don't want to simply say I can show you how they do it, I don't want to give viewers the safety of the easy answer. It's more powerful. Its appeals to the imagination, whereas straightforward debunking does not.'

With those final words, Derren says he must go. My time with the cold reading maestro, albeit brief, has been highly beneficial. There's now only one piece of preparation left to undertake. The next morning I practise talking to myself in the mirror while shaving. I'm told that this will either make or break me as a psychic performer. 'I can feel your energy,' I coo at my reflection. 'You are a troubled soul. I have a memory of an accident when you were young and no one looked after you properly.' This man in the mirror clearly knows me too well. It's spooky.

And then the day for my own psychic performance arrives. I can't be late for my first reading. You can just imagine it, can't you?

Me: 'Really sorry I'm late.'

Her: 'But you're psychic. Didn't you predict you needed more time to get here?'

Me: 'Oh, yeah. Sorry. I'll just go then.'

I'm going to call the woman I'm reading for Linda. I don't know what it is about psychics, but every time I speak to an ordinary person about their beliefs, they get all excited, tell me how they think they have a sixth sense, and then lean in close and say conspiratorially: 'But you'll change my name, right? I don't want this getting out.'

But I understand Linda's concern about wanting to remain anonymous. Using my advanced psychic ability I might reveal something deeply personal about her. I'd want my name changed too, if I was having a reading from me. She opens the front door of her house in a north London suburb. She's 28, pretty, with long dark hair. I walk in and shake her hand in a long, slow, reassuring way.

'You have good energy,' I say, amazingly keeping a straight face.

Her face brightens up. 'I've always wanted a psychic reading,' she tells me, smiling. 'So you're at psychic school?' she asks.

'I am – just there honing my abilities, you know,' I say cryptically.

She nods.

We head into the back room and sit on the sofa. I ask for a piece of jewellery or a watch. She hands me her watch, and I rub it in my hands and close my eyes.

'Hmmmm,' I say. 'Right, yes, that's very interesting.' Clearly my practice sessions in front of the mirror have paid off because when I open my eyes, Linda's hanging on my every word.

First off, I go for something general. 'I feel that you are ambitious, but that you are only motivated by what is important to you. I feel,' pausing to rub her watch again, 'I feel that you have deep values, and that you are very creative but often lose interest in what you're doing because your standards are so high.'

She looks at me and shakes her head. 'Yes,' she says.

'It's the energy. You've got loads of it.'

She smiles. While she does this, I make a surreptitious scan of the room. I see photos of family members and one of those large picture frames full of photos of 'mad' and fun times with her friends. I don't see a picture of a boyfriend.

I close my eyes. 'I'm getting a feeling that you've recently finished a relationship and it was painful,' I say.

'No, not recently,' she replies, a cloud forming across her face. But I don't let it linger, because I've got a Derren Brown cold reading technique tucked up my sleeve. 'What I mean is that you *feel* it's still very recent. It was a painful split,' I say.

She nods. 'Yes it was.' She looks puzzled. 'How did you know that?'

I just smile mysteriously and close my eyes again. 'You've been worried all this time, and nervous of seeing other men because you think it will happen again.'

She nods. 'Yes. He was a bastard,' she says suddenly.

'I know,' I say, using the information she has provided to bolster my own psychic abilities. 'And your sisters have been there for you too, haven't they?' I'm looking at the photo on the mantelpiece of her with two other young women and hoping they aren't friends.

'Yes, they've been amazing,' she tells me. I think I can see her eyes beginning to water. This moment changes everything. I become suddenly uncomfortable giving this young woman information about herself just to see whether I can get any hits. I'm beginning to pry into her relationships and I don't want to. So I revert to the sweet old Betsy Lee school of psychic readings.

'But you're a strong person and very loving. Your friends respect you and men find you very attractive. People only hurt you because they don't know what they're doing. You're far too good for them.'

She nods.

I want to finish now. I really don't feel like carrying on. I've proved a point, so I give her one last line before I draw to a close.

'I can see that your future will be positive and happy. You are also self-reliant. I can feel deep down that you don't need strangers telling you what to do. You have the strength to make those decisions for yourself. And when you do,' I say, 'you'll feel happier and more in control.'

She smiles. 'Yes, I feel that,' she says, pausing for a moment. 'I didn't tell you that I invited you here today because I was curious.'

'Right,' I say, feeling confused.

'I'm afraid Rachel [our mutual friend] let it slip that you're not a real psychic, but I have to say this, you certainly had me fooled. Are you sure that psychic school isn't working?'

I laugh. 'Well, I don't know, maybe it is.' But Linda doesn't laugh. She looks at me in a curious way as though I've just peered deep down in her soul.

I return her stare. 'Listen, I'm really not psychic. Honestly.'

'Well, you say that, but you never know,' she says. 'The world works in mysterious ways.'

'Right, I'd best be off now.' I shuffle to the door, feeling uncomfortable that somehow, despite my best intentions, I've just convinced someone I'm psychic.

Bugger.

18

The James Bond of psychics

JOE MCMONEAGLE IS no ordinary psychic. He's the 007 of the world of psychic spies, recruited in the 1970s by the American military to use his extra-sensory powers to spy on the Soviets. He has his own call number – remote viewer 001. He was the first, the original, and the best. He was awarded, and I find this rather mind-blowing, the Legion of Merit for his efforts. The US military gave McMoneagle one of their highest awards for using his psychic powers. So, could he be a real, fully tested and effective psychic? My brain is blowing circuits just thinking about it.

What's more, McMoneagle claims to be able to see the future as well. In fact, he was the psychic that Dean Radin recruited to leap into the future and bring back a design for his 'psi switch'.

The Legion of Merit award states that McMoneagle was a Special Project Intelligence Officer for the SSPD (Security Strategy and Policy Division). It then goes on to say that 'while with the SSPD, he used his talents and expertise in the execution of missions for the highest echelons of our military and government, including such national level agencies as the Joint Chiefs of Staff, DIA, NSA, CIA, and the Secret Service', and, significantly, 'producing critical intelligence unavailable from any other sources'.

It seems from that citation, at least, that respect for McMoneagle went to the highest levels of government. It's a little more complicated than Professor Wiseman had me believe when I mentioned psychic spying to him all those months ago. He suggested that psychic spying was just a ruse by the CIA to protect its real spies: the Russians wouldn't hunt them out if they thought the CIA was getting the leaked information from psychics instead.

But the Soviets, it appears, were at it just as much as the US. According to an internal CIA document written in 1977 by Dr Kenneth Kress, the CIA was being shown 'films of Soviets moving inanimate objects by "mental powers"' as early as 1972. There was also evidence that the Russians were spending $500 million on psychic spying experiments, and that the Red Army was successfully using telepathy and remote viewing. The US intelligence agencies, already paranoid about 'Reds under the bed', had a collective seizure at the idea of Commies in their heads, able to read their 'free world' thoughts.

According to McMoneagle, psychic spying went to the very top, sponsored by senators and generals. Even President Carter was photographed with a secret file compiled using information gathered by McMoneagle and other remote viewers during the Iranian hostage siege in the late 1970s.

So if the US military, a president, various generals and the CIA were willing to spend money and actually use psychic spies, then they must know something that we don't, right? If so, what do they know, and what does it say about the power of psychics? Are there really a very few, I mean literally just one or two, special people with unworldly powers?

I've got to get a handle on Joe McMoneagle. Who is he, and is he really a psychic remote viewer who can see the future? I call him up in Virginia where he runs his company Intuitive Intelligence Applications, which offers businesses his remote viewing powers to help them find mineral deposits and reveal financial information about the stock market.

'We are still vulnerable from the threat of remote viewing,' Joe tells me, when I ask whether he believes the US is at risk from psychic Russian spies stealing secrets. 'I absolutely know that the Russians are still using remote viewers. I have visited where they work and have met them,' he tells me.

So it's not that secret then, I think, if they've let in the US's best remote viewer to check out the competition.

'The best Russian remote viewer is a woman,' Joe says. 'She was awarded the equivalent of my Legion of Merit.'

According to Joe McMoneagle, the Russians used remote viewers in the Chechnyan war, with this Russian female strapped into the front of a tank finding military targets with her special powers. 'This is not flighty stuff,' he says, 'this is serious business that soldiers are doing.'

McMoneagle himself has first-hand experience of soldiering. He joined the US Army during the Vietnam war 'when it wasn't a popular thing to do', was attached to Special Ops and posted to Vietnam, where he was assigned to an Army intelligence company in the central highlands of Pleiku. His tour included five major offensives, including the Tet offensive of 1968.

'It cranked up my psychic ability and increased my sensitivity to other forms of information transfer,' he writes in his autobiography, *The Stargate Chronicles – Memoirs of a Psychic Spy*.

He came to rely on his gut or intuitive nature in Vietnam. He instinctively knew when he wasn't safe. He always listened to his inner voice, which became louder, it seems, as the threat got closer. 'I did whatever it suggested and did it without question,' he says.

'If I felt an urge to get into a bunker, I did so immediately. If it was a gut feeling to zig rather than zag, then that's what I did. I once abandoned a Jeep and walked back to the base camp on advice from my internal voice. To the consternation of my first sergeant, the Jeep was never seen again,' he recalls in his memoirs.

There was an occasion in a listening post in Tay Ninh, where he had an urge to move fast. It was night, there was no natural light, but he moved anyway. He could hardly see where he was going. It took almost an hour to move him and his two reluctant fellow soldiers. They moved about 60 yards west, and then at 4.00am two grenades exploded in the area they had been in.

'So what did you think when the grenades exploded – phew, lucky me?' I ask him.

'To be honest I wasn't thinking about anything,' he tells me. 'I just didn't want to be where I was. You don't think, "Wow, that was a great decision," the only thing you remember is the elation at not being killed. In the Tet offensive, death was all around. It was pretty overwhelming. In those kind of operations you are just terrified.'

Yet it wasn't until 1978 that he was approached by two military intelligence officers working for the 902nd Military Intelligence Group, located at Fort Meade, Maryland. He was taken to a quiet room, where they showed him classified documents about psychics.

Their job was to recruit possible remote viewers to test the degree to which remote viewing could be taught, organised and used for intelligence-collection purposes.

The project was kept secret on a need-to-know basis, which basically prevented the sceptics in the military finding out and banging their heads against sensitive equipment in disbelief.

Or as McMoneagle puts it: 'We knew the Russians were working with psychics. I suppose others were concerned that if they got wind of what we were doing they would try to neutralise the facility.'

He was eventually introduced to Dr Hal Puthoff and Russell Targ, two civilian researchers working on the project for the military at the world-renowned Stanford Research Institute (SRI). McMoneagle was shown a video of a retired policeman, Patrick Price, who used his remote viewing skills to do spooky things, such as describe buildings he'd never been to. The implications for spying on the enemy were vast.

And then, according to McMoneagle, the chief of staff for intelligence began to get scared. The remote viewers were providing details of ongoing intelligence operations that they shouldn't know anything about.

In November 1979, things got serious. McMoneagle was pulled out of bed at 4.00am to start work, with immediate effect, on the hostage crisis at the American embassy in Iran. He had to identify the hostages, the rooms they were in, and what they were doing. He got confused by the amount of information he was asked to produce, and found it hard to distinguish between what his imagination was telling him and what his remote viewing was showing. He says that 'the descriptions of the floor layouts and rooms were accurate enough to amaze people brought in who had just left the country and who had previously worked in them'.

I have no way of checking McMoneagle's account, other than looking at the history of the crisis to see what happened. I'm on the hunt not just for a real-world psychic, but one who can change the course of history. I'm looking for what Professor Wiseman called utility. That means I need to know whether Joe McMoneagle really was useful to the US Army or whether he just thinks he was. So I read about the Iran hostage rescue attempt and discover it ended badly, very badly, when a US rescue helicopter crashed into a refuelling tanker, killing eight servicemen. The crisis was eventually resolved through diplomatic channels, Iran suffering badly from sanctions and a sudden invasion by Iraq. So McMoneagle's drawings of rooms, despite some people thinking they were accurate, did nothing to help end the crisis. I'm also intrigued about how Joe McMoneagle's ability fits into Dean Radin's theory that we are more likely to get a sense of something from the future if it's highly emotional. Well, you can't get more emotional than a crash between a helicopter and an aeroplane. Why didn't McMoneagle sense this?

McMoneagle gives another example of his remote viewing skills. He claims that by using his extra-sensory powers he was able to locate a downed Soviet bomber in Zaire in the late 1970s. The bomber was carrying either nuclear weapons or information about them, so it was essential to get hold of it before terrorists did.

Search after search failed in the inhospitable terrain, so McMoneagle and a team of remote viewers were brought in to help. The team 'placed the aircraft in a specific area of Zaire … Search teams were sent into the area and the plane was located within a kilometre of the location given by the SRI remote viewer,' says McMoneagle.

'This one case was publicly known to have reached a presidential level of interest. It also belies claims that remote viewing information was never used as standalone information, or used at national levels of intelligence importance,' he says.

I don't know what to make of this. McMoneagle and his fellow remote viewers already knew to look in Zaire, but it's still impressive to get within one kilometre, even if they didn't locate the plane exactly, isn't it? Wanting to double-check, I do what most people do in moments of doubt: I contact the CIA in Langley, Virginia. Marie in the public affairs department tells me about Kenneth A. Kress's internal newsletter, which I'd already read, and then tells me that McMoneagle was given his Legion of Merit by the Army, so I should try them. So, not having any luck with the foremost intelligence operation in the world, I try the Army. I email Wayne V. Hall at the Pentagon and ask him about McMoneagle's citation.

'All I can say is that Chief Warrant Officer 2 Joseph W. McMoneagle retired from the Army Aug. 31, 1984, after completing 20 years of service,' he says. 'As far as the claims the individual makes, there is no copy of the award citation in his records, which is quite common.'

But I've read the citation. Even I was able to locate that. It's at the back of McMoneagle's memoir. I'm finding it weird that such a high-level honour could be awarded for psychic spying without the Army being aware of it.

'And what about the plane crash in Zaire?' I ask Wayne.

'I would recommend that you contact the US Army Intelligence and Security Command Public Affairs Office,' says the ever-helpful Wayne, leading me on to yet another level of bureaucracy.

So I do. And while I wait for the intelligence office to think about my request, I decide to take a closer look at the research that backs up McMoneagle's claims. Why did the US military and the CIA pump millions of dollars into funding tests on remote viewers?

Both Brian Josephson and Dean Radin have complained bitterly that research into psychics and psi isn't given a fair hearing. Prestigious scientific journals don't touch paranormal science, they claim. Well, somewhat to my surprise, it appears the first-ever study of remote viewing was published in *Nature* in 1970. This is possibly the most prestigious science periodical in the world, which boasts that many of its published papers have led to Nobel Prizes. And it published a paper about remote viewing which led directly to the US military getting involved.

The researchers behind the paper were Russell Targ and Hal Puthoff, the two scientists whom Joe McMoneagle was introduced to at Stanford Research Institute HQ. Targ and Puthoff claimed in the paper to have shown that remote viewing is both a 'powerful and reliable phenomenon that defies reason or logic'.

They claimed the methods they used to test remote viewers were watertight and foolproof. All of their experiments had been successful and were easily repeatable. From the time this paper was published, it certainly looked as though all the hard years of searching for the existence of extra-sensory perception had paid off. The experiments were simple. Ex-police commissioner Patrick Price, sitting in a room at SRI, would use his special psychic powers to describe in a drawing or in writing one of twelve locations that a researcher was standing in. That was it.

The drawings and descriptions were then handed to an independent judge called Dr Arthur Hastings to decide how accurate they were. It was calculated that Price's accuracy went against chance by something in the order of 1 in 1 billion. Considering that the odds of winning the National Lottery jackpot are 1 in 13 million, you get an idea of how significant that is. Exit stage right Targ and Puthoff to rapturous applause. They had achieved what hundreds of researchers before them had not – proof of psychic power.

But enter stage left Dr David Marks, a tenacious English psychologist, to undertake one of the most penetrating and well-researched investigations into remote viewing ever. He wanted to test Targ and Puthoff's claims by repeating the experiments and checking the data for even the tiniest flaw.

At first Dr Marks was flummoxed by the findings, saying in his book *The Psychology of the Psychic* that 'these mind-boggling results defy any of the usual, simple explanations that might be raised to account for them'. 'The experimenter who stayed with the subject couldn't have cued him/her or led him/her to a correct description because he, like the subject, was blind to the target.'

Unlike other experiments that have attempted to find psychic ability, Targ and Puthoff's experiments didn't rely on psychics with special gifts. They could be repeated at will by anyone. The ESP effect was not something that disappeared through performance anxiety, as Dean Radin might suggest. Anyone could do it at any time. So Dr Marks, taking them at their word, did so.

While he was teaching at the University of Otago in New Zealand, he and his late colleague Richard Kammann ran a series of 35 experiments between 1976 and 1978, replicating Targ and Puthoff's apparently flawless tests. His results didn't match their findings. In fact, they were no better than you would expect from chance. Dr Marks admits that 'there was not a single significant result'.

Confused as to why he had failed when Targ and Puthoff had succeeded, Dr Marks did a bit of digging. He discovered a subtle flaw in the design of their experiment. I mentioned before that Patrick Price's descriptions of the remotely-viewed locations were handed to an independent judge called Dr Arthur Hastings, who would decide how accurate they were. Dr Hastings was handed twelve descriptions for twelve remotely-viewed locations that had taken place on different days. The problem was, Dr Hastings shouldn't have known which description was for which day, because for the test to work, they had to be mixed up and be 100 per cent random. Instead, Targ and Puthoff had dated the descriptions and even included hints to signal which site it was describing – in other words, making it easier for Dr Hastings to award points for accuracy. Imagine being given twelve descriptions and having to decide which one matched a picture of, say, London Bridge. Two of them might mention water, three might mention a curved structure, and another two might say bricks. That's generally how specific remote viewers' descriptions tend to be. Faced with that choice, you'd probably scratch your head, whimper, and give up. Yet if you were handed only one of these descriptions and asked whether it matched a picture of London Bridge, and the description contained words in it like arch, water, and bricks, you'd give it at least a few marks for accuracy. The latter method is what Targ and Puthoff were doing. The first purely random experiment is what Dr Marks was doing. No wonder he couldn't get any positive results and they could.

I'm sure, like me, you're furrowing your brow and saying 'So what?' But it was this subtle flaw that made the difference. And yet Dr Marks found this problem in only one of Targ and Puthoff's studies. The reason? They wouldn't release the rest for independent scrutiny. Marks realised that he needed to get hold of the full transcripts in order to check whether these kinds of cues were present in all of them. This could explain the reason for the study's success.

Eventually the independent judge, Dr Arthur Hastings, handed over a few more. Then Dr Marks set up the final climactic scene and, using only the cues he had discovered in the transcripts (and there were plenty), he matched the remote viewers' descriptions with the locations visited by the experimenters. He did it, five out of five. He repeated this again and again and every time got them all correct. Dr Marks was thousands of miles away in New Zealand, hadn't visited the locations in California, and didn't have a psychic bone in his body, yet there he was performing just as well as a remote viewer. Final curtain descends to rapturous applause.

Suddenly, but predictably, the whole edifice of the remote-viewing tests began to crumble. The results in *Nature* were based on a series of flawed scientific tests rather than the brilliant psychic talents of Patrick Price. Yet it was these flaws that ensured that the US military would spend close to $20 million on remote viewing and that Joe McMoneagle, who hadn't been involved in the original tests, would be recruited.

Having access to data is the key, says Dr Marks. Without independent verification it stops being science and stops being trustworthy. 'It is scientific practice for researchers in the same field to have access to their original data. When researchers consistently refuse to allow colleagues such access, something important is being signalled,' claims Marks.

But did they believe that what they were doing was real science? Subjective validation could be behind this, Marks believes. 'This occurs when two unrelated events are perceived to be related because a belief, expectancy, or hypothesis demands or requires a relationship,' he says. According to Marks, Targ and Puthoff believed in what they were doing so much that they ignored any problems that came up.

It's the same reason why remote viewing was endorsed in the military for so long. Certain senators and presidents have famously believed in the paranormal – President Reagan used an astrologer to help him decide when to arrange meetings, and Senator Claiborne Pell was known to support psychical research, spending $48,000 a year hiring C.B. Scott Jones, a UFO expert, to research paranormal phenomena in the national interest.

But what about McMoneagle? He told me that he considers himself only 20 per cent effective. Yet he believes that even at this level of accuracy, he's useful. 'It's at least as effective as any other information-gathering system,' he told me, referring to real spies on the ground. Yet the CIA clearly weren't convinced in the end, and after having spent millions of dollars of US taxpayers' money, they closed down the programme in the early 1980s, concluding that 'there is no adequate evidence … for the existence of the remote viewing phenomenon'.

When the programmes were declassified in 1995, Robert Gates, the former Director of the CIA and now Secretary of Defence in President Obama's administration, said that the programme was funded due to pressure to match the Soviets' psychic research, and thanks to the beliefs of a few senators and congressmen. Senator Pell may well have been one of these. Indeed, the programmes were declassified just after he announced his retirement. Gates also said that remote viewing had never been 'critical to national interest' and 'at no time had … ever been used as standalone material,' contradicting McMoneagle's claim that the finding of the downed Russian aeroplane in Zaire was due to remote viewers alone.

Still without word from the US military intelligence unit (I'm beginning to wonder what they spend their time thinking about), I'm stuck on McMoneagle's Legion of Merit, though. So I ask Dr Marks about this, confused that if the CIA finally admitted that remote viewing was useless, why did McMoneagle get a gold star from the military for it? Like a true scientist without the full facts, he refuses to be drawn on the subject. 'Presidents do not select people for the award of Legion of Merit. These come up though the service,' he tells me.

Suddenly a lightbulb pops in my head and I remember reading in McMoneagle's memoir about a General Stubblebine who was in charge of INSCOM (the US Army Intelligence and Security Command, the very people I'm waiting to hear from) and head of the psychic spies when McMoneagle was awarded his Legion of Merit. I've just remembered where I've heard General Stubblebine's name before. At the beginning of Jon Ronson's brilliant book *The Men Who Stare at Goats*, Ronson retells the tale of the general leaving his desk and walking towards the wall in his office, in an attempt to do something quite extraordinary:

He is almost at a jog now.

What is the wall mostly made up of? General Stubblebine thinks.

Atoms! All I have to do is merge the spaces. *The wall is an* illusion. *What is destiny? Am I destined to stay in this room? Ha, no!*

Then General Stubblebine bangs his nose hard on the wall of his office.

Damn, he thinks.

When you have a general and the head of intelligence in the US Army trying to walk through a wall (and failing), suddenly a high-level award for psychic spying doesn't seem that much of a surprise any more.

19

My sister's prediction –
a last rescue attempt

ASTROLOGER JONATHAN CAINER is driving along in his BMW, dictating his answers to my questions with precision.

'There are many things that remain unproven about astrology and are likely to remain so for all time, comma, not that this in itself compromises the validity of the subject, full stop.'

That's the grammar taken care of, now I just need to get to the bottom of why astrology wants to drown my sister and my niece. In order to do that, I've got to understand it, and that's not as easy as you'd think. If anyone can sort this mess out, it's Cainer, who's probably the best and certainly the best-known astrologer in the business. He does so, brilliantly.

I mention that some critics of astrology say that since a philosopher called Ptolemy wrote down the fixed astrological houses in the sky in about 100 BC, new planets have been discovered and the earth's rotational axis has shifted 26 degrees. This surely means astrology is useless.

'What! So they think we didn't notice that?' Cainer exclaims. 'The fucking numpties. They did it knowing that there would be an elliptical problem, and they found a way around it.'

Yeah, they are numpties, aren't they? Call anyone a numpty in my presence and my rational brain melts. He's nearly won me over.

'That is why we have a fixed system and an equal division of the elliptical path. It beggars belief that we made a deliberate decision to use a particular system precisely to avoid the problems, only to be told by some ignoramus and highly biased pseudo-scientist that, "Oh look, it must all be rubbish because of the way things have slipped."'

Although that goes nowhere towards understanding why my sister and her daughter are on death row.

I talked with Cainer the day after I'd spent an hour or so rowing around the Serpentine in Hyde Park with my sister and niece. It's a safe way to get them back on the water together. It's not deep, the sides are always nearby, and – this is the clincher – I'm a very bad rower. We skirt the edges like kerb-crawling ducks on the lookout for passers-by throwing bread. Still, it's the thought that counts.

But rowing is the least of our worries. I didn't realise just how much the astrological prediction has affected my sister. It's deeply upsetting to hear that a small gift has caused so much misery.

'I had horrible nightmares about me and Elly on a boat that capsizes,' she says. 'I didn't think about it at first, not when I read mine, but when I saw it in Elly's, then I just couldn't stop thinking about it.'

'You're joking.'

'No, I'm not. Maybe it's not true, but it just gets inside you. You can't stop thinking about it. Watch the swans there,' she says, as I nearly mow down a family of cygnets.

'Oh yeah, sorry.' I lift my oar out of the way. 'You do know it's rubbish, don't you,' I say, hoping that the research I plan to undertake the following week will back up my assumption. If not, and the astrologer's right, I think I might just leave the country.

'I just don't want to tempt fate,' she says, looking at Elly who's trying to attract the attention of a passing goose.

'Tempting fate? What do you mean? How are you tempting fate?'

'Well if it's written in your horoscope that you're more likely to have an accident in water, then you should avoid going on water. It's like being told you'll break your leg if you go walking up a mountain, but you go anyway, and you break your leg,' she says.

I row on in silence, looking at the people walking along the edge of the lake, all of them oblivious to the life-and-death struggle taking place in our battered rowing boat.

'You're tempting the fate of nothing,' I say, suddenly irritated with my sister. 'There's nothing in this. How can you be more likely to have an accident in water, if your risk is the same as anyone else's? Having an astrological chart done doesn't mean you're more likely to die,' I say, accidentally slipping on an oar and sending a splash of water over Elly and Sarah.

'Well, I hope that wasn't an omen,' she says, wiping water from her face.

I sigh. The astrology chart may have given Sarah a few bad dreams, but has it really stopped her doing things?

'I didn't get that night ferry, we flew to France instead,' she says.

'And what about sailing? Have you booked up to go sailing?'

'No. I don't mind going swimming with Elly, and this, but not sailing.'

I feel increasingly exasperated. Sarah can sail. She's good at it. It's something she can share with Elly. I can't believe that my sister has stopped doing one of the things she loves because of what this astrologer has said. Yet she hasn't been given any more information about the nature of astrology, other than the birth chart. All she has is her brother telling her it's rubbish. It's just an opinion.

I didn't realise until today quite how deep a reading like that can go. It's no longer a passing curiosity; it's deeply affecting my sister's life. Knowing that I haven't got much time to convince her that she should stop worrying about the chart before her next holiday, I hit the books hard as soon as I'm home. I've got to find out if astrology can really do what it says on the tin.

Astrology, I find, has a long, distinguished history and was once considered a science. The ancient Babylonians and Sumerians first started looking at the sky for omens, but they were random one-off events – an eclipse, for instance, might mean bad things for the local king. There was no mapping of regular cycles of the stars or planetary movements. This came later, and not surprisingly, it started with the Greeks.

It was Euktemon, a Greek philosopher, who first identified the solstice and the equinox points in the 5th century BC. Prudence Jones, writing in *The World Atlas of Divination*, reveals that these discoveries created a 'framework of observation within which an exact solar calendar could be drawn up. This framework of observation, known as the ecliptic, or the sun's annual path against the constellations as seen from earth, is also the framework for astrology.'

So the ancient astrologers had worked out the path of the sun in the sky, and they knew when it was at its highest and lowest (summer and winter solstice) and the points where it cuts the equator in the spring and autumn (the equinoxes).

They had begun observing the planets and how they moved, which is the basis of astronomy. Yet this wasn't some stone-age man, chewing on a piece of gristle and scratching his thoughts onto the wall of a cave. I'm talking about the fathers of the modern world — Plato and Aristotle. As Nicholas Campion writes in his book *What Do Astrologers Believe?*: 'Plato asserted that the entire cosmos was arranged according to perfect mathematical and geometrical proportions, and that astrology's primary purpose was political: for the preservation of order.' Plato was quite into order, suggesting in his most famous tract, the *Republic*, that every citizen has his pre-ordained role in society — you were either a Guardian, who ruled, an Auxiliary, who policed and defended, or an Artisan, who produced goods and rendered services. No upward or downward mobility. If you were born to sell oranges, you sold oranges until you died. It was similar with astrology — the planets had a hierarchy and their role was to transmit 'God's will to humanity'. In fact, said Plato, 'as one ascended from earth through the planets to the stars, one passed from imperfection to ever increasing levels of perfection.' Plato's followers believed that astrology was a way to control fate and was a route to enlightenment, rather than the other way round. It was to help make life choices, rather than be dependent on the whims of the gods. As Campion says: 'Plato's belief is that each of us has a soul which is tied to the stars and inhabits a mathematically predictable universe.' After that, life must have become suddenly less anxious and unpredictable.

These philosophical musings by the great man were soon underpinned by astrologers who split the path of the sun into twelve houses – twelve 30-degree sectors – starting at the spring equinox, which is Aries, the Ram. Ancient astrologers reckoned that if they could understand the stars, they might avoid wars and keep order, very much in line with Plato's way of thinking.

But no one could decide whether to study the constellations – the fixed stars in the sky – or the movement of the sun – the elliptical path. Claudius Ptolemy, living in the 1st century AD, tried to put some order into astrology. In the *Tetrabiblos*, which became the most important astrological textbook until the 1700s, Ptolemy explained precession, which is the slow wobble of the earth's axis over about 26,000 years, and used this to show why the signs of the zodiac no longer coincided with the constellations. He favoured developing a system based on the elliptical path of the sun, and not the planets. Ptolemy was a great astronomer and astrologer, but that doesn't mean he knew whether his system really did influence life on earth.

I look through my vast pile of textbooks and try to find something that will give me some quick answers. I find it. Not only does its title *Debunked* sound suitably encouraging, but its author Georges Charpak won the Nobel Prize for physics. Charpak reveals that astrological predictions made using just the path of the sun are not based on a constant elliptical path, because the sun is never in the same place year in, year out. He calculates that for people born on the same day, but years apart – say 9 January 1924 and 9 January 1960 – the position of the orbit of the sun would have shifted 780,000 miles.

Charpak suggests that most astrologers aren't practising astrology at all. 'Today's "tropically-based" astrologers just blindly apply rectangular sign-zones, empty boxes that have nothing to do with anything and are devoid of any consistency or correspondence with the stars,' he says. They practise 'something we've got to call the study of emptiness — voidology, or astrology in a vacuum'.

But telling my sister it's just 'voidology' isn't going to change her mind, even if it's a Nobel laureate saying it. That's how belief works — it's stubborn. There's now only one solution left. I've got to track down the astrologer who gave my sister and my niece that reading all those years ago and force him to retract his prediction. Actually, I can't force him. He's got to believe that what he said isn't true. That could be difficult, and I just hope I can keep my cool with him.

I track him down using the web address printed on my sister's birth chart and arrange to meet up. I tell him I'm writing a book about astrology and that I want to pick his brains; I don't mention that I mean that literally. We're sitting in a loud bar in north London, surrounded by early evening drinkers. My plan is to come out with it, tell him he's ruined my sister's life, and see him squirm. But he's got a technique of self-defence that's my worst nightmare. He's boring. I've had visions of being stuck in rooms with people like him and they never end well. He starts a long spiel about the first trip he made to India some years ago:

'All things psychic happened to me in India, what's the word, er, the whole civilisation evolved out of, er, it's a very tough place, it's the place to go really, you know,' he tells me, taking a sip of his drink. I try to interrupt him and get him to explain how astrology can be a divination tool. But he's on a roll and he ploughs straight over my questions.

I slip, slowly but irrevocably, into a coma. I take a slug of red wine, pinch myself on the cheek and every so often hit my ankle with my foot to keep myself awake. But he goes on and on about his hippy wanderings through India.

I'm going to call the astrologer Pete. It's not his real name. I feel obliged to protect him, because he needs it. It's not Pete that's done the bad thing, but belief in the powers of astrology. To make him a scapegoat would be irrational. Besides, he's in his late fifties and wears an old woolly jumper and a working-man's jacket of a kind that I haven't seen since the 1980s. I feel sorry for him. His old-fashioned jacket makes me think of someone stuck on a picket line in cold weather.

He drones on about something that happened in Delhi. I think he may have had an illness, and then took a truck ride somewhere. I don't know. Maybe my horoscope says that I will succumb to a slow, painful death on this very day.

But I finally get him back on topic. I tell him I've heard about people who have been given predictions about their future.

'Oh, I don't do that any more because it worries people,' he says.

I tell him, smiling, drawing him in, that my sister had an astrological chart that predicted her death.

He looks at me and guffaws loudly.

'Christ, I bet that freaked her out!'

'Yes it did,' I reply.

He's still laughing, so I tell him.

'The prediction was made by you, for both my sister and her daughter. They both think they're going to die thanks to the birth chart that you wrote.'

He looks at me, and then at the door. I'm not being menacing. I just pick up my glass of wine and look back at him across the small table as I take a sip.

'I, er … it would be difficult to give you the full background to the predictions without looking at both of their charts,' he says, shifting in his seat.

I look down at my notebook. 'In the part of the chart where the prediction was made, both of them had something aspected with Scorpio. With Sarah it was Jupiter and with Elly it was Mercury,' I say, as though I know what I'm talking about. For all I care, Sarah's chart could have been aspected with a tin of dog food, but I'm hoping the extra information might jog Pete's memory.

'Oh, that's a star sign linked, among many other things, to water and death experiences. If the planets involved were badly aspected, then it could easily produce predictions like those you have mentioned,' he says, trying to reassure me but failing dismally. 'As regards death, there usually needs to be a whole constellation of negative influences in the chart for it to come into effect,' he adds.

'Right,' I say, but think, 'Wrong'. Wrong thing to say, big time. Clearly Pete is in no state of mind to be convinced that astrology can't make these kinds of predictions. He's a true believer and has been for more years than I've been alive. A quick chat over a glass of wine isn't going to change that. So I feed him some slack. I ask whether he'd mind running the birth charts again and telling me what he finds.

He agrees, a little too quickly. I leave Pete to finish his glass of wine and go to the bar to pay the bill. I look back to the table while the bartender swipes my card. Pete's gone. Vanished.

Done a runner. I've a feeling that's the last I'll be seeing of the donkey jacket.

'I re-ran your sister's chart,' the opening line of Pete's email reads when I get home. To my amazement, the new-age wanderer has followed through on his promise after all. I scan through it quickly. 'The warning about being careful around water is very much a general one, there is not much to back up this general warning, so it is just a reminder to be careful while travelling. I did note an interest in areas like yoga and meditation which could help prolong the lifespan,' he writes.

'Please reassure her there is not much to worry about, there is plenty of highly positive input in the chart and there is no such thing as a perfect chart in any case,' he continues, before adding that my sister has a tendency to worry.

Really? No, she doesn't, I think.

'I had a look at Elly's chart and like her mother's this was a very general warning about taking care while travelling, nothing too much to worry about at all, quite a positive chart overall,' he concludes.

Of course, this is welcome news. But his about-face won't fill my sister with confidence, I'm sure. Beliefs are deep-set, so I want to make sure I'm fully armed with all the facts before I reveal Pete's new findings to Sarah. I've got to get more perspective on this, so I've decided to head to the only place that can provide real answers about the stars – the Royal Observatory in Greenwich – to meet Rebecca Higgett, the curator of the history of science and technology.

I had the impression that astronomers didn't think much of astrology, but I recently read that an 'astrological election' was made for the birth of the Royal Observatory itself, drawn up by John Flamsteed, the first Astronomer Royal, in 1675. An astrological election uses the alignment of the planets to select the most favourable time to start a venture. Flamsteed's plan reveals the most auspicious time for the Observatory's foundation stone to be laid – 10 August 1675, 3.14pm. Was Flamsteed, a respected and intelligent astronomer, using the stars to ensure that the Royal Observatory had a successful life?

'He was making a joke,' says Rebecca, as we head down to the underground vault where the Observatory stores its ancient star-gazing instruments.

She shows me a copy of Flamsteed's original election, and the inscription he wrote on it: 'May this keep you laughing my friends.' The wise old bird, I think, as I hand it back.

In fact, Flamsteed tried to publish some serious critiques of astrology. 'The most important thing for him was being able to get a good, accurate mapping of the stars,' Rebecca tells me. 'I think that's what got him excited,' she adds, showing me an astrolabe, a 15th-century navigational instrument that was also used for astronomy and astrology.

Rebecca describes how Flamsteed's mission in life was to try to get accurate astronomical data in order to improve navigation at sea. It was a far more urgent problem in the 17th century than trying to use the stars to foretell the future. Flamsteed tried to discover the longitude of places – their exact position east and west – while at sea and out of sight of land, by using astronomy. In 1714, Parliament established a panel of experts, the Board of Longitude, and offered a massive £20,000 reward (equivalent to about £2 million today) to anyone who could solve the problem of finding longitude at sea. It took nearly 60 years for the prize to be claimed. In the end it went not to a famous astronomer, scientist or mathematician, but to a little-known Yorkshire carpenter turned clockmaker, John

Harrison, who invented a highly accurate portable clock that could be taken on ships. And in all this there was not a word about astrology. Clearly, doubt had already set in, even in the 17th century.

At this time, says Rebecca, there was a clear rupturing of the link between astrology and astronomy. The latter was science, the former just superstition. Huge advances in the understanding of the universe were being made. They were no longer based on theories like Plato's hierarchical view of the cosmos, but on precise mathematical calculations and observations. Polish astronomer Nicolaus Copernicus had found that the sun, rather than the earth, was at the centre of the solar system. Galileo, looking through his telescope, had observed sunspots and realised that the sun's action didn't correspond to that on earth. It acted independently, suggesting that the universe wasn't a giant mechanical system.

Other discoveries that came fast on the heels of Copernicus were the principles of planetary motion by Johannes Kepler and the formulation of the laws of motion and gravitation by Isaac Newton. In 1750 Thomas Wright suggested that the universe was made up of numerous galaxies. Later that century, William Herschel undertook the first thorough telescopic survey of the heavens and established the foundations of modern stellar astronomy.

What's more, around this time the foundations of modern science were being constructed. 'There was a shift in scientific methodology towards a desire to establish the truth of accepted knowledge by doing repeatable experiments and testing knowledge, which is why you've got someone like Francis Bacon saying that we should collect data on astrology, and find out how it works,' Rebecca tells me.

Francis Bacon, living in the late 16th and early 17th centuries during the reigns of Elizabeth I and James I, was the father of empirical natural philosophy and set about changing the way science was practised. He gave short shrift to Aristotle's ideas that you could reach a scientific truth just by argument, which meant that the cleverest words won the day. Bacon argued that truth required evidence from the real world, and he published his ideas in his *Novum Organum* (1620), which gave an account of the correct method of acquiring natural knowledge.

Eventually, Bacon turned his attention to astrology, saying that the 'methods' of these 'disciplines' were based on occasional insights but didn't command strategies to reproduce the natural effects under investigation. Basically, what he meant was, 'Stop believing in this nonsense unless you've got evidence'. After Bacon got stuck in, astrology began falling out of favour with the ruling classes. Rebecca puts it best, saying that 'astrology just fell off the radar, really'.

In fact, by 1670 astrologers were stripped of their right to make political statements affecting the Church or State. Up to this point, astrology had played an enormous role at court, with Elizabeth I relying on John Dee to examine the birth charts of potential suitors – all of them failing – and kings and queens across Europe asking their own astrologers for political advice.

However, despite Bacon's efforts to expose the lack of evidence for any real meaning behind astrology, it still had popular appeal, with almanacs selling in their thousands during the 18th and 19th centuries. And today astrology is akin to a new world religion based on popular beliefs rather than elitist churches. It's been nearly 400 years since Bacon's death. Surely in that time we must have scientifically proved whether astrology really works or not?

Astrophysicist Rhiannon Buck says there are only two possible explanations for why the planets might have an effect on us – gravity or electromagnetism. 'Gravity may sound like a good candidate; after all, it does work over an infinite distance. But unfortunately it also weakens rapidly as the distance increases from a source of mass,' she says. This means that if you start to move away from the surface of a planet, by the time you are twice as far from it as you were when you started, gravity will be four times weaker. Three times the distance from where you started, and gravity will be nine times weaker.

Electromagnetism also rapidly drops off with distance. 'Any electromagnetic radiation that was emitted from a planet would be dominated by that of the sun,' Rhiannon explains. 'The sun would also override any negligible magnetic effects from the few planets that have magnetic fields. In a way, the sun and moon are the only celestial bodies to affect life on earth, for example by causing weather variations and tidal cycles.'

It's important to understand that the planets in astrology have taken on their individual meanings due to ways of thinking in the past that have leaked and stained the present, and not from any mystical reasoning. For instance, the planets in our solar system take their names and characteristics from ancient gods of classical mythology – Mars is aggressive, while Venus is love. Nicholas Campion, in his book *What Do Astrologers Believe?*, suggests that the relationship between 'heaven and earth became increasingly complex in medieval times. Theologians elaborated a "great chain of being" to explain the hierarchy of the universe, which included not just angels and archangels, but all natural objects, from the sun and the stars to clouds, animals, trees and rocks.'

Links were created by the similarities of appearance or effect of different objects, revealing deep sympathies between them. For instance, Mars, due to its reddish hue, ruled the blood, soldiers, dry weather and hot-tempered people, while Saturn was melancholy and Jupiter was jolly.

Yet it wasn't until the 1890s that astrologer Alan Leo started writing detailed descriptions of personality traits, again based on the characteristics of classical gods. So Aries is assertive and self-interested, while Virgo is self-sacrificing. I remember when I was younger blaming my star sign every time I hit my head. I'm an Aries and I read somewhere that my head would be prone to accidents. This kind of thinking is similar to how my sister was allowing her reading to affect her life.

Even Jonathan Cainer is concerned about the self-perpetuating impact of this. 'We know all too well what the power of planting suggestion can do in the back of some-one's mind. We do not want the responsibility. If I tell you that I think you are going to die on Wednesday week, I vastly increase the likelihood of you kicking the bucket on that very day — especially if you are poorly already,' he tells me. 'The fact that we are all terribly suggestible doesn't invalidate astrology, but it does make it bloody hard to tell the predicted chicken from the self-fulfilling egg.'

Cainer also said that to really ascertain whether astrology affected people, we'd have to test it. Luckily, this has already been done.

In 2006, Dr Peter Harmann published in the journal *Personality and Individual Differences* one of the largest studies of the possible link between human traits and astrology. It found little if any connection between the traditional sun signs of the zodiac and people's characteristics.

Over in Australia, former astrologer Geoffrey Dean also researched the possible scientific validity of astrology, tracking over 2,000 people who were born within minutes of each other. The study, published in 2003 in the *Journal of Consciousness Studies*, spanned several decades and covered over 100 different characteristics like marital status, IQ, anxiety and temperament. Dean concluded that date of birth does not affect an individual's personality. He found no evidence of the similarities that astrologers would have predicted.

Feeling fully informed about the fact that astrology won't actually harm my sister or my niece in any way, I call up Sarah and break the good news to her.

'Are you sure?' she asks.

'Yes. I've been through every piece of research I can, and none of it suggests that your prediction will come true,' I tell her.

She mentions something about tempting fate again, and that it would be better not to go on water just in case.

'But I just told you, there's nothing to worry about,' I tell her again.

'I know, but I've been living with this idea that something might happen for a long time. I can't just switch it off like that,' she says. 'If it was just about me, then maybe, but it's also about Elly, and I'd just rather not risk it.'

I understand what she means. Look at me and my palm reading from that young witch at that party all those years ago. Part of my brain that I had no control over just dwelt on it and wouldn't let me forget.

I then tell Sarah about astrologer Pete's change of mind. She sounds relieved, but she wonders whether he changed his mind because I was putting pressure on him. She also latches onto the news that she's a worrier.

'I went with mum to see a medium, years ago now,' she says.

'You didn't tell me.'

'It was in the early nineties. I've always felt that Nan was around me, you know, after she died, looking out for me. This medium told me that there's an older woman around me, my maternal grandmother, and she told me not to worry so much,' Sarah says.

So now, as well as thinking she'll die in a water accident, my sister now believes she's a worrier. She isn't. She worries about the same as everyone else. In fact, I think she worries less than anyone else. It's only with this astrology chart that she's shown concern, and that's understandable.

'You do know that that's a very general statement,' I tell her, doing my best Richard Wiseman impression. 'Everyone worries, so to say you're a worrier is like telling a dog that he likes sniffing other dogs' backsides.' Actually, Professor Wiseman wouldn't quite put it like that.

Despite all my hard work to right the wrong of giving her the astrological birth chart, I know that my sister still has lingering doubts about the prediction. Even though she took a ferry to the Isle of Wight recently with Elly, she's still concerned about flying over the Atlantic next year when they go to Disneyland. Not because she's scared of flying, but because there's an awful lot of water on the way.

So I go to the top, the very top: Sir Martin Rees, the Astronomer Royal. Whatever he says, I'm going to take for gospel on this. I discover that he has described astrology as 'absurd', adding: 'There is no place for astrology in our scientific view of the world; moreover its predictive claims cannot stand any critical scrutiny.'This is backed up by a statement, signed by 186 astronomers including eighteen Nobel Prize-winners, outlining their collective concern about 'the increased acceptance of astrology in many parts of the world'.

'There is no scientific foundation for its tenets,' they say. And because they're nice, caring scientists, they also offer some worldly advice themselves:'In these uncertain times many long for the comfort of having guidance in making decisions. They would like to believe in a destiny predetermined by astral forces beyond their control. However, we must all face the world, and we must realise that our futures lie in ourselves, and not in the stars.'

These are wise words, but have I become over-reliant on science in my quest? To prove how open-minded I am on this journey, I've been secretly undertaking my own personal experiment into astrological birth charts. Last year I asked an astrologer to draw up a chart for the year ahead, based on the time, place and date of my birth. Sitting on my desk in front of me is a booklet of the chart, with a string of predictions for the last twelve months contained inside. I'm intrigued about what I'll find when I open it up. Considering my sister and niece's predictions, it's a potentially life-threatening move.

I read through the whole chart, and then turn the last page over and start again. I take a sip of my now-cold cup of tea, and look out of the window at the darkening sky. I can't make any sense of it.

The chart reveals, for instance, that some time between 25 February and 1 April 'recent events in your career and public life may have "taken you down a peg or two"'. This won't, however, be a serious problem, so goodness knows why it was mentioned. My life is also vague, fluid and uncertain. Between 11 February and 26 February an unusual friendship makes life a little bit more exciting. I'm really not sure what that means. Unusual? What, like with a frog or the next-door neighbours' cat? There are so many ambiguous and generalised gems in my reading, it's difficult to know how to use them to guide me in my life. At times my freedom expands, then it's curtailed. My relationship flounders, and then it bounces along. My finances are in ruins, but wait a minute, I'm suddenly loaded. The most perceptive piece of advice is that I'm struggling to control my destiny. You bet I am. I close the birth chart and suddenly feel a weight lift from my shoulders. I know it's me again that's back in charge of my life.

I'll leave the last word to the greatest living astrologer, Jonathan Cainer.

'You know the reason I'm successful as an astrologer?' he asks me.

'I don't,' I reply.

'I hate having my fortune told,' he told me. 'I loathe and detest fortune-telling. I find it intrusive, disempowering and insulting to the intelligence. It's a strange thing to say from someone who is basically a glorified fortune-teller.'

It is, but he's not finished yet.

'I'm very conscious of all the bad ways in which this potential gift from the universe can be abused,' he tells me.

Well, he said it, I didn't.

20

Bomber Command gets all superstitious

It's September 1940 and the skies above the south coast of Britain are the scene of the fiercest fighting in the country's last-ditch defence against the German Luftwaffe. The Battle of Britain is in its final, frenetic phase. It would be reported after the war that in these few months, the RAF came close, closer than anyone dared contemplate, to total collapse. Yet today all thoughts of defeat are far from everyone's thoughts. It's a clear morning, the grass carpeted with dew, and nineteen-year-old Geoffrey Wellum, the youngest fighter pilot in the RAF, waits in the dispersal tent at Biggin Hill – the front line of the battle. Broken Spitfires and Hurricanes lie in ruins everywhere, hangars are barely standing up, filled-in craters litter the runway. It's a scene of total devastation, but somehow the station is fully operational, and pilots like Geoffrey are able to get airborne.

Geoffrey's been up since 4.30am and has been waiting for nearly two hours when the phone call comes to scramble. Within four minutes, the twelve Spitfires in his squadron are flying east to meet more than 150 enemy aircraft over Dungeness. Minutes later, he's in the thick of a dogfight with German Messerschmitt 109s which are escorting the Dornier and Heinkel bombers.

The scene is one of complete chaos. Aeroplanes are flying in every direction, gunfire whizzes past, oil streaks smear the air as planes are hit, parachutes fill the sky. It's a near-impossible feat not hitting one of his own planes in the confusion. He opens fire, turns, banks left, opens fire, turns. There's little precision, just sheer panic.

'Confusion: more yells on the R/T, "Watch 109s at eight o'clock high." I look up and see them as they half roll and start to come down into the dogfight, fresh for the fray. God, is there no end to them?' Geoffrey Wellum recounts in his vivid and searingly honest memoir, *First Light*.

He has no time to think what he's doing as commands and advice fill the cockpit.

'Watch that bastard behind you, Yellow 2. He's close, boy, real close. Break Yellow 2, break you clot, break!'

A 109 is on his tail and he tries desperately to shake him off.

'Since the fight started I've been flogging the Merlin like mad; too bloody frightened to do anything else.' He pulls the Spitfire into a desperate hard turn that makes him black out from the G-force.

'As I watch the 109, I now know the meaning of the word "fear", real stark staring fear, the sort of fear that few people possibly ever experience.'

Breaking loose, he arrives back at the landing strip in one piece, just. No one knows who will make it back with him. Geoffrey doesn't know, yet he doesn't need statistics to tell him that 51 per cent of airmen were killed on combat operations during the war. He's a witness to the high death toll every day. Waking that morning, he'd glanced over to see if his friend John was awake, 'but, of course, his bed will be empty; collided yesterday with Bill Williams attacking a Dornier,' he remembers. There are too many dead already to bear thinking about.

It will be the same for the German pilots, the Italians fighting in North Africa, the French, Poles and Americans. The young men will all be feeling the same fear, the same anguish. These feelings are not restricted to the British pilots; they are universal.

Who determined the fate of these men? Was it the ground crews ensuring that the aeroplanes were fit to fly? Or the RAF strategists who kept rotating the squadrons to keep them fresh? Or was it the skill of the fliers? Was it that the British pilots were fighting on home turf, while the Germans travelled further before they had to fight? Or was it something else, something beyond their control that was dictating their chances of survival – their fate? Whatever it was, with so much stress, so much death and so many unknowns, it's a wonder that they didn't all go insane.

'It was stressful,' Geoffrey tells me from his home in Falmouth. 'But we were resigned to what we did. You felt part and parcel of the aeroplane and you just got on with it. There was no alternative,' he says.

Now in his late eighties, Geoffrey still sounds bright and intelligent and recalls the events that occurred over 60 years ago with clarity and precision. 'You felt scared when they were shooting at you, trying to throw them off your tail. You were so preoccupied, with eyes in the back of your head. I don't know, I think you just became an automaton. I threw the aeroplane all over the sky and shot at whatever I could to try to stop them,' he tells me. 'It was always the German you didn't see that shot you down. If I could see him, I could out-fly him,' he says.

There's no doubt about Geoffrey's tremendous flying ability. The fact that he survived is testament to that. But there was something else that helped him: his lucky mascot Eeyore.

'I kept him in my map case and I never flew without him,' Geoffrey tells me. 'I had a girlfriend when I was in training and she sent it to me and told me it would bring me luck. I was shot up badly three times and always got away with it each time.' Many of the pilots in Fighter and Bomber Command kept mascots to help them ward off death, or at least the anxiety of death. Geoffrey believes that Eeyore ensured this good luck never ran out.

It was a small thing, but like many of the other pilots, it helped him cope with the intense life-and-death situations he was thrown into, not just daily, but sometimes seven or eight times a day. 'It was a private thing that we did. We didn't really talk about it,' he says.

There were other coping mechanisms too. 'You didn't ever show that you were panicked or worried. It was stiff upper lip. There was a certain calmness. You suppressed thoughts about those who had not returned, who were missing and unaccounted for. You didn't think about it. If you thought about it, you'd get so upset you'd shoot yourself.'

Even though stories of the war are around us constantly, it's still strange to remember that people were fighting for their lives just a few miles from where we live today. In the present, war happens in other places and to other people. For us, it's a protest march or a clip from the evening news. So talking to Geoffrey Wellum about his experiences shifts the perspective, makes his experiences more real, and puts into context his superstitious belief that a small toy could help control his fate. It's not funny, it's not ridiculous; it's deadly serious.

So far in my journey I've focused on trying to find the best and most powerful psychics, such as Joe McMoneagle, and on trying to find some scientific evidence for the existence of psi. I've overlooked the idea that superstitions can play a real and powerful role in people's lives. It's not about counselling. It's about trying to control our destiny.

'Given the survival statistics of operational flying, it's easy to understand why aircrew developed a host of superstitions, rituals and supernatural beliefs to try to increase their chances of survival; to give them something to believe in or a prop to help get them through,' says historian Dr Vanessa Chambers, an expert on the rise of superstitious beliefs in British society.

Dr Chambers has undertaken one of the most detailed investigations of belief in wartime and found that even the smallest ritual could help ward off anxiety. In the First World War, for instance, the third light was considered unlucky. This refers to the person whose cigarette is third in line to be lit from the same match. In this case, however, the superstition was based in reality – the flame from the match was a clear target for enemy snipers, and the longer it was alight, the easier it was to get shot.

But superstitions also changed to reflect the new technology of aviation. Unlike in the First World War when soldiers relied on traditional 'props' to help get them through the anxiety, such as putting coins in their pockets over their hearts, the RAF pilots developed gremlins.

'Gremlins were initially perceived as small, mischievous, malevolent, imp-like creatures who were deemed responsible for things going wrong, especially, but not confined to, mechanical or electrical faults,' Dr Chambers writes in her thesis on the subject. 'Their pranks [were deemed] responsible for a large number of accidents which would otherwise be inexplicable except as lapses on the part of the pilots,' she says.

Chambers has also collated numerous examples of the RAF's superstitions and charms, including one airman's lucky dog mascot, which was split open during an operation. 'My mascot is still split because the crew thought the luck came from inside the dog (the luck was flowing out) and wouldn't let me have it stitched,' he told Chambers.

'They would delay take-off unless they had done their rituals, like peeing on the back wheels or spitting on the rudder. There was a crew-member that had a life-sized duck made from wool, which they once forgot while on the way to the aircraft. They went running back to the base for it, refusing to fly unless they got it. Flying without the duck would have made them uncertain and anxious,' she tells me.

This kind of thinking isn't born out of irrationality, it's an all-too-human way of coping in a crisis. Wouldn't we all react like that in similar circumstances? The men faced with their own death, like Geoffrey Wellum, were simply trying to bring order to the chaos of combat.

In fact, Chambers points out that these superstitions and rituals were not ridiculed but accepted by all the airmen as a way of getting through the 'ordeal of staying alive and staying sane'.

But not everyone reacted in that way. It may have been due to the circumstances of being a pilot, but soldiers, it seems, were less prone to superstition. I call up the British Legion in Putney to speak to George Brownly, a member of the British Airborne Division during the Second World War.

'Brownly,' he barks down the phone at me after picking up the receiver. I don't feel like I'm speaking to someone in their late eighties. I actually sit up to attention.

'I was part of the Airborne, parachuted behind enemy lines on D-Day. I was an anti-tank gun operator,' he says. 'I also fought in the Battle of the Bulge and took part in the largest airborne operation in the world, using gliders to try and cross the Rhine at Arnhem.'

He really was in the thick of it. These battles saw some of the fiercest fighting of the war.

'My glider was shot down. I was the only one who survived. I was in a German hospital for some months before the Canadians came to liberate us,' he says.

'How did you deal with the stress?' I ask him. 'Were you superstitious? Did you have any good luck charms?'

Brownly's silent for a moment before he barks again. 'Of course not. We were the Parachute Regiment. You trained with people for years, you got to know them. My mates were in the same position and we always looked after each other. That's how we survived. You looked after your mates. And you'd look at them and think, if he can do it, well then I can do it, and to hell with everyone else.'

And as suddenly as the conversation started, it stops. 'Is that it?' he asks.

'Yes, I think so,' I say.

'Right. Thank you. Goodbye,' he says, hanging up.

Putting down the phone, I have a feeling that they don't make them like George Brownly any more.

Dr Chambers, with her years of research into the subject, doesn't think that Brownly's response is representative of all soldiers' experiences. 'I'm not convinced that soldiers as a whole did not believe in any lucky mascots or fate,' she says. 'I certainly have evidence to show that they did. Maybe the "tough" Airborne Division were made up of professional soldiers rather than recruits or conscripts. Military archives or museums I have contacted always tell me they have no evidence, they don't like to admit that soldiers were superstitious. However, when you dig a little deeper you find that in fact soldiers believed in astrology and fortune-telling as much as anyone else.'

But superstition isn't the preserve of the military. Civilians are also more likely to act in a superstitious way when they're subject to danger. Professor Giora Keinan of Tel Aviv University found that during the first Gulf War, magical beliefs were more widespread in cities like Tel Aviv and Ramat Gan, that were exposed to Scud attacks, than in places that weren't targeted. A study quoted in *Quirkology*, a book by Richard Wiseman (yes, the professor not only single-handedly fights off irrational beliefs but also writes), reveals that people in these areas were more likely to shake hands with someone they considered a lucky person or to carry a lucky charm.

New types of superstitious behaviour had developed since the start of the attacks. Since the early 1980s, new houses in Israel had been built with a plastic lining in order to protect the owners from gas attacks. To increase their luck and ward off an attack, people were more likely to step into this room with their right foot first. They also believed that they were more likely to avoid an attack if they were in the same room as someone whose house had already been targeted.

These superstitious beliefs, while not a surprise, are certainly challenging my ideas. Superstition is clearly not restricted to primitive peoples who have no other way of understanding how the world works, though these people can show us how superstition actually functions. Take the Trobriand islanders of Melanesia, off the coast of New Guinea, studied by Polish psychologist Bronislaw Malinowski in the 1900s. Malinowski found that when events were outside the islanders' control they resorted to superstition. While observing the fishermen at work, he noticed that when sailing in lagoons or close to the shore, the men relied entirely on their skill and experience to control their boats and locate fish. On venturing into the open sea, however, these same fishermen began using magical rituals, faced as they now were with unpredictable hazards – exactly the type of superstitious behaviour in the face of anxiety and uncertainty that is very much alive today.

And it's certainly not only uneducated and vulnerable people who are prone to superstitious beliefs, as Jenny Thompson, a 22-year-old former student at one of the UK's leading universities, confirms.

'I had a lucky pen and a lucky scarf,' she tells me, looking sheepish, glancing at the couple sitting next to us in the café in case they've overheard. She leans in and whispers: 'I had a panic attack the day of my last exam. I couldn't find the pen that I'd used in every exam since my A-levels.'

'A panic attack? What, you started screaming?' I ask.

'No,' she says, rolling her eyes at the suggestion, 'but I hyperventilated. I couldn't catch my breath. I trashed my room trying to find it. I even thought about not going to the exam. I mean, what would be the point? I was going to fail without it,' she says.

'So all your intelligence and revision notes were held in that pen?'

'No,' Jenny tells me sternly. 'It was because I was so anxious, I couldn't concentrate.'

But despite not finding the pen, Jenny still managed to get her act together, went to the exam and came out with a high 2:1.

'What did you study?'

'English Literature,' she says. 'Why?'

'Oh, nothing,' I reply, sipping my coffee.

My question wasn't innocent. It confirmed a theory I'd read in Stuart Vyse's book *Believing in Magic*. A study undertaken by psychologists Laura Otis and James Alcock found that while professors were generally found to be more sceptical than their students, who had the same level of belief as the general public, English professors were more likely to believe in ghosts, psychic phenomena and fortune-telling. Basically, social and natural scientists were more sceptical than humanities, arts and education students and professors. According to Vyse, this could be attributed to the substance of their subjects — literature, art and poetry frequently refer to paranormal beliefs, whereas they never feature in science classes.

Reading Vyse's book, I realised that it was telling me something about myself that I didn't know. It made me look back over my history and reassess my beliefs. It made me recognise that I'm a humanities student, steeped in fantasy, ghost stories and tales of magic. It's true that I base my experience of reality on stories and anecdotes, and this is very different to a scientific education, where facts are rigorously tested and ghost stories just don't figure, ever.

It makes me think back to other people I've met on this long journey to the future. I remember Guy Lyon Playfair, the famous psychic investigator, telling me that belief in the paranormal was unquestioned, if not encouraged, in his upbringing.

He suggested that the only way to encourage belief was to be around other people who believed.

'I expect childhood's got a lot to do with it. If you grow up in surroundings where this kind of thing is taken for granted, which luckily I did, you don't have any resistance at all,' he told me. 'On the other hand, if you were brought up by someone like Richard Dawkins you'd live in a different gestalt where these things not only don't exist, but they're not allowed to exist.' Yet my meeting with Dawkins had suggested quite the opposite. He was open-minded about psychic abilities, he just wanted real proof.

Yet Vyse doesn't stop there. He says that research shows that those who 'endorse common superstitions are more likely to show features of emotional instability,' revealing that 'the other personality dimensions associated with superstition are similarly negative (depression, anxiety, low self-esteem, and low ego strength – that is difficulty responding constructively to stressful or challenging events)'.

Yet while painting this picture of dependency and vulnerability, Vyse also makes an astonishing find. People with a very strong belief, such as psychics or people who regularly attend psychic fairs, develop a stronger sense of personal control over their lives. This is quite the opposite of the fretful, anxious person with low confidence that I imagined. He actually goes as far as saying that their beliefs may make their problems appear, at least, less difficult and more solvable. It gives them a perception of control over unpredictable events and a sense that they can influence political decisions.

The world certainly has become a far more depressing place recently, with 24-hour news cycles constantly churning out their favourite topics – death, destruction and corruption. As news agendas are obsessively focused on negative and destructive stories, it's little wonder that belief in superstition, a natural way of controlling fear and anxiety, has increased.

I contact Vyse to see whether he agrees that people are more superstitious today because they feel out of control. 'I think a society's overall level of superstitiousness varies with conditions,' he told me from the US. 'In times of trouble, people grasp at various forms of comfort in an effort to gain control.'

'We are now in a period when people are likely to turn to superstitions and psychics to give them a sense of predictability – illusory though it is – about their lives. Scientific thinking and logic are foreign to many people who seem to be more comfortable with intuitive and emotional reasoning processes. Our culture is much more likely to reward belief than scepticism and critical thinking,' he says.

The current financial turmoil and wars overseas aren't helping, according to Vyse. 'The world is much more uncertain than it was a few months back. For many people the stakes are very high. Levels of anxiety and fear are bound to rise and, with them, the urge to find sources of control outside ourselves.'

But what's more shocking is that the people who are to blame for the worst financial meltdown since the First World War are the most superstitious of the lot. 'Traders often engage in superstitious behaviour, such as wearing lucky clothes or engaging in job-related rituals, as a means of controlling their anxiety in a volatile high-stakes occupation,' Vyse tells me.

I had recently read a newspaper article that confirmed this. It included a quote from Christeen Skinner, an astrologer who works with businesses, saying that rather than traders and stockbrokers turning away from psychic predictions in a crisis, they were more likely than ever to seek them out.

'The financial crisis has ensured that I'm busier than ever,' she said, talking to a journalist from the *Daily Mail*. 'People in the City need to know what is just around the corner. I can help with that.'

'Desperate to avoid financial meltdown in the ongoing "credit crunch" and to spot fashions and consumer trends before they start,' the newspaper article stated, 'these institutions have turned to the stars to divine the future.'

I call up Christeen and she tells me that one trader phones her on a daily basis for advice. He calls asking her views about particular stocks, supplementing his 'talent' birth charts of the businesses he's interested in.

I don't want to hear any more. I've already had my mum on the phone this morning, fretting because she has all her savings in HBOS and is anxious that she's going to lose them all. I tell her what I know. That the government will insure up to £35,000 of savings (upping the limit to £50,000 a few weeks later), and that she should put the rest in National Savings until the crisis blows over.

The irrepressible Richard Wiseman undertook an experiment a few years ago in which he asked an independent analyst, a financial astrologer (actually, Christeen Skinner), and, wait for it, a sweet four-year-old girl called Tia to try to make a quick buck on the stock market. The analyst used his experience and skill, Christeen Skinner relied on the stars, and little Tia just chose companies randomly. Tia won hands down. The three invested £5,000 over twelve months, and Tia's was the only portfolio that made a profit, up 5.8 per cent, while Christeen Skinner's investment, relying on the movement of the planets, fell 6.2 per cent. The financial analyst slipped by a rather embarrassing 46.2 per cent. Tia even outperformed the FTSE 100, which dropped 16 per cent in the same period.

Taking this in, I turn back to Vyse's book and am struck by something he says: 'Superstitious behaviour wastes time, effort and money and prolongs ineffective responses to uncertainty.' It seems that just at the moment when people need to keep their heads, they lose them. By turning to superstitious behaviour at a time of anxiety in order to control it, they make it worse. Vyse tells me what they should be doing instead: 'They should be reducing uncertainty by learning about their investments and finding ways to reduce their debts and increase their job security. In general, those who are feeling out of control should become more active in their efforts to take steps, even if they are small ones, towards greater security.'

Yet, just as I think that Vyse has found a solution, I uncover another problem. The work of people like Richard Dawkins, Richard Wiseman and Stuart Vyse might all be in vain because, according to Bruce Hood, a psychologist at Bristol University, superstition is a natural response, hard-wired into the human psyche. And frankly, it ain't gonna go away, no matter how hard we try to refute it. It's within us like the chewy centre of a mint humbug – without it, we'd lose the best and most interesting bit and we'd crumble in on our hollow centres.

Hood reveals that humans have evolved over thousands of years to be susceptible to magic and supernatural beliefs. He reckons that the human brain has adapted to make up patterns and meanings about events and processes we don't understand, like gravity or why the sun moves across the sky. He calls this intuitive thinking, as opposed to reason. It's why the early Greeks thought the sun was Apollo charging his chariots through the ether. They were hoping to make sense of it.

'I don't think we're going to evolve a rational mind because there are benefits to being irrational,' said Professor Hood, quoted in *The Times* and speaking at the British Association Festival of Science in Norwich. 'Superstitious behaviour – the idea that certain rituals and practices protect you – is adaptive. If you remove the appearance that they are in control, both humans and animals become stressed.'

Professor Hood even challenges Richard Dawkins' idea that supernatural beliefs are formed by religions taking advantage of young, gullible minds: 'Rather, religions may simply capitalise on a natural bias to assume the existence of supernatural forces.' As a result, beliefs in the supernatural and superstition will never die out, he concludes, no matter how scientific we become.

Well, Richard Dawkins wouldn't like that line of reasoning, I think to myself. Then something out of the corner of my eye catches my attention.

Oh shit.

I've noticed the witches' herbal spell jar sitting forlornly in a corner of my desk. I've forgotten to keep adding coins to it.

Shitshitshit.

I reach over and pick up a 5 pence piece, but I notice there's a 50p coin lying next to it on my desk. I'm suddenly in two minds as to what to do. I haven't stuck to the witches' rule to put in a piece of silver every day for seven days, so, making up my own logic, I decide to add the 50p, hoping it'll override the previous lack of silver deposits.

Feeling relieved, I head into the kitchen, put the kettle on and think about taking the afternoon off. I take my tea and sit down in the lounge and wonder what I'm going to do with the rest of the day. I deserve a rest, I think. I've been working all morning without a break. I can see the witches' jar on my desk. I sit back, relax, and put my feet up.

I drift off. Five minutes later my mind begins reasoning all by itself and sends a shot of adrenaline coursing through my body. I suddenly sit bolt upright, wired and panicked. I rush over to my desk and grab the witches' jar. I take it outside to the bin, and having poured out all the potent herby ingredients and rescued my silver coins, I smash it into its depths.

I go back to my desk, open up Vyse's book and read again his prophetic words: 'Superstitious behaviour wastes time, effort and money and prolongs ineffective responses to uncertainty.'

Taking in their full meaning, I turn on my computer and finish a piece of work I've been putting off for weeks. At least this will earn me some money, I think, as I look at the pile of coins reclaimed from the jar. What's more, Professor Hood might think superstitious beliefs are hard-wired into my system, but I'm sure as hell going to try to rewire them.

21

The time machine

I'VE FOUND IT – a way to see into the future. I really have. I've discovered a man who can get me there. It's mind-blowing in its simplicity but painfully troubling in its complexity.

All I wanted to do was test out Dean Radin and Brian Josephson's claims that scientists don't like putting their reputations on the line. Scientists might believe in fanciful ideas, but if they dare mention them in polite company their colleagues fall about in fits of laughter before carting the offending scientist off to the glue factory. Trying to test that idea, I found a hidden passageway down the backstairs of the scientific community, and when I emerged I wasn't anywhere I'd ever been before. I realised that scientists can believe in crazy things and get away with it. In fact, so long as they can prove it, the crazier the better. What's more, there are scientists who have dreams and imaginations wilder than any mystery writer. Science, I've found, is no longer boring and painful, but exciting.

Professor Ronald Mallett, a theoretical physicist from Connecticut University in the US, is one such scientist with a brilliantly vivid imagination. Yet it didn't stop him worrying about his reputation being torn to shreds when he delivered a lecture to some of the world's leading physicists at a conference on relativity theory a few years ago.

'I was about to reveal in detail my plan for finally realising my lifelong goal. It would not be enough for me to tell them my belief that this century will be the century of time travel just as the 20th century was the century of air and space travel. No, this audience would want the nuts and bolts,' he says, describing the day that he told the world about his designs for a time machine.

The audience at Howard University in Washington wouldn't be satisfied with anything less than scientific rigour. As Professor Mallett says in his book *The Time Traveller*: 'This audience would expect to see the equations and solutions that led me to believe I had made a theoretical breakthrough that could lead to the design of the world's first working time machine.'

It was a daunting prospect, even for a professor. 'Should I make a mistake in calculation and veer off course, I would be interrupted mid-speech and subjected to in-your-face critiques – "Professor, your equations are wrong" – rather than any gentle, instructive words of advice. This is the world of physics; we are after all scientists, not psychotherapists.'

Professor Mallett, rather than spending his time like Dean Radin turning entanglement theory into a metaphor for psychic ability, had undertaken some very difficult mathematical equations, anchored in Einstein's theory of relativity. In fact so difficult were they that you get a feeling, reading his story, that Professor Mallet was on the edge of either a revolutionary breakthrough or a nervous breakdown.

For weeks he had spent twelve to fifteen hours a day working non-stop on his calculations in order to be fully prepared. His work took over his life. He ate and slept when he remembered, and more often than not was still working when the early morning birds started singing. His health had become secondary to working out one of science's most difficult problems: how to travel through time.

Professor Mallett was risking his hard-fought academic status for his dream. It could all end in tragedy. Yet the very reason he had come this far was because his dream had been caused by a tragedy in the first place.

'Time stopped for me in the middle of the night on May 22, 1955,' Mallett writes. His father, a hard-working electronics whizz and TV repairman, whom he idolised, died in his sleep from a heart attack aged just 33.

'My father was a handsome, robust man with a soft baritone voice. He had natural warmth with people, and possessed a gentle manner and keen curiosity. Although he put in long hours, he was never too tired to answer my questions about how things worked,' he says.

He was devastated. He sought comfort in reading, and one book, H.G. Wells' *The Time Machine*, fired his imagination and offered an unusual source of comfort. The twelve-year-old Mallett read with heart-stopping awe the words: 'Scientific people know very well that time is only a kind of space. We can move forward and backward in time just as we can move forward and backward in space.'

They were the 'most incredible and wonderful things I had ever heard; these words filled my wounded heart with hope,' he said.

Soon after finishing the book, using old tubes, wires and electrical parts, he tried desperately to build his first time machine in order to see his father again. It's this unyielding desire that has driven him on throughout his life ever since.

While many people resort to mediums and psychics for comfort when people die, Professor Mallett was motivated by learning all he could about science to achieve his dream. This eventually led to an obsession with physics and Einstein's theory of relativity. Rather than resorting to the supernatural, Mallett turned to hard work.

Yet he often had to put his desire for designing the time machine on the back burner as he tried to build a solid reputation.

'My reason for keeping mum about my interest in time travel was one of practicality: to advance up the academic ladder, from assistant to associate to full professor, and in order to eventually attain tenure (meaning one cannot be dismissed without cause), it is best not to be pegged within or outside your department as a crackpot,' he says.

His plan was sensible and foolproof: 'As I progressed in my academic career … my time travel work would be my own business. Afterwards, when I was a tenured full professor, I would feel freer to publicly work on, and speak out about, the subject that had caused me to go to college, study hard, and become a physicist in the first place.'

So, when Professor Mallett finally stood up in front of all those physicists, he had calculations that only someone with an advanced grasp of physics could understand. He'd also published them in one of the world's leading journals, *Physics Letters*. His science was watertight.

His ideas aren't easy to understand; a simple metaphor isn't going to build a time machine. What Mallett had to get to grips with was Einstein's discovery that gravity is a bending of space and time. 'The sun is bending the empty space (or matter around it) and the earth is moving along the curved empty space created by the sun,' he says. The sideways motion of the planets prevents them plunging into the sun. The gravitational force of attraction is essentially just the bending of empty space by a massive object.

Einstein also found that clocks run slower in the gravitational field close to a large object, like a planet, than they do in outer space. So if an object of large mass, such as the earth, is sent spinning, it drags space and time around it, creating a whirlpool. This is a bit like spinning a stick in bathwater – the water is dragged after the stick. If you keep spinning the large object, time and space will be diverted from their straight path and eventually be twisted into a loop. This is the crucial bit. You can then go back in time to the point when the loop was created. So, if you created a loop in time on Tuesday at 11.00am outside your local Indian restaurant, then at any day in the future you'd be able to walk back around to the restaurant and arrive again on Tuesday at 11.00am. It's like returning to the same spot on a running track.

Mallett's revolutionary theory, based on some advanced calculations, was to bend photons (or light beams) into a circular path, creating a whirlpool in space and time. Through this vortex, you could then head straight back to the past. But could he really use this to meet his father again?

At the end of Mallett's presentation to the assembled physicists he told them about his initial motivation – his father's death.

'There was a silence from the audience that lasted somewhat longer than I would have liked. I wasn't sure how to take it,' Mallett says, believing that his sudden personal touch had moved even this bunch of hard-nosed theoretical physicists. Then, after the applause, Bryce DeWitt, the legendary co-founder of the theory of quantum gravity and someone whom Professor Mallett was in complete awe of, walked up to the front of the lecture hall and put his arm around him.

'I don't know if you'll ever see your father again,' DeWitt said, looking at him intensely. 'But I do know he would have been proud of you.'

Fascinated by Mallett's story and his designs for a real, working time machine, I call him up at his home in Connecticut. For a man with big ideas and a complex understanding of physics, he's remarkably self-deprecating. He's just a very clever, very hard-working and very nice man. I want to ask him whether he has yet turned his designs into a functioning time machine. It seems that he's still trying to secure funding, which he's in the middle of doing when I call. It also won't hurt that Spike Lee has bought the rights to his book and will be making his life story into a movie. Mallett admits that the machine won't be built for another five to ten years, and, disappointingly, it won't be able to send a person back in time, just information. But then that's all that psychics can do, after all – receive garbled information from the future that generally doesn't make any sense. I get the impression that Professor Mallett would send back information that can be fully understood.

However, his invention becomes a time machine only from the moment it's switched on. In other words, if Professor Mallett switched on his time machine next Tuesday, people from the future would be able to travel back only to next Tuesday. The rest of history would be out of bounds. This provides an answer to the people who say that we'll never invent a time machine because there aren't any time travellers knocking on the front door right now. Actually, we don't have any visitors from the future because the first machine hasn't been switched on yet.

As soon as it is, future generations will start sending back messages to us.

'I think one of the benefits for mankind would be to use it as an early warning system. I've already provisionally patented this idea. If we have information sent from the future to the present, we could save thousands of human beings from disaster,' he tells me, suggesting that we could be told about tsunamis or earthquakes before they happen.

'We will use information from the future to control mankind's destiny,' he says. I listen in awe to a man who really is creating a way of seeing the future. 'You'd send back binary codes, 1s and 0s, depending on which direction the particle was spinning,' he explains. Despite the complexity, I'm really excited about his discovery.

'So this would be the first fortune-telling machine?' I suggest, expecting him to tell me not to be so silly.

'Yes it is,' he says, surprising me. 'Fortune-telling will become a real science allowing us access to information from the future.'

Professor Mallett is the first real fortune-teller I've met, and he doesn't claim to be psychic. Now that's where reason can get you.

He also has an idea for how we could go back even further into the past. 'If we came across another civilisation in the universe more advanced than ours, then they could have started their machine before we did. In that case, theoretically, we would be able to go back to that time,' he says.

Professor Mallett's hard work has inspired me to hit the books for the final time. No, I'm not going to make my own time machine, I just want to check some of Dean Radin's assumptions. So far, his idea about how entanglement theory explains precognition and fortune-telling is the most convincing I've come across. Radin believes that because sub-atoms can communicate over large distances in both space and time, then so can our minds. I want to double-check that it works the way he says it does.

I tell Professor Mallett about Radin's ideas concerning entanglement. For someone who's pursuing his own dream, I expect a full endorsement. But I have a surprise.

'I don't buy into that,' he tells me, saying Dean Radin's use of entanglement as a metaphor for psi is not the same as what he has done. 'It's a whole different thing. I'm not saying that I just have an idea, I've also done the maths. I have systematically developed a mathematical model. My papers and theories were peer-reviewed in published and referenced journals. To understand finally what I have done would require several years of advanced physics,' he says.

I tell Professor Mallett that I've come across suggestions that writers like Jules Verne and H.G. Wells were somehow psychic themselves, basing their stories on a reading of what they'd seen in the future.

I think I hear him rolling his eyes down the line at this notion. 'It's an abuse of the scientific tradition,' he tells me. 'I wanted to build a time machine as a child. I was inspired by science fiction writers like Jules Verne and H.G. Wells, but without learning the necessary maths and physics to show how this could become reality, it's little more than speculation and it must stay in that realm. Without going into the lab and reproducing those results again and again and again, well, I think it's outside the domain of science,' he says, sounding a little annoyed for the first time that what he has achieved could possibly be compared with other people's fictionalised ideas about quantum physics.

Despite Mallett's outright dismissal of Dean Radin's theory, I want to know what he thinks about all those sub-atoms in our brains communicating with sub-atoms in the rest of the universe. I've spent the whole of my quest trying to kick-start mine with little effect.

'Consciousness is an emergent interaction of neurones that we don't completely understand,' he tells me, suggesting that the brain is too warm and wet for quantum activity such as entanglement to exist.

Too warm? So the idea of entanglement affecting our brains in spooky ways is further from reality than I thought. Yet not quite wanting to give up hope entirely, I do my own form of repeatability. I get a second, then a third and then a fourth opinion. The responses are all depressingly similar.

First off is David Deutsch, the professor in quantum physics at Oxford University. I contact him about entanglement and psychics and he gets back with such speed that I realise this subject really gets under his skin.

I ask him whether entanglement could explain precognition, presentiment and telepathy.

'Even if those things existed, they could not possibly be due to entanglement, as it exists according to the laws of quantum mechanics and the experiments corroborating them – which are, after all, our only reason for believing that entanglement exists at all,' Professor Deutsch tells me.

'But what about the fact that two atoms can communicate over large distances? That's surely evidence enough that something odd is happening?'

'Just because you can entangle two sub-atoms, doesn't mean that this is happening in the brain. Entanglement is very unstable and the brain is too wet and hot for entanglement to take place,' he says, echoing Professor Mallett.

I really do want to give Dean Radin's ideas a fair hearing. They're my last hope for a real scientific explanation for psychic energy.

'Okay,' I say, 'but Dean Radin reckons that we're all entangled in a quantum web of reality, and that our brains are constantly aware of what's happening in time and in space, and sometimes this is communicated into thoughts in our heads.'

'It's ruled out by the laws of quantum mechanics,' Deutsch says abruptly. 'Sloppy thinking about so-called "quantum non-locality" has caused a lot of confusion about this, even among some physicists.'

Next, I read the latest book by Robert L. Park, a professor of physics at the University of Maryland. He sounds even angrier than Professor Deutsch. I imagine all this pent-up angst might have something to do with spending too long thinking about quantum mechanics. In his book *Superstition* he argues that quantum mechanics 'was a godsend for the paranormal community. It provided scientific cover for every New Age fantasy from telepathy to feng shui. New Age technobabble was sprinkled with "quantum non-locality", "entanglement", and "collapsing wave functions" ... To the question, "How can that be?" the standard answer became "quantum mechanics."'

Marcus Chown, the cosmology consultant for *New Scientist* magazine, puts it best in his book *Quantum Theory Cannot Hurt You*. For me, Chown nails the coffin shut on the idea that entanglement or quantum theory can explain psychic powers. It's simple really. Atoms are entangled in the microscopic world of the sub-atom only because they are isolated from the environment. As soon as another atom smashes into it, the effect is destroyed. 'The price of quantum schizophrenia is therefore isolation,' says Chown, easing the pain in my head with every word I read. 'However, in the large-scale world in which we live, it is nearly impossible, with countless quadrillions of photons bouncing off every object every second,' Chown writes lucidly. In that case, how can a person who lives in the big, real world ever get close to a sub-atom without it whimpering out of existence in a flash?

Dean Radin also compared psychic entanglement to the building of a quantum computer. But scientists have found, according to Chown, that it's not that easy to build a quantum computer because it has to be isolated from its environment too. 'So far, the biggest quantum computer they have managed to build has been composed of only 10 atoms, storing 10 qubits. Keeping 10 atoms isolated from their surroundings for any length of time takes all their ingenuity. If a single photon bounces off the computer, 10 schizophrenic atoms instantly become 10 ordinary atoms,' he says.

But the problem I have with this debunking of entanglement theory is that Dean Radin proved through his unique meta-analysis that extra-sensory perception and precognition really exist. So the theory may be wrong but the effect is still real, isn't it?

Robert Todd Carroll, author of *The Skeptic's Dictionary*, creator of skepdic.com and also the chairman of the philosophy department of Sacramento City College in California, is my next port of call. Carroll has an unnerving ability to unpick complex arguments and research that at first reading look watertight.

Just to remind you, 'meta-analysis is a type of data analysis in which the results of several studies, none of which need find anything of statistical significance, are lumped together and analysed as if they were the results of one large study,' says Carroll.

Dean Radin undermines criticism that suggests researchers can get positive results for psi only by hiding their negative findings in a file drawer, thus skewing the evidence in their favour. For one such positive meta-analysis, Radin suggests there would have to be 423 unreported studies in order to undermine the result. That's fifteen unpublished studies for each study that was published, and one big drawer to hide them all in. Radin is clearly suggesting that no one would have the time to undertake, let alone bury, so much bad news. Yet Bob Carroll looked at Dean Radin's meta-analysis and found something entirely different. He found that there would have to be only '62 studies in the drawer, which amounts to only a little over two unpublished studies for each study that was published'. The idea of researchers hiding their negative results suddenly looks less time-consuming.

Carroll then reveals something that leaves me feeling uncomfortable. He quotes an experiment that psychologist Susan Blackmore exposed as clear fraud, and finds it within the meta-analysis that Dean Radin used to show that ESP existed.

Carroll also questions the reliability of Radin's rescue of J.B. Rhine, the original researcher from Duke University who produced studies proving the existence of precognition and telepathy in the 1930s. Carroll suggests that Rhine, while a nice guy, didn't realise he was being duped by his subjects.

In fact, none of Rhine's experiments has ever been repeated successfully, including trials at Princeton, Johns Hopkins, Colgate, Southern Methodist and Brown universities. The only person who successfully repeated them was the University of London mathematician Samuel Soal, and, as we've seen, his experiments were found to be a clear case of fraud. So does that make Dean Radin's claims unfounded? Carroll says that Radin's use of meta-analysis is consistently odd and unreliable. For instance, Radin quotes from 142 articles published between 1880 and 1940 and claims that they represent 3.6 million individual trials by 4,600 subjects in 185 experiments, thereby proving beyond doubt the existence of ESP. Yet these studies came from a time when scientists still believed that ectoplasm was real and that you could levitate a table by looking at it. Not exactly the most reliable period on which to base your evidence. But most importantly, Dean Radin doesn't mention the fraudster Soal, thus ignoring the best piece of evidence for the non-existence of psychic ability.

If Dean's meta-analysis is doubtful, and that's the only basis on which psychic ability is shown to exist, then what are we left with? The best place to start looking for answers is in the brain. I want the last stop on my perilous journey to the future to be the brain itself. I want to literally rip the lid off and have a good poke around inside. It's big, it's messy, it's complex, but my main worry is that when I take a closer look at what's inside my head, I might not find anything at all.

22

Taking the lid off

I'm STARING AT a magnetic resonance imaging (MRI) picture of the human brain with 50 other people in a small room at the Eastman Institute, near King's Cross in London. It's full of funny colours and doesn't look too healthy. But this is far from an unhealthy brain. This is an amazing brain, as Colin Blakemore, producer of the BBC2 series *Mind Machine* and professor of neuroscience at the universities of Oxford and Warwick, is telling the assembled crowd.

I'm sitting in the audience of the annual lecture for Sense, a charity for deaf and blind people, listening to one of the world's foremost authorities on brain functioning, but I'm not liking everything I hear. Sure, the brain is truly phenomenal, but it also seems to work like one of those old Commodore 64 personal computers from the early 1980s. They took a year to upload games using a tape recorder, and then all you could play was ping-pong. What's more, the human brain, our biggest ally in this fretful journey we call life, doesn't seem the most supportive of friends. It can play tricks on us. In fact, it plays tricks on us all the time. If I had the choice, I'd drop my brain. But it looks like I'm stuck with it.

'It turns out that an awful lot of what we do with our eyes is not conscious and never enters consciousness. We're totally unaware of most of our reactions to events in the world,' Professor Blakemore says at one point in the lecture. I'm looking at him and I'm seeing him. I'm wondering what he means. What's in front of me that I can't see? Well, it seems, just about everything.

'At any one time, we only really see and are aware of a tiny fraction of the information that's being processed by our brains,' says the professor. 'This means that what we really see is only what we're attending to, and the rest is all made up. It's a very scary feeling, but looking around this room, you think you're seeing it all, the people, the faces, the room and the shape and everything, but imagine that the lights suddenly went out completely and you were quizzed as to exactly what the colour of the jacket of the person in front of you was, precisely how many people there were, what the colour of the walls of the room was, you couldn't possibly do it. It's all imagined; it's not real, I'm afraid,' he says matter-of-factly. I'm never going to be able to see the same way again after this.

'You know you're in a room because you come in and you take a few snapshots here and there, but you're synthesising it,' he explains. The brain is drawing nice pictures for us rather than allowing us to be overwhelmed by information. He's basically suggesting that our brains are computers or virtual reality machines, creating reality rather than viewing it.

But what Professor Blakemore says next suddenly puts everything I've learnt on my journey to the future into perspective. 'Lawyers know perfectly well that eye-witness recall, which is always a very important source of evidence in trials, is extremely unreliable because people are remembering so little in reality, and what we're doing is inventing the rest on the basis of expectation.'

He means we just see things because we want to see them, rather than because they are there – which goes some way to explaining why all those witches at Hallowe'en thought they were seeing ghosts in the woods. They expected to. In fact, they wanted to. And their brains obliged by filling in the details. It also might explain why mediums and psychics believe they're getting messages from the spirit world.

The brain seems to have a life of its own. After the Sense lecture I'm desperate for another view, so I pick up a copy of *New Scientist* and read something even more worrying. 'Though many may find it troubling, it is now clear that few of the active processes occurring in our brains ever impinge on our awareness. In other words, we do most of our "thinking" without ever being conscious of it,' writes Professor Chris Frith, a neuroscientist at the University of London, leaving me wondering just who's in control, me or my brain. Who's in charge of the free will control pad – me or that spongy mass lurking in the top of my head?

But that's the big question – do we feel conscious and in control of our destinies because we know what we're thinking about? If we believe that, then our brains making stuff up all the time must surely raise questions about the reliability of our beliefs. Are we experiencing something that's real – such as a ghost that we see with our own eyes or a spirit voice in our head – or believing in a version of the world created by our brains? It's like our brain is a TV channel giving us access to TV programmes that we mistakenly believe are reality. The ghosts that the witches saw in the woods were really just an episode of *Most Haunted*. And that's why I couldn't see them. Not because I'm not psychic, but because my brain didn't want me to watch that channel. I was clearly tuned into BBC spoilsport science, while the witches were watching ITV paranormal world.

I call up Professor Blakemore to get some clarity. He's been looking inside brains for more than 25 years so he should know what he's talking about. 'Our senses invent experiences,' he tells me. 'And our brain also incorporates our model of the world into what we see. So if we expect to see ghosts because we read ghost stories, then our brain will trigger devices that make a hypothesis about the world based on our expectations.'

The brain does this because it isn't very efficient, struggling with the small amount of energy the body gives it. It sounds like what the world will be like when the oil runs out. 'The brain has to limit the amount of information it takes in and sorts it on a statistical basis,' Blakemore says.

In fact, as I scour for information to support these views, I come across more and more research that shows that the brain works a bit like a malfunctioning computer. One study found that people with high levels of dopamine, the pleasure hormone that rewards one activity over another, are more likely to believe in the paranormal and are more likely to believe a psychic. The reason for this is that they're more likely to find coincidences and patterns where there are none. Neurologist Peter Brugger from the University Hospital in Zurich asked twenty believers and twenty sceptics to distinguish real faces from scrambled faces as the images were flashed up briefly on a screen. Believers were much more likely than sceptics to see a face when there wasn't one.

Brugger then gave the sceptics high levels of dopamine and they became worryingly less sceptical, making more mistakes under the influence of the drug. The drug had no effect on the believers. They already had enough dopamine swishing around in their brains.

I then discover why the people on the ghost walk were freaking each other out all the time. It had nothing to do with seeing ghosts, but everything to do with that pesky brain of ours working of its own accord. Scientists have found that 'fear' resides in the amygdala, a section of the brain that controls emotions. More than ten years ago, Professor Ray Dolan at the Institute of Neurology in London found that the amygdala can 'see' fear in the face of another person, when we don't. It sees it unconsciously, and we have no idea it's doing it until we start jumping around from all the adrenaline being pumped through our bodies. Our brain, it seems, is the best and most effective house of horrors there is.

There's also research to prove that what we think is psychic intuition is just our brain again, working quietly behind the scenes. Rather than our minds picking up information from our sixth sense, it's information that our brain already has but didn't tell us about. It chose to release the information only when it, rather than we, thought it was important. For instance, we often make a decision because we feel it's right, a precognitive hunch or a gut feeling. It's not our sixth sense, but our brains picking up on subliminal messages that have escaped our conscious attention. An example could be observing a poker player's 'tell', a facial signal about the hand they've been dealt. While you didn't notice, because you're a bit slow, your unconscious brain did. Rather than tell you this, it just gives you an uncomfortable feeling in your stomach, which turns out to be right. You think, what a hunch, I must be psychic. No, it was your brain being subtle, and we don't like subtlety.

Yet, evidence has shown that leaving unconscious brains to make decisions for us might be the best thing anyway. For instance, faced with an overload of information, it's better to rely on gut instinct rather than think through the information rationally. This is because your unconscious mind is far more rational than you'll ever be.

The brain, I've discovered, is drip-feeding us all these false ideas about ghosts, psychics and superstitions so we don't break down under the anxiety of life. It knows the truth, it just isn't telling us about it. If I were you, I'd have a serious word.

23

My final future

Professor Michael Kinnear was a towering intellect. Growing up, he came top of every subject at school. He was bright, quick and most of his teachers were in awe of him. He went to the best universities, and was the youngest professor in a generation. Then something happened which made him realise he wasn't that clever after all. He fell off a stage, literally. Professor Kinnear had fallen for the 'conditioning the professor' routine by a lecture room full of third-year psychology students. The students, who were also very clever, but not quite as clever as Professor Kinnear, knew that human behaviour could be conditioned unconsciously. They also knew that lecturers' behaviour is encouraged by positive reinforcement. So every time Professor Kinnear moved to his right, they smiled and nodded, encouraging the professor's brain to think, 'Wow, that feels good, what if I do it again? Ohh, that's nice, I feel sort of all warm and gooey inside. And again? Oooh, yes.' So Professor Kinnear shuffled onwards, unaware of his fate, while his brain basked in the warm glow of all the friendly faces in the audience. Arriving at the edge of the platform, his brain gave one last gurgling sigh of delight. Moments later, the professor plunged out of sight. Despite the size of his brain, Professor

Kinnear's future, like mine and yours, wasn't as easy to predict as we all thought.

You might yourself be basking in the knowledge that nothing like that could happen to you, but you've just been fooled as well. While the 'conditioning the professor' experiment really does exist and professors have indeed fallen for it, or fallen over because of it, Professor Kinnear is a figment of my imagination. Like the ghosts in the wood and the fortune-telling predictions of the psychics, he's just an anecdote based on false information. But I bet your brain was already picturing what he looked like. Did he have a beard? Was he fat or thin? Was he in colour or black and white? You may well have been feeling a bit inferior because of Professor Kinnear's impressive intellectual abilities. Personally, I can't stand the man.

Thinking about what went on in the professor's brain, I realise I've gone as far as I can in my quest to discover the future. In my search, I've found no evidence that people who claim to be psychic are channelling energies, talking to dead people, or bobbing along on a sub-atomic entangled universe. Not one of my many futures, whether from Sylvia Browne, Alice at Mysteries or sweet old gypsy Betsy Lee, has been consistent or foretold something that has taken place. The only consistent reading I received was that I would have to dump my girlfriend either just after or, confusingly, just before I made her pregnant. Neither has happened. Yet I've found out something far more interesting and compelling. I've discovered that the human mind is so powerful that it can make us believe in something when it doesn't exist. It does this by looking back to the past, and building a virtual reality world out of our past experiences and our expectations. Our world is the one that we choose to create for ourselves. Our brains do not tap into mysterious energies through a sixth sense, yet they do absorb information in mysterious ways – not by hanging out with the worldwide web of universal collective consciousness, but by picking up on signals and retaining information that we hadn't consciously noticed ourselves. That is truly awe-inspiring.

But because psychics don't do what's written on the tin, should we stop believing in them? That really is up to you. I'm not going to tell you what to think. The point of this book has been to think through the meaning of our belief in foreseeing the future in an open-minded way. I really had no agenda, no preconceptions. If anything, I had the background, the education and the belief system to be converted more thoroughly than most people to believe in voices from the spirit world predicting the future. But I tried to look at the evidence in a fair and unbiased way. I assumed that quantum physics really would explain fortune-telling, and I really did think that I would find the one true psychic, because it would be so much more interesting if people really could detect events in the future.

What I've discovered on my journey is that the false hope given by psychics isn't always harmless. I feel uncomfortable that some of my cleverest and most charming friends will sit in the pub and tell me about how numerology or astrology can determine the character of their next boyfriend. Looking across the wine-stained table, I don't understand why this amazing and resourceful person wants to defer their intelligent judgement to something that doesn't work. Is that what belief really is – putting your critical faculties and initiative on hold? They search the stars and the souls of psychics, avoiding the one true path to happiness. The future's not out there, it's inside. Those who have worked that out somehow seem more content and fulfilled with life. Yet that doesn't mean that non-believers live a heartless existence without any belief at all. I believe in the warm, tingling feeling I get when I'm with a group of friends talking and laughing together, and the satisfaction of working something out for myself. And I also believe that people can change the future together and for themselves.

There's an old lady I know. She's in her eighties. For a long time, few people visited her, although she was friendly and very interesting to talk to. She just got forgotten about. Her friends died. Her family moved away and wouldn't make the effort to visit. Eventually social services found out and, through something called Home Care, sent round a woman to help the old lady clean herself and do her cooking. Soon, after weeks of chatting over the noise of bubbling vegetables, they became friends. The Home Care woman realised that what the old lady needed wasn't just a quick wash every few days. What she needed was a life. So they went out. They visited the seaside. They went to bingo. The Home Care woman's young granddaughter drew some pictures to decorate her wall. She visited for dinner. The woman's husband fitted the old lady's new bathroom, and the woman painted her kitchen. The old lady's future, her life, was irrevocably changed for the better through an act of human kindness, and not through the predictions of an astrologer or a psychic. The old lady's name is Flo, the Home Care woman is my mum. Flo's just spent Christmas Day at our house, making merry, laughing at my niece's silly antics and my embarrassing inability to play a basic computer game. My mum's not a psychic, but she's certainly shown a lot of 'spirit' in helping Flo change her fortunes.

Whether you really need psychics, tarot cards and crystal balls to help you get through life's anxious moments is really up to you as well. But ask yourself these questions. How come not everyone else needs them? What is it that this belief gives me? And what has actually changed because of it?

My sister had a prediction of her death. If you believe that the future can be foretold, no ifs and no buts, then my sister has to die in a water accident with her daughter. You can't pick and mix what you want to hear, ignoring the unsavoury items of information on the way. From that innocent present I bought my sister all those years ago, my future has changed too. I now have to live with the fact that, despite working hard to present my sister with evidence that astrology has no influence over hers or Elly's lives at all, she will still avoid trips over water and won't play water sports. And she still suffers nightmares. Okay, maybe it's not a big deal. She hasn't lost her life, although at one time she thought she would. She's not like Shawn Hornbeck's parents who were told he was dead when he was alive, or that poor African man Derren Brown told me about who killed himself to save his son. But if I hadn't bought that astrology chart, my sister wouldn't have worried, Elly would get to do more fun things involving water, and I ... well, I wouldn't have written this book.

So what is my final future? As Richard Dawkins the arch-sceptic suggested, my future is down the pub, with a packet of crisps, a pint of beer and some warm, friendly words for whoever wants to join me. We can chat and argue about the reality of psychics and fortune-tellers, but that won't stop me believing in something that I've learnt on this rocky road to tomorrow. No matter what you say, not for one second will you change my mind that the future is yet to take place. And when it does, it will be made by you. And only you. You are your own best fortune-teller, and if you can't see that coming, then no one else can.

Acknowledgements

I WOULD LIKE TO THANK everyone who allowed me to interview them for this book, particularly Anu Anand, Dr Susan Blackmore, Derren Brown, Jonathan Cainer, Robert Todd Carroll, Dr Vanessa Chambers, Professor Richard Dawkins, Angela Donovan, Professor Chris French, Christine Holohan, Professor Brian Josephson, Dr Ciarán O'Keeffe, Diane Lazarus, Professor Ronald Mallett, Annette Martin, Joseph McMoneagle, Sally Morgan, Marilyn Payne, Guy Lyon Playfair, Dean Radin, Captain Fernando Realyvasquez, Stuart Vyse, Georgina Walker, Geoffrey Wellum, Professor Richard Wiseman and Tony Youens. And thanks also go to those rechristened anonymous interviewees – in particular the not-so-wicked witches of Sussex.

Thanks also to Lorella Belli, my agent, for her sound advice, Duncan Heath, my editor at Icon Books, for his elegant editing, and everyone at Icon for their work on the book – Najma Finlay, Simon Flynn, Andrew Furlow and Sarah Higgins.

Special thanks go to Nikki for her enthusiasm and support, and also her desire to read on even when she had better things to be doing; to ffinlo for showing me the tarot, bandana optional; to my mum and dad, Anne and Graham, for their support and for laughing at my bad jokes; and all other friends and family for their stimulating and entertaining conversations about the curious world of psychics. The last and biggest thanks, and a sort of belated apology, go to my sister Sarah and my niece Elly

– thank you and I'm really sorry. I promise we'll all go sailing one day and survive!

Bibliography

I REFERRED TO many books and materials in my research. The most helpful were: James Alcock et al, *Psi Wars – The Journal of Consciousness Studies*; Tony Allen's *Prophecies*; Anthony Aveni's *Behind the Crystal Ball*; Susan Blackmore's *The Adventures of a Parapsychologist*; Deborah Blum's *The Ghost Hunters*; Derren Brown's *Tricks of the Mind*; Nicolas Campion's *What Do Astrologers Believe?*; Robert Todd Carroll's *The Skeptic's Dictionary*; Marcus Chown's *Quantum Theory Cannot Hurt You*; David Marks' *The Psychology of the Psychic*; Stuart Vyse's *Believing in Magic – The Psychology of Superstition*; Dean Radin's *Entangled Minds*; Geoffrey Wellum's *First Light*; Michael Shermer's *Why People Believe Weird Things*; Robert L. Park's *Superstition*; Ronald Mallett's *The Time Traveller*; Jon Ronson's *The Men Who Stare at Goats*; Richard Wiseman's *Quirkology*; and Danah Zohar's *Through the Time Barrier*.